CAMBRIDGE
EDUCATIONAL SERVICES®

AMERICA'S #1 STANDARDS-BASED SCHOOL IMPROVEMENT

ACT • PLAN • EXPLORE
Science Reasoning Victory

Teacher's Guide

ACT•PLAN•EXPLORE•SAT•PSAT•SATII•GRE•GMAT•LSAT•MCAT•TOEFL•GED•PRAXIS•PSAE•ITBS•CollegePrep™

Copyright © 2005, 2004 by Cambridge Publishing, Inc.
Published by Cambridge Publishing, Inc.
All rights reserved
including the right of reproduction
in whole or in part in any form.

Cambridge Educational Services, Inc.
2720 River Road, Des Plaines, IL 60018
(847) 299-2930

Portions Copyright © 2005 by Thomas H. Martinson.
All rights reserved
including the right of reproduction
in whole or in part in any form.

Manufactured in the United States of America.
2 3 4 5 6 7 8 9 10
Edited by Julie M. Lengle and David P. Waldherr.

CAMBRIDGE
EDUCATIONAL SERVICES®

AMERICA'S #1 STANDARDS-BASED SCHOOL IMPROVEMENT

Dear ACT • PLAN • EXPLORE Science Reasoning Teacher,

Welcome to the Cambridge School Improvement Program for the ACT, PLAN, and EXPLORE!

In your materials, you will find the *Cambridge ACT • PLAN • EXPLORE Science Reasoning Victory Student Textbook* and this *Cambridge ACT • PLAN • EXPLORE Science Reasoning Victory Teacher's Guide*. The teacher's guide contains an overview for teaching each step of the Cambridge Six-Step Approach™. In addition, the Introduction contains pertinent information about the first class procedures, instructor responsibilities, and Cambridge teaching methods.

Every step begins with a Course Concept Outline that reviews the instruction method for that step, as well as student and instructor progress reports to monitor each student's progress through each step of the program. In addition, Step Three's Course Concept Outline lists the concepts and testing methods for the Science Reasoning lesson, cross-referenced with the Section One—Science Reasoning Review questions in the student textbook. At the end of the Science Reasoning lesson is a Strategy Summary Sheet, which summarizes question formats, concepts, and strategies for attacking the problems. Completing the lessons associated with each step of this teacher's guide, you have everything you need to deliver a comprehensive school improvement plan.

You must review all of the course materials before your first class. After reviewing the materials, call our Teacher Hotline at 1-800-444-4373 (1-800-HIGHER ED) for your phone orientation and to answer any questions that you might have regarding initial class procedures, course format, or instruction. You should complete your certification process by attending a regional or on-site professional development in-service. We look forward to speaking with you and hope to maintain a personal relationship.

Sincerely,

The Cambridge Curriculum Committee

ACT • PLAN • EXPLORE SCIENCE REASONING
Teacher's Guide
Table of Contents

INTRODUCTION
- Cambridge Course Concept Outline—Introduction iii
- Teaching the Cambridge Program v
- 15 Key Ways to Increase Attendance and Homework Completion xxiv
- The Cambridge Top 20 TestPrep PLUS™ Tips xxvi
- Error Corrections, Suggestions, and Comments Form xxix

STEP ONE: DIAGNOSTIC TESTING AND ASSESSMENT SERVICE
- Cambridge Course Concept Outline—Step One 3
- Step One Overview 5
- ACT • PLAN • EXPLORE Diagnostic Pre-Test Student Progress Report 19
- ACT • PLAN • EXPLORE Diagnostic Pre-Test Instructor Progress Report 21
- Proctoring Instructions 23

STEP TWO: SKILLS REVIEW
- Cambridge Course Concept Outline—Step Two 31
- Step Two Overview 33
- ACT • PLAN • EXPLORE Science Reasoning Step Two Student Progress Report 39
- ACT • PLAN • EXPLORE Science Reasoning Step Two Instructor Progress Report 41
- Science Reasoning Skills Review Games and Activities 43
- Answers and Explanations 47
  - Exercise 1—Basics of Experimental Design 47
  - Exercise 2—Data Organization in Controlled Experiments 47
  - Exercise 3—Presentation of Conflicting Viewpoints 47
  - Exercise 4—Science Reasoning Passages 48

STEP THREE: PROBLEM-SOLVING, CONCEPTS, AND STRATEGIES
- Cambridge Course Concept Outline—Step Three 53
- Step Three Overview 57
- ACT • PLAN • EXPLORE Science Reasoning Step Three Student Progress Report 63
- ACT • PLAN • EXPLORE Science Reasoning Step Three Instructor Progress Report 65
- Section One—Science Reasoning Review 67
- Section Two—Science Reasoning Problem-Solving 88
- Section Three—Science Reasoning Quizzes 94
  - Quiz I 94
  - Quiz II 95
  - Quiz III 95
- Strategy Summary Sheet—Science Reasoning 97

STEP FOUR: PRACTICE TEST REINFORCEMENT
    Cambridge Course Concept Outline—Step Four 103
    Step Four Overview 105
    ACT Science Reasoning Step Four Student Progress Report 109
    ACT Science Reasoning Step Four Instructor Progress Report 111
    Answers and Explanations 113
        ACT Science Reasoning Practice Test I 113
        ACT Science Reasoning Practice Test II 116
        ACT Science Reasoning Practice Test III 119
        ACT Science Reasoning Practice Test IV 122

STEP FIVE: FINAL EXAM, ASSESSMENT REPORT, AND REVIEW
    Cambridge Course Concept Outline—Step Five 131
    Step Five Overview 133
    ACT • PLAN • EXPLORE Diagnostic Post-Test Student Progress Report 139
    ACT • PLAN • EXPLORE Diagnostic Post-Test Instructor Progress Report 141

STEP SIX: PERSONAL STUDY PLAN
    Cambridge Course Concept Outline—Step Six 147
    Step Six Overview 149
    ACT • PLAN • EXPLORE Science Reasoning Step Six Student Progress Report 153
    ACT • PLAN • EXPLORE Science Reasoning Step Six Instructor Progress Report 155
    ACT • PLAN • EXPLORE English Step Six Student Progress Report 157
    ACT • PLAN • EXPLORE English Step Six Instructor Progress Report 159
    ACT • PLAN • EXPLORE Mathematics Step Six Student Progress Report 161
    ACT • PLAN • EXPLORE Mathematics Step Six Instructor Progress Report 163
    ACT • PLAN • EXPLORE Reading Step Six Student Progress Report 165
    ACT • PLAN • EXPLORE Reading Step Six Instructor Progress Report 167

CAMBRIDGE
EDUCATIONAL SERVICES

ACT • PLAN • EXPLORE
SCIENCE REASONING

INTRODUCTION

CAMBRIDGE
EDUCATIONAL SERVICES

AMERICA'S #1 STANDARDS-BASED SCHOOL IMPROVEMENT

Cambridge Course Concept Outline
INTRODUCTION

I. TEACHING THE CAMBRIDGE PROGRAM (p. v)

A. ABOUT THIS TEACHER'S GUIDE AND COURSE MATERIALS (p. v)

B. USING THIS BOOK WITH THE CAMBRIDGE SIX-STEP APPROACH™ (p. vi)
1. STEP ONE: DIAGNOSTIC TESTING AND ASSESSMENT SERVICE (p. vi)
2. STEP TWO: SKILLS REVIEW (p. vi)
3. STEP THREE: PROBLEM-SOLVING, CONCEPTS, AND STRATEGIES (p. vii)
4. STEP FOUR: PRACTICE TEST REINFORCEMENT (p. vii)
5. STEP FIVE: FINAL EXAM, ASSESSMENT, AND REVIEW (p. vii)
6. STEP SIX: PERSONAL STUDY PLAN (p. viii)

C. SUPPLEMENTARY COURSE MATERIALS (p. viii)
1. THE COURSE CD-ROM (p. viii)
2. THE WEB COURSE (p. viii)
   a. SELF-STUDY MODEL (p. ix)
   b. CONFERENCE MODEL (p. ix)
   c. CLASSROOM MODEL (p. ix)

D. ACT • PLAN • EXPLORE COURSE FORMATS (p. ix)

E. ACT • PLAN • EXPLORE TESTPREP™ REVIEW COURSE SCHEDULES (p. x)

F. ADVERTISING AND PROMOTING YOUR COURSE: THE SUPPORT CENTER (p. xvii)

G. TEACHER RESPONSIBILITIES AND CLASS PROCEDURES (p. xvii)

H. TEACHING CAMBRIDGE TESTPREP™ (p. xviii)
1. FIRST CLASS PROCEDURE (p. xviii)
2. YOUR ROLE AS INSTRUCTOR (p. xviii)
3. CLASSROOM LESSONS (p. xix)
4. CLASS BREAKS (p. xx)
5. HOMEWORK (p. xx)
6. P.A.L.PREP™ TEACHING METHOD (p. xxi)
7. GRADING TESTPREP™ COURSES (p. xxii)
8. ACCOUNTABILITY (p. xxii)
   a. IN-CLASS PORTFOLIOS (p. xxii)
   b. PROGRESS REPORTS (p. xxii)

INTRODUCTION

II. 15 KEY WAYS TO INCREASE ATTENDANCE AND HOMEWORK COMPLETION (p. xxiv)

III. THE CAMBRIDGE TOP 20 TESTPREP PLUS™ TIPS (p. xxvi)

TEACHING THE CAMBRIDGE PROGRAM

The Cambridge ACT • PLAN • EXPLORE TestPrep™ Review Course is designed to provide students with a review of the important tested skills, concepts, and strategies in preparation for the ACT, PLAN, and EXPLORE exams. Because the ACT is aligned with state standards, it examines concepts that should already be a part of your school's curriculum. While teaching this course, you are supplementing skills that students are learning in the classroom with powerful test-taking strategies. You are giving your students the tools that they need to effectively demonstrate their learned knowledge and to perform up to their true ability levels. Ultimately, a successful program will help students raise their skills, get into the college or university of their choice, and earn valuable grants and scholarships. A combination of your teaching abilities with the materials in both the student textbook and this teacher's guide will help students to succeed.

You are giving your students an incredible opportunity with this class. For decades, students in the highest income brackets have had these powerful test-taking strategies and concepts made available to them. However, students in the lower socioeconomic stratum have historically been denied these opportunities, making the testing gap more pronounced. The Cambridge program helps to level the playing field. More importantly, it gives your students valuable life-long skills that go far beyond the ACT.

Many "test prep" programs focus only on certain test-taking strategies, or "tricks." It is assumed that student skills are generally at a level meeting that of a college-bound student. However, not all of your students may be considering college, and even those who are considering college may still have skill gaps in specific content areas (not to mention students who may be performing at the lower percentiles). Step Two: Skills Review makes up a vital part of this course since there is no singular, defining ACT student characteristic. Whether your students cover the Skills Review content in class or as homework, they must have this foundational knowledge before moving on to the more advanced test-taking strategies.

This program also has specific activities and drills for students who are performing at higher levels and display mastery of the core content areas. These students may end up skipping most, if not all, of Step Two: Skills Review, focusing more on the strategies and concepts that are detailed in Step Three: Problem-Solving, Concepts, and Strategies and the application of those strategies to the four included practice tests.

Even the most skillful teacher who is equipped with the best test preparation materials can be made ineffective by a lack of student motivation. Look to the motivation techniques that are included in this Introduction to help you keep your students motivated throughout the course. Remind students of everything they have to gain by attending the class, and what they have to lose by not attending. There is no simple way to raise student scores. Students have to come to class and do the work to improve their scores. Your students should know, however, that with your help and their hard work, scores will increase and doors will open for them.

It is important to note that the PLAN and the EXPLORE are simply scaled-down versions of the ACT—they test the same skills and concepts as the ACT but are geared for 10th grade and 8th grade, respectively. Therefore, students taking the PLAN and the EXPLORE will be prepared after studying the ACT materials.

A. ABOUT THIS TEACHER'S GUIDE AND COURSE MATERIALS

The *ACT • PLAN • EXPLORE Science Reasoning-Only Teacher's Set* includes the *Cambridge ACT • PLAN • EXPLORE Science Reasoning Victory Student Textbook* and the *Cambridge ACT • PLAN • EXPLORE Science Reasoning Victory Teacher's Guide*. The *Cambridge ACT • PLAN • EXPLORE Science Reasoning Victory Teacher's Guide* is designed to follow the Step Three: Problem-Solving, Concepts, and Strategies questions in the student textbook, detailing explanations, material concepts, and strategies. The teacher's guide also provides a teaching structure for all six steps of the Cambridge program, as well as answers and explanations for Step Two: Skills Review and Step Four: Practice Test Reinforcement.

In the teacher's guide, Step Three begins with a Cambridge Course Concept Outline, listing the concepts and testing methods for the Science Reasoning lesson, cross-referenced with the Section One—Science Reasoning Review

INTRODUCTION

questions. Following the Science Reasoning lesson's Review section are answers and explanations to the Problem-Solving and Quizzes sections. At the end of the lesson is a Strategy Summary Sheet, which summarizes the question formats, concepts, and strategies for attacking the problems.

Step Three: Problem-Solving, Concepts, and Strategies in the *Cambridge ACT • PLAN • EXPLORE Science Reasoning Victory Student Textbook* combines a review of tested skills and concepts, easy-to-difficult problem-solving, and timed quizzes. Step Three in the teacher's guide supports the textbook Science Reasoning lesson with complete substantive reviews of the ACT, PLAN, and EXPLORE testing materials, using detailed explanations of the textbook problems, powerful test-taking strategies, and TestPrep™ shortcuts. The Step Three review of substantive concepts and skills, strategies, tips, and explanatory answers is given in class (and is not repeated in the student textbook), so students must attend each class.

Pages marked "Notes and Strategies" are provided in the *Cambridge ACT • PLAN • EXPLORE Science Reasoning Victory Student Textbook* for student note-taking. Important notes and strategies are set-aside in a boxed format throughout this teacher's guide. Be sure to go over these points with your students, reminding them to keep notes in their student textbooks.

Please call your Cambridge representative at (847) 299-2930 with any questions about your student or teacher materials or the teacher hotline at (800) 444-4373 with any questions about the content or teaching method of the course.

B. USING THIS BOOK WITH THE CAMBRIDGE SIX-STEP APPROACH™

The Cambridge Six-Step Approach™ is the proven test preparation model that has worked for thousands of students at thousands of schools. Each of the six steps plays an integral role in helping students reach their maximum score improvement. The following brief overview of the six steps will help clarify how to use this book as the primary tool for score improvement and greater academic achievement. At the beginning of each step, there is an extended and more detailed overview of its contents. Be sure to read through these extended overviews in this teacher's guide, as they explain how to best use each step as a teaching tool.

1. STEP ONE: DIAGNOSTIC TESTING AND ASSESSMENT SERVICE

The first step is to have your students take a diagnostic pre-test. Cambridge recommends administering an official ACT, PLAN, or EXPLORE test (not included with this package). If your program has chosen to use the Cambridge Assessment Service, the Assessment Reports Request Form will indicate which of the official tests your students should take as a pre-test. After submitting your students' completed tests to the Cambridge Assessment Service, you will receive student summaries and item analyses with the pre-test results. The student summary reports will dictate which sections in Step Two: Skills Review students need to review most, and the item and error analyses will allow you to pinpoint the areas of the test on which you need to focus the most in Step Three: Problem-Solving, Concepts, and Strategies. A high, medium, low error analysis also helps locations that are ordering more than 150 student sets to target specific content areas that will have the greatest impact on student achievement.

If your program is not using the Cambridge Assessment Service, it is still necessary to administer a pre-test, using the results to determine which sections students need to review most in Step Two: Skills Review and which areas of the test require the most attention in Step Three: Problem-Solving, Concepts, and Strategies. If you are not using the Cambridge Assessment Service, students should use the Pre-Test Bubble Sheet on page 17 in the *Cambridge ACT • PLAN • EXPLORE Science Reasoning Victory Student Textbook*.

If your students are also using the Cambridge Adaptive CD-ROM or Cambridge Web Course, they should use the computerized pre-test that is included with both. This pre-test provides additional preparation for the practice tests.

2. STEP TWO: SKILLS REVIEW

Building on Step One, the second step is Skills Review. In the *Cambridge ACT • PLAN • EXPLORE Science Reasoning Victory Student Textbook*, Step Two: Skills Review includes the Science Skills Review. In this teacher's guide, Step Two includes a description of the Science Skills Review and how to use the exercises to enhance instruction. Additionally, this step includes a review of innovative Science Reasoning Skills Review games and activities. Answers and explanations to Step Two: Skills Review are included in both the student textbook and teacher's guide.

If students answer less than 50 percent of the questions correctly on any section of the diagnostic pre-test, then you should assign those students Step Two: Skills Review for added preparation. Also, encourage all of your students to use the Skills Review exercises to reinforce their existing skill sets or to provide extra practice. These review exercises can be done in class or assigned as homework, depending on the duration of your program.

If your students are also using the Cambridge Adaptive CD-ROM, they can use the included adaptive skill-builders for added skills review. For the Cambridge Web Course, students should use the included Skills Review lessons.

3. STEP THREE: PROBLEM-SOLVING, CONCEPTS, AND STRATEGIES

Once students have mastered the necessary skills in Step Two: Skills Review, they are ready to begin learning the strategies that will help them improve their pre-test scores. The majority of this teacher's guide focuses on Step Three: Problem-Solving, Concepts, and Strategies, with detailed lecture material for the Science Reasoning section of the ACT, PLAN, and EXPLORE. As you review strategies and problem-types for the ACT, PLAN, or EXPLORE in class, students will complete Science Reasoning reviews, problem-solving exercises, and quizzes to build familiarity with the test formats and question-types. If you used the Cambridge Assessment Service for the diagnostic pre-test, the error analyses will help guide you as you prepare to teach this material. Focus most of your time and attention on the test areas with which students had the most trouble on the pre-test but which are attainable at the next skill level as indicated by the high, medium, low error analysis.

With the Cambridge Adaptive CD-ROM, students may also use the included adaptive skill-builders to reinforce the problem-solving, concepts, and strategies lectures. For the Cambridge Web Course, students use the included problem-solving, concepts, and strategies lesson online.

4. STEP FOUR: PRACTICE TEST REINFORCEMENT

After learning the key ACT, PLAN, and EXPLORE test-taking strategies, it is necessary for students to complete practice tests to reinforce what they have learned. For this step, students should use the four ACT Science Reasoning Practice Tests in Step Four of the *Cambridge ACT • PLAN • EXPLORE Science Reasoning Victory Student Textbook*. This step may be completed, in part or whole, as homework or in class, depending on the duration and nature of your program. Answers and explanations to ACT Science Reasoning Practice Tests I-IV are included in both the student textbook and teacher's guide.

If using the Cambridge Adaptive CD-ROM or Cambridge Web Course, students should complete the tests in their textbook before completing the tests on the CD-ROM and Web Course. Use those additional tests for further practice after taking all four tests in this book.

5. STEP FIVE: FINAL EXAM, ASSESSMENT REPORT, AND REVIEW

Step Five measures, with a post-test, how far students have come since the diagnostic pre-test in Step One. If your program has ordered two official ACT, PLAN, or EXPLORE tests, use the second test that has been designated as a post-test by the Cambridge Assessment Service. The data on the post-test assessment report will not only document each student's improvement, but it will also prepare students for the final step—a personal study plan to further review any test areas in which students are still not performing as well as they would like.

As with Step One, if you are not using the Cambridge Assessment Service, it is still necessary to administer a post-test in order to obtain maximum score improvement. Students should use the Post-Test Bubble Sheet on page 177 in the *Cambridge ACT • PLAN • EXPLORE Science Reasoning Victory Student Textbook*.

In Step Five of this teacher's guide, you will also find valuable information on how to interpret assessment data. This information will help to ensure that you make the most of the data that the pre- and post-tests reveal.

For the Cambridge Adaptive CD-ROM and Web Course, use the official test (if possible) for your post-test, and then use the tests on the CD-ROM and/or Web Course as additional practice during Step Four: Practice Test Reinforcement.

6. STEP SIX: PERSONAL STUDY PLAN

Finally, meet with students individually to discuss their performances, and to help them develop a personal study plan that focuses most of their time and attention on the test areas with which they had the most trouble on the post-test. There is usually not much time between the course and the real test, so they should review material very selectively.

C. SUPPLEMENTARY COURSE MATERIALS

1. THE COURSE CD-ROM

All Cambridge software begins with a detailed tutorial of how the test is structured and how the CD-ROM works. We recommend that students work with the CD-ROM in parallel with the classroom course. Many students look to the classroom or to the CD-ROM as the exclusive source of information and practice. However, our data show that combining classroom instruction with at-home review and practice using the CD-ROM is the ideal model for maximizing test score improvements.

In addition to the Homework Progress Report Forms, there are four key software reports that students should print and file in their course performance portfolios to allow you to effectively monitor their progress: Diagnostic, Performance, Content, and Difficulty.

The Diagnostic Report is on the first page of the reports for the CD-ROM ACT Diagnostic and Practice Tests. It indicates how well the student performed on the Science Reasoning section of the exam and gives a recommendation as to whether to study Step Two: Skills Review in the *Cambridge ACT • PLAN • EXPLORE Science Reasoning Victory Student Textbook*.

The Performance Report is also on the first page of the reports and provides estimated test scores based on the ACT 1-36 score scale. This gives a general idea of the student's performance compared to other test-takers.

The Content Report is on the second page and shows the percentage of questions that are answered correctly for the Science Reasoning test section. It also shows the percentage of questions that are answered correctly according to difficulty level.

The Difficulty Report is the final report. It lists the difficulty of each item presented to the student during the test and whether the item was answered correctly.

2. THE WEB COURSE

The Cambridge Web Course can be used in combination with the live Cambridge TestPrep™ Review Course both by providing additional material to supplement the class sessions and as an opportunity for students to make up any missed classes. The online Web site also provides a Cambridge TestPrep™ Review Course alternative for students who are not attending class sessions.

The Cambridge Web Course offers unique descriptions of the strategies that are covered in the live Cambridge TestPrep™ Review Courses, providing the students with another Science Reasoning lesson from a "visiting professor." This Web Course can be utilized either before or after class. If students listen to the corresponding Web Course lesson before each class, you can then review the Science Reasoning lesson using the *Cambridge Web Course Textbook*, testing students' knowledge with the extra textbook problems. Alternatively, students can use the Web Course lesson following each class session to reiterate and firmly establish the material reviewed in class. Students can also use the Web Course lesson to make up any missed class sessions. Students can log on to the Web site to review material similar to that covered in class.

Finally, the Cambridge Web Course can be offered independently as a course alternative for students who are not attending a live Cambridge TestPrep™ Review Course. The Web Course includes an online grade book that stores students' pre- and post-test scores, allowing you to track the improvement of students over the duration of the course. The Web Course also includes Basic Skills Review. Students can complete the Basic Skills Review online.

We recommend that school administrators choose one of the following three Cambridge Web Course models. The Classroom Model, or "blended model," has been shown to be the most effective at increasing test scores.

a. SELF-STUDY MODEL

Students are responsible for completion of coursework at their own pace. They can complete the lessons in any order and at any time. This model is strengthened by having a teacher at your school who is available to respond to any questions from the students. Students with questions can also contact their school or Cambridge directly via the online *E-mail Contact Form*.

b. CONFERENCE MODEL

Course expectations are set during an initial student/teacher conference. Further accountability is achieved through student/teacher interactions during the course via e-mail and several follow-up conferences. You should discuss course expectations, assignments, and homework with each student. Additionally, track and record the students' progress in a grade book.

c. CLASSROOM MODEL

Students individually use computer terminals in the school's classroom to complete the Web Course lessons at their own pace. Discussion of homework and major TestPrep™ strategies is done together as a class, integrating all of the available course materials. Monitor the students' completion of homework assignments and course progress to ensure that every student successfully completes the course.

Use the extra problems in the *Cambridge Web Course Textbook* to reinforce the strategies reviewed during the problem-solving, concepts, and strategies lesson. The *ACT • PLAN • EXPLORE CD-ROM* should be used for additional skill-builders, practice tests, and homework assignments.

D. ACT • PLAN • EXPLORE COURSE FORMATS

The Cambridge ACT • PLAN • EXPLORE TestPrep™ Review Courses are highly structured and standardized—in order for the program to continue to provide positive results, the format and content should not be altered. Unless your program administrator has altered your course, our standard course formats should be followed, including the presentation of classroom lessons and the homework assignments. The five standard Cambridge Course Formats are described below.

Any questions and comments regarding course content and format should be addressed directly to Cambridge (Teacher Hotline: 1-800-HIGHER-ED). Contact us to take advantage of the unique opportunity to shape your class lessons and to have an impact on the future developments of our materials.

The benefits of and criteria for each type of Cambridge TestPrep™ Review Course format are as follows:

1. **STANDARD FORMAT:** The standard review course format presents the class lessons in the optimal order. This format should be used if test preparation is for one standardized test and classes are offered after school, on weekends, or during the school day (semester-long course). We recommend the standard review course format for locations with high enrollments in all of their Cambridge TestPrep™ Review Courses.

2. **OVERLAPPING FORMAT:** The overlapping review course format combines class lessons common to separate courses into a single class: The same instructor teaches the same subject at the same time for different courses. For instance, you can teach EXPLORE, PLAN, and ACT students together because of the overlapping Science Reasoning subject area. This format minimizes instruction costs and eliminates course cancellations. We recommend the overlapping review course format for locations with low enrollments (seven or less) in their Cambridge TestPrep™ Review Courses with common class lessons.

3. **REVOLVING FORMAT:** The revolving review course format presents the class lessons in a continually revolving schedule. This format gives your students maximum scheduling choices, allowing students to begin the course at any time and to attend class on consecutive weekdays, weekends, or evenings. The revolving review course format dramatically increases enrollments in the Cambridge TestPrep™ Review Courses, while lowering

INTRODUCTION

the number of students that are present in any one class. Diagnostic and Practice Tests cannot be overlapped, so test administration must be done at the beginning and end of each complete set of class lessons, either in a school lab or as homework.

4. **MULTI-YEAR FORMAT:** The multi-year review course format allows schools to cover a greater depth and breadth of material with their students by starting earlier and covering materials with students over several years. For instance, start a multi-year review course in 8th grade with an EXPLORE pre-test, covering basic skills in this first year. Then, in subsequent years, advance through the book and through PLAN and ACT official tests. This format has seen the greatest gains in scores and skills, as it builds upon each year's progress.

5. **INTENSIVE/PREMIUM EMBEDDED FORMAT:** The intensive/premium embedded review course format offers the intensive review course (pre- and post-tests are taken at home) embedded in the premium review course (pre- and post-tests are administered in class). Premium course students will pay more tuition for classes that start on an earlier date (pre-test) and end on a later date (post-test/post-test review). Intensive course students will pay less tuition and attend only the Science Reasoning content lesson.

For courses including in-class administration of the pre-test and post-test, it is important to simulate actual testing conditions when you administer these exams. Use official time limits and have students record their answers on the official test answer forms. If students are to take the exams at home, advise them to simulate testing conditions by using the time restrictions. Collect the ACT • PLAN • EXPLORE Diagnostic Pre-Test Instructor Progress Report and the ACT • PLAN • EXPLORE Science Reasoning Step Four Instructor Progress Report (*Cambridge ACT • PLAN • EXPLORE Science Reasoning Victory Student Textbook*, pp. 15 and 113, respectively) from students after each exam is completed and graded.

E. ACT • PLAN • EXPLORE TESTPREP™ REVIEW COURSE SCHEDULES

ACT Semester-Long Format

Sessions (30 minutes each)	In-Class Lesson	6-Step Approach	Materials[†]
Sessions 1-9	ACT DIAGNOSTIC TEST and ASSESSMENT	Step 1	*Official ACT Test I*
Sessions 10-30	SCIENCE REASONING REMEDIATION Science Reasoning Skills Review	Step 2	• Science Skills Review (*Cambridge ACT • PLAN • EXPLORE Science Reasoning Victory Student Textbook*, Step Two)
Sessions 31-40	SUBJECT LESSON Science Reasoning	Step 3	• Science Reasoning Review, Problem-Solving, and Quizzes (*Cambridge ACT • PLAN • EXPLORE Science Reasoning Victory Student Textbook*, pp. 61, 76, 94) • Step Three Science Reasoning (*Cambridge ACT • PLAN • EXPLORE Science Reasoning Victory Teacher's Guide*, p. 67)
Sessions 41-55	PRACTICE DRILLS Science Reasoning Practice Tests and Explanations	Step 4	• ACT Science Reasoning Practice Tests I and II (untimed) (*Cambridge ACT • PLAN • EXPLORE Science Reasoning Victory Student Textbook*, Step Four) • ACT Science Reasoning Practice Tests III and IV (timed) (*Cambridge ACT • PLAN • EXPLORE Science Reasoning Victory Student Textbook*, Step Four)
Sessions 56-64	ACT • PLAN • EXPLORE FINAL PRACTICE TEST and ASSESSMENT	Step 5	*Official ACT Test II*
Sessions 65-73	POST-TEST REVIEW and CUSTOM STUDY PLAN	Steps 5 and 6	*Official ACT Test II Explanations*

[†] The number of class sessions may be shortened by assigning remediation (Step 2) and practice drills (Step 4) as homework. To lengthen class to multi-year, use additional Cambridge Educational Services materials and official ACT tests.

ACT • PLAN • EXPLORE SCIENCE REASONING TEACHER'S GUIDE

PLAN Semester-Long Format

Sessions (30 minutes each)	In-Class Lesson	6-Step Approach	Materials†
Sessions 1-9	ACT • PLAN • EXPLORE DIAGNOSTIC TEST and ASSESSMENT	Step 1	Official ACT • PLAN • EXPLORE Test I
Sessions 10-30	SCIENCE REASONING REMEDIATION Science Reasoning Skills Review	Step 2	• Science Skills Review (Cambridge ACT • PLAN • EXPLORE Science Reasoning Victory Student Textbook, Step Two)
Sessions 31-40	SUBJECT LESSON Science Reasoning	Step 3	• Science Reasoning Review, Problem-Solving, and Quizzes (Cambridge ACT • PLAN • EXPLORE Science Reasoning Victory Student Textbook, pp. 61, 76, 94) • Step Three Science Reasoning (Cambridge ACT • PLAN • EXPLORE Science Reasoning Victory Teacher's Guide, p. 67)
Sessions 41-55	PRACTICE DRILLS Science Reasoning Practice Tests and Explanations	Step 4	• ACT Science Reasoning Practice Tests I and II (untimed) (Cambridge ACT • PLAN • EXPLORE Science Reasoning Victory Student Textbook, Step Four) • ACT Science Reasoning Practice Tests III and IV (timed) (Cambridge ACT • PLAN • EXPLORE Science Reasoning Victory Student Textbook, Step Four)
Sessions 56-64	ACT • PLAN • EXPLORE FINAL PRACTICE TEST and ASSESSMENT	Step 5	Official ACT • PLAN • EXPLORE Test II
Sessions 65-73	POST-TEST REVIEW and CUSTOM STUDY PLAN	Steps 5 and 6	Official ACT • PLAN • EXPLORE Test II Explanations

† The number of class sessions may be shortened by assigning remediation (Step 2) and practice drills (Step 4) as homework. To lengthen class to multi-year, use additional Cambridge Educational Services materials and official ACT • PLAN • EXPLORE tests.

EXPLORE Semester-Long Format

Sessions (30 minutes each)	In-Class Lesson	6-Step Approach	Materials†
Sessions 1-9	EXPLORE DIAGNOSTIC TEST and ASSESSMENT	Step 1	Official EXPLORE Test I
Sessions 10-30	SCIENCE REASONING REMEDIATION Science Reasoning Skills Review	Step 2	• Science Skills Review (Cambridge ACT • PLAN • EXPLORE Science Reasoning Victory Student Textbook, Step Two)
Sessions 31-40	SUBJECT LESSON Science Reasoning	Step 3	• Science Reasoning Review, Problem-Solving, and Quizzes (Cambridge ACT • PLAN • EXPLORE Science Reasoning Victory Student Textbook, pp. 61, 76, 94) • Step Three Science Reasoning (Cambridge ACT • PLAN • EXPLORE Science Reasoning Victory Teacher's Guide, p. 67)
Sessions 41-55	PRACTICE DRILLS Science Reasoning Practice Tests and Explanations	Step 4	• ACT Science Reasoning Practice Tests I and II (untimed) (Cambridge ACT • PLAN • EXPLORE Science Reasoning Victory Student Textbook, Step Four) • ACT Science Reasoning Practice Tests III and IV (timed) (Cambridge ACT • PLAN • EXPLORE Science Reasoning Victory Student Textbook, Step Four)
Sessions 56-64	EXPLORE FINAL PRACTICE TEST and ASSESSMENT	Step 5	Official EXPLORE Test II
Sessions 65-73	POST-TEST REVIEW and CUSTOM STUDY PLAN	Steps 5 and 6	Official EXPLORE Test II Explanations

† The number of class sessions may be shortened by assigning remediation (Step 2) and practice drills (Step 4) as homework. To lengthen class to multi-year, use additional Cambridge Educational Services materials and official ACT • PLAN • EXPLORE tests.

INTRODUCTION

ACT • PLAN • EXPLORE 8th-11th Grade Multi-Year Format

8th GRADE

Sessions (30 minutes each)	In-Class Lesson	6-Step Approach	Materials[†]
Sessions 1-9	EXPLORE DIAGNOSTIC TEST and ASSESSMENT	Step 1	*Official EXPLORE Test I*
Sessions 10-30	SCIENCE REASONING REMEDIATION Science Reasoning Skills Review	Step 2	• Science Skills Review (*Cambridge ACT • PLAN • EXPLORE Science Reasoning Victory Student Textbook*, Step Two)
Sessions 31-36	EXPLORE FINAL PRACTICE TEST and ASSESSMENT	Step 5	*Official EXPLORE Test II*
Sessions 37-42	POST-TEST REVIEW and CUSTOM STUDY PLAN	Steps 5 and 6	*Official EXPLORE Test II Explanations*

[†] The number of class sessions may be shortened by assigning remediation (Step 2) and practice drills (Step 4) as homework. To lengthen class to multi-year, use additional Cambridge Educational Services materials and official ACT • PLAN • EXPLORE tests.

9th GRADE

Sessions (30 minutes each)	In-Class Lesson	6-Step Approach	Materials[†]
Sessions 1-9	PLAN DIAGNOSTIC TEST and ASSESSMENT	Step 1	*Official PLAN Test I*
Sessions 10-29	SUBJECT LESSON Science Reasoning	Step 3	• Science Reasoning Review, Problem-Solving, and Quizzes (*Cambridge ACT • PLAN • EXPLORE Science Reasoning Victory Student Textbook*, pp. 61, 76, 94) • Step Three Science Reasoning (*Cambridge ACT • PLAN • EXPLORE Science Reasoning Victory Teacher's Guide*, p. 67)
Sessions 30-35111	ACT • PLAN • EXPLORE FINAL PRACTICE TEST and ASSESSMENT	Step 5	*Official ACT • PLAN • EXPLORE Test II*
Sessions 36-41	POST-TEST REVIEW and CUSTOM STUDY PLAN	Steps 5 and 6	*Official ACT • PLAN • EXPLORE Text II Explanations*

[†] The number of class sessions may be shortened by assigning remediation (Step 2) and practice drills (Step 4) as homework. To lengthen class to multi-year, use additional Cambridge Educational Services materials and official ACT • PLAN • EXPLORE tests.

10th GRADE

Sessions (30 minutes each)	In-Class Lesson	6-Step Approach	Materials[†]
Sessions 1-9	ACT DIAGNOSTIC TEST and ASSESSMENT	Step 1	*Official ACT Test I*
Sessions 10-39	PRACTICE DRILLS Science Reasoning Practice Tests and Explanations	Step 4	• ACT Science Reasoning Practice Tests I and II (untimed) (*Cambridge ACT • PLAN • EXPLORE Science Reasoning Victory Student Textbook*, Step Four) • ACT Science Reasoning Practice Tests III and IV (timed) (*Cambridge ACT • PLAN • EXPLORE Science Reasoning Victory Student Textbook*, Step Four)
Sessions 40-48	ACT FINAL PRACTICE TEST and ASSESSMENT	Step 5	ACT Practice Test (*ACT CD-ROM*)
Sessions 49-54	POST-TEST REVIEW and CUSTOM STUDY PLAN	Steps 5 and 6	ACT Practice Test Explanations (*ACT CD-ROM*)

[†] The number of class sessions may be shortened by assigning remediation (Step 2) and practice drills (Step 4) as homework. To lengthen class to multi-year, use additional Cambridge Educational Services materials and official ACT tests.

Photocopying not allowed without Cambridge licensing agreement.

ACT • PLAN • EXPLORE SCIENCE REASONING TEACHER'S GUIDE

11th GRADE

Sessions (30 minutes each)	In-Class Lesson	6-Step Approach	Materials†
Sessions 1-45	ACT PRACTICE TESTS and ASSESSMENTS	Step 5	Official ACT Tests II, III, and IV ACT Practice Tests (ACT CD-ROM)
Sessions 46-120	POST-TEST REVIEWS and CUSTOM STUDY PLAN	Steps 5 and 6	Official ACT Tests II, III, and IV Explanations ACT Practice Test Explanations (ACT CD-ROM)

† The number of class sessions may be shortened by assigning remediation (Step 2) and practice drills (Step 4) as homework. To lengthen class to multi-year, use additional Cambridge Educational Services materials and official ACT tests.

ACT • PLAN 9th-11th Grade Multi-Year Format

9th GRADE

Sessions (30 minutes each)	In-Class Lesson	6-Step Approach	Materials†
Sessions 1-9	PLAN DIAGNOSTIC TEST and ASSESSMENT	Step 1	Official PLAN Test
Sessions 10-30	SCIENCE REASONING REMEDIATION Science Reasoning Skills Review	Step 2	• Science Skills Review (Cambridge ACT • PLAN • EXPLORE Science Reasoning Victory Student Textbook, Step Two)
Sessions 31-36	ACT • PLAN • EXPLORE FINAL PRACTICE TEST and ASSESSMENT	Step 5	Official ACT • PLAN • EXPLORE Test
Sessions 37-42	POST-TEST REVIEW and CUSTOM STUDY PLAN	Steps 5 and 6	Official ACT • PLAN • EXPLORE Test Explanations

† The number of class sessions may be shortened by assigning remediation (Step 2) and practice drills (Step 4) as homework. To lengthen class to multi-year, use additional Cambridge Educational Services materials and official ACT • PLAN • EXPLORE tests.

10th GRADE

Sessions (30 minutes each)	In-Class Lesson	6-Step Approach	Materials†
Sessions 1-9	ACT DIAGNOSTIC TEST and ASSESSMENT	Step 1	Official ACT Test
Sessions 10-29	SUBJECT LESSON Science Reasoning	Step 3	• Science Reasoning Review, Problem-Solving, and Quizzes (Cambridge ACT • PLAN • EXPLORE Science Reasoning Victory Student Textbook, pp. 61, 76, 94) • Step Three Science Reasoning (Cambridge ACT • PLAN • EXPLORE Science Reasoning Victory Teacher's Guide, p. 67)
Sessions 30-35	ACT FINAL PRACTICE TEST and ASSESSMENT	Step 5	ACT Practice Test (ACT CD-ROM)
Sessions 36-41	POST-TEST REVIEW and CUSTOM STUDY PLAN	Steps 5 and 6	ACT Practice Test Explanations (ACT CD-ROM)

† The number of class sessions may be shortened by assigning remediation (Step 2) and practice drills (Step 4) as homework. To lengthen class to multi-year, use additional Cambridge Educational Services materials and official ACT • PLAN • EXPLORE tests.

INTRODUCTION

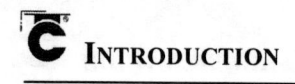

		11th GRADE		
Sessions (30 minutes each)	*In-Class Lesson*	*6-Step Approach*	*Materials†*	
Sessions 1-9	**ACT DIAGNOSTIC TEST and ASSESSMENT**	Step 1	*Official ACT Test*	
Sessions 10-39	**PRACTICE DRILLS** Science Reasoning Practice Tests and Explanations	Step 4	• ACT Science Reasoning Practice Tests I and II (untimed) (*Cambridge ACT • PLAN • EXPLORE Science Reasoning Victory Student Textbook*, Step Four) • ACT Science Reasoning Practice Tests III and IV (timed) (*Cambridge ACT • PLAN • EXPLORE Science Reasoning Victory Student Textbook*, Step Four)	
Sessions 40-85	**ACT PRACTICE TESTS and ASSESSMENT**	Step 5	*Official ACT Tests III and IV* ACT Practice Tests (*ACT CD-ROM*)	
Sessions 86-161	**POST-TEST REVIEW and CUSTOM STUDY PLAN**	Steps 5 and 6	*Official ACT Tests III and IV* Explanations ACT Practice Test Explanations (*ACT CD-ROM*)	

† The number of class sessions may be shortened by assigning remediation (Step 2) and practice drills (Step 4) as homework. To lengthen class to multi-year, use additional Cambridge Educational Services materials and official ACT • PLAN • EXPLORE tests.

ACT 10th-11th Grade Multi-Year Format

		10th GRADE		
Sessions (30 minutes each)	*In-Class Lesson*	*6-Step Approach*	*Materials†*	
Sessions 1-9	**ACT DIAGNOSTIC TEST and ASSESSMENT**	Step 1	*Official ACT Test I*	
Sessions 10-30	**SCIENCE REASONING REMEDIATION** Science Reasoning Skills Review	Step 2	• Science Skills Review (*Cambridge ACT • PLAN • EXPLORE Science Reasoning Victory Student Textbook*, Step Two)	
Sessions 31-50	**SUBJECT LESSON** Science Reasoning	Step 3	• Science Reasoning Review, Problem-Solving, and Quizzes (*Cambridge ACT • PLAN • EXPLORE Science Reasoning Victory Student Textbook*, pp. 61, 76, 94) • Step Three Science Reasoning (*Cambridge ACT • PLAN • EXPLORE Science Reasoning Victory Teacher's Guide*, p. 67)	
Sessions 51-56	**ACT FINAL PRACTICE TEST and ASSESSMENT**	Step 5	ACT Practice Test (*ACT CD-ROM*)	
Sessions 57-62	**POST-TEST REVIEW and CUSTOM STUDY PLAN**	Steps 5 and 6	ACT Practice Test Explanations (*ACT CD-ROM*)	

† The number of class sessions may be shortened by assigning remediation (Step 2) and practice drills (Step 4) as homework. To lengthen class to multi-year, use additional Cambridge Educational Services materials and official ACT tests.

ACT • PLAN • EXPLORE Science Reasoning Teacher's Guide

11th GRADE			
Sessions (30 minutes each)	*In-Class Lesson*	*6-Step Approach*	*Materials*†
Sessions 1-9	**ACT DIAGNOSTIC TEST and ASSESSMENT**	Step 1	*Official ACT Test II*
Sessions 10-39	**PRACTICE DRILLS** Science Reasoning Problems and Explanations	Step 4	• ACT Science Reasoning Practice Tests I and II (untimed) (*Cambridge ACT • PLAN • EXPLORE Science Reasoning Victory Student Textbook*, Step Four) • ACT Science Reasoning Practice Tests III and IV (timed) (*Cambridge ACT • PLAN • EXPLORE Science Reasoning Victory Student Textbook*, Step Four)
Sessions 40-85	**ACT PRACTICE TESTS and ASSESSMENT**	Step 5	*Official ACT Tests III and IV* ACT Practice Tests (*ACT CD-ROM*)
Sessions 86-161	**POST-TEST REVIEW and CUSTOM STUDY PLAN**	Steps 5 and 6	*Official ACT Tests III and IV* Explanations ACT Practice Test Explanations (*ACT CD-ROM*)

† The number of class sessions may be shortened by assigning remediation (Step 2) and practice drills (Step 4) as homework. To lengthen class to multi-year, use additional Cambridge Educational Services materials and official ACT tests.

INTRODUCTION

CAMBRIDGE
EDUCATIONAL SERVICES®

AMERICA'S #1 STANDARDS-BASED SCHOOL IMPROVEMENT

Need help customizing your Cambridge School Improvement Program?
Photocopy and fax us the following information.
(fax: 847-299-2933)

School Name: _____

Tests Covered: ☐ ACT   ☐ PLAN   ☐ EXPLORE

Please indicate course schedule(s), including class days and time and course start and end dates:

_____
_____

Total number of hours in Cambridge TestPrep™ Review Course (content hours): _____

Total class hours per week (average by week if varied): _____

Number of classes per week and minutes per class (*e.g.*, 5 classes/week, 55 minutes/class): _____

At how many locations is the course taught? _____

Are there any off-campus locations? ☐ No   ☐ Yes   If yes, how many? _____

Number of teachers per Cambridge TestPrep™ Review Course: _____

Number of Cambridge TestPrep™ Review Courses planned for your school's academic year: _____

Will elective credit be given?	☐ No	☐ Yes
Will a course grade be given?	☐ No	☐ Yes
Will any software be used?	☐ No	☐ Yes If yes, what software? _____
At home?	☐ No	☐ Yes
In school lab?	☐ No	☐ Yes
Will there be a brochure?	☐ No	☐ Yes

Will parents receive a *Course Expectations* letter (if applicable)? ☐ No   ☐ Yes

How will course information and homework be communicated to parents (if applicable)? _____

_____

How will homework progress be monitored? _____

Photocopying not allowed without Cambridge licensing agreement.

ACT • PLAN • EXPLORE SCIENCE REASONING TEACHER'S GUIDE

F. ADVERTISING AND PROMOTING YOUR COURSE: THE SUPPORT CENTER

The Cambridge Ed Support Center allows you to develop new strategies for organizing and promoting your TestPrep™ Courses.

All Cambridge Partner Schools may request a user name and login after their first order of student textbooks and teacher guides. Go to **www.CambridgeEd.com** to request a user name and ID and to login to the Support Center using your school's user name and password.

The Support Center allows you to do several things. First, you can create a customized schedule using ScheduleMaker. By providing a course start date or course finish date, ScheduleMaker will generate a customized schedule based on standard course formats. You will have a selection of possible formats—from short, simple course formats to advanced, multi-year formats.

Additionally, you will be able to view and download sample brochures and letters. These promotional materials have been used with great success by other schools and may help you improve course enrollment and course effectiveness. Included in these materials are sample letters to parents that will help you outline the goals of the course and enlist their support in holding students accountable for attendance and homework. Our studies show that students who complete assigned homework show 30 percent greater score improvements than students who do not complete assigned homework. Parents are indispensable in helping students to value and respect the TestPrep™ course that you provide.

G. TEACHER RESPONSIBILITIES AND CLASS PROCEDURES

After you have reviewed all of the Cambridge ACT • PLAN • EXPLORE TestPrep™ Review Course materials, we ask that you call Cambridge with any questions regarding the first class procedures, course format, course materials, or teacher instruction. Our Teacher Hotline number is 1-800-HIGHER ED—contact us any time you have questions, comments, or concerns. All first-time instructors are required to call the Cambridge Teacher Hotline before teaching their first class.

Instructors who call the Cambridge Teacher Hotline well in advance of their first class:

- ☎ Reduce their preparation time
- ☎ Reduce their anxiety level about the class
- ☎ Are better prepared to customize the class for their students
- ☎ Learn the latest test information and updates

We will help you with:

- 👍 The Cambridge Six-Step Approach™ to score improvements
- 👍 Customizing material for different class schedules
- 👍 Utilizing specific formats and remediation for students who are weak in Science Reasoning
- 👍 Using skill-builders and homework forms
- 👍 Copying useful lesson outlines for students
- 👍 The P.A.L.Prep™ method of instruction

We have built a great deal of flexibility into the Cambridge ACT • PLAN • EXPLORE TestPrep™ Review Course. Our materials can be adjusted to allow for any number of test administrations (diagnostic test, midterm assessment, and final practice exams) and for any degree of basic to advanced skills review. Any questions and comments concerning changes in course presentation and coverage should be discussed in advance with Cambridge.

INTRODUCTION

Remember that we do not merely provide you with test preparation course materials but with an entire educational service, from customized courses to one-on-one teacher training.

Contact your school's ACT • PLAN • EXPLORE program administration on the day before the first class of each course to confirm class enrollment and classroom location. You will be given an enrollment roster to check attendance. It is imperative that your program administrator has an accurate attendance list to account for each set of student materials. Also, before the first class, determine where, when, and how the student materials will arrive. Unless otherwise directed by your program administrator, do not distribute materials to students who owe tuition.

Arrive at least 15 minutes early to each class to allow time for checking attendance and answering any homework questions. Collect the ACT • PLAN • EXPLORE Science Reasoning Step Four Progress Reports at the beginning of each class. If the classroom location changes, then post a notice on the door with the new location. Also, contact your program administrator for procedures on how to return unused sets of student materials.

You must notify your program administrator at least two weeks before a class absence. The Cambridge ACT • PLAN • EXPLORE TestPrep™ Review Course is a short, cumulative review—this means that it is very important for *you* to teach every class. If more than one teacher instructs a course, it is difficult both for students to adjust to different teaching styles and for a teacher to satisfactorily answer questions about another instructor's lesson.

H. TEACHING CAMBRIDGE TESTPREP™

1. FIRST CLASS PROCEDURES

Depending on the course length, the first class will consist of either the administration of a Diagnostic Test or the presentation of the ACT • PLAN • EXPLORE Science Reasoning lesson. Whichever format, always begin the first class with an introduction to the ACT, PLAN, and EXPLORE; the *Cambridge ACT • PLAN • EXPLORE Science Reasoning Victory Student Textbook*; and the Cambridge ACT • PLAN • EXPLORE TestPrep™ Review Course. Remind students that they are responsible for test registration.

Your overview of the Cambridge ACT • PLAN • EXPLORE TestPrep™ Review Course should include the order and coverage of in-class lessons, what students can expect from you and the course, and what you expect from the students, such as attendance and completed homework assignments. Introduce the different parts of the *Cambridge ACT • PLAN • EXPLORE Science Reasoning Victory Student Textbook*: Step One: Diagnostic Testing and Assessment Service (Diagnostic Pre-Test), Step Two: Skills Review (Science Skills Review), Step Three: Problem-Solving, Concepts, and Strategies (Science Reasoning lesson), Step Four: Practice Test Reinforcement (four simulated ACT Science Reasoning Practice Tests for assignment as homework practice drills), Step Five: Final Exam, Assessment Report, and Review (Diagnostic Post-Test), and Step Six: Personal Study Plan.

If you have classroom rules, you should review them with your students at the beginning of the first class. Do you allow eating in class? When are the class breaks? Will you tolerate students arriving late or leaving early? If grades will be given for the course, how will they be determined?

2. YOUR ROLE AS INSTRUCTOR

At this point, the success of the Cambridge ACT • PLAN • EXPLORE TestPrep™ Review Course—and the success of your students—is in your hands. Years of hands-on research and in-class experience at more than 2,000 schools nationwide have proven the quality and effectiveness of Cambridge TestPrep PLUS™. As a TestPrep™ instructor, you make the connection between our test preparation materials, the classroom lessons, and student achievement.

Your appearance and demeanor can have an effect on students, conveying your ability and professionalism. Commanding respect and authority through your presentation and professional manner allows you to focus on the materials at hand.

3. CLASSROOM LESSONS

Although shorter courses (less than 36 hours) may only focus on Step Three: Problem-Solving, Concepts, and Strategies and assign Step Two: Skills Review and Step Four: Practice Test Reinforcement as homework, most semester-long and multi-year courses will cover all steps in class.

With Step One: Diagnostic Testing and Assessment Service, you administer and proctor the official ACT, PLAN, or EXPLORE diagnostic test. After devoting time to review of skills based on the pre-test results, you may return to the official test, using the Cambridge Unofficial Guide to the Official Test™ explanation guide to aid you. Using the official test as a teaching tool links students' work with the real test.

During Step Two: Skills Review, you will review the basic skills and content that are being tested by the exam. The lessons and exercises in the Science Skills Review help students to build and retain the skills they will need when taking the ACT. The Science Skills Review has a review section of the core content on the ACT. Oftentimes this may be what you have taught or are already teaching in your curriculum. These lessons merely boil down the test to its essentials and offer review exercises that are presented in a similar format to the test. These exercises help students become capable of exhibiting their learned knowledge on the test when confronted with this content in the test format. In most cases, you will want to spend part of the class reviewing the concept lessons and part of the class reviewing the material through the use of these exercises.

During Step Three: Problem-Solving, Concepts, and Strategies, you will review the concepts and skills tested by the exam, demonstrate key points and strategies using illustrative "Review" questions, work through difficult "Problem-Solving" items with students, and administer short, simulated "Quizzes." These problems are located in Sections One, Two, and Three, respectively, of the Step Three lesson in the *Cambridge ACT • PLAN • EXPLORE Science Reasoning Victory Student Textbook*; problem explanations and related materials are in the Science Reasoning lesson's corresponding Step Three *Cambridge ACT • PLAN • EXPLORE Science Reasoning Victory Teacher's Guide* chapter. Also, take time to answer any questions that students may have regarding the materials and homework assignments—it is important to address the questions in addition to reviewing all of the course materials in the allotted time.

With Step Four: Practice Test Reinforcement, you will have students complete the four ACT Science Reasoning Practice Tests contained in the *Cambridge ACT • PLAN • EXPLORE Science Reasoning Victory Student Textbook*. Each test should be completed in one sitting so that students learn to work through all of the problems at once. Plan on spending two class sessions reviewing each test, or twice the amount of time given for each test. Before focusing entirely on pacing and timing, first let students learn to answer as many questions correctly as possible by not setting time limits for the first two practice tests. Then, however, have students complete ACT Science Reasoning Practice Tests III and IV with the prescribed time restrictions so that they can learn the necessity of proper pacing. This step is vital to help students learn how to effectively apply their knowledge.

Step Five: Final Exam, Assessment Report, and Review, like Step One, includes the administration of an official, retired ACT, PLAN, or EXPLORE test. This should be done under strict testing conditions. Here, too, you can use the official test as a teaching tool, alongside the students' data, to target students' areas of weakness and where they have a good chance of advancing to the next skill level. You should refer to the Cambridge Unofficial Guide to the Official Test™ to help you with this review.

Step Six: Personal Study Plan is typically the last class session. You should work with students, using the Step Six Study Plan provided in this teacher's guide, to identify any remaining areas of study and where to find that material in the student textbook. Here, for instance, you might tell a student who displayed weakness with Conflicting Viewpoints passages to return to the Science Skills Review in the student textbook and review the material dealing with that subject. By creating customized study plans for students, you are creating "road maps" for them to work from until the actual test.

An effective method for tying together the course materials with the exam is to draw examples from the Diagnostic Test that students take at the beginning of each course. Use these additional problems to illustrate the tested concepts, skills, and strategies that are discussed in the Science Reasoning lesson. It is much easier for students to learn new concepts and strategies when they are illustrated by using problems with which the students are already familiar.

INTRODUCTION

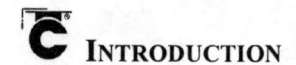

Your teaching style can have a significant impact on students' mastery of the course content. The P.A.L.Prep™ Method was designed by Cambridge to increase students' interest in and retention of the course materials by increasing in-class involvement. This highly successful method is marketed as part of the Cambridge TestPrep PLUS™ program, and we recommend that you use this teaching method in your classes, as discussed on page xxi.

4. CLASS BREAKS

Class breaks are essential for students to refresh their minds so they are better able to concentrate for the remainder of class. For a three-hour class, plan on at least one 15-minute break halfway through the class. Breaks must be structured into your class lesson plan. Do not interrupt yourself in the middle of discussing a specific point, but neither should you expect students to wait for a break until the last hour of class. Watch your students for insight—it will be obvious when a break becomes necessary!

5. HOMEWORK

As with the classroom lessons, there are many discrepancies in the content coverage of shorter courses (less than 36 hours) and longer courses. A longer course may not assign any homework from the student textbook. Rather, these courses may work through all material in the student textbook in class.

However, for shorter courses, it cannot be stressed enough how important it is for students to complete the homework assignments. Simply attending class will not prepare students for the exam—they must practice the content, concepts, and strategies that are reviewed in class. The homework assignments are practice drills of two designs: timed and untimed problem-solving using the four ACT Science Reasoning Practice Tests in Step Four of the *Cambridge ACT • PLAN • EXPLORE Science Reasoning Victory Student Textbook*. Untimed practice drills using problems from ACT Science Reasoning Practice Tests I and II allow students to review and master the materials at their own pace and to build test-taking skills and confidence. After completing untimed practice drills, problems from ACT Science Reasoning Practice Tests III and IV are used for timed practice drills. It is important for students to first master the concepts and strategies before working with time restrictions. Advanced practice using time restrictions develops the ability to work with speed and accuracy while under stress.

Another key source of homework for shorter courses is remaining material from Step Two: Skills Review in the *Cambridge ACT • PLAN • EXPLORE Science Reasoning Victory Student Textbook*. In fact, for students scoring below 50 percent on any test subject, completing the Skills Review, even as homework, is more vital to their success than completing all four practice tests. As with anything, there is a balancing act between test practice and exposure and the knowledge of the ACT core content.

The classroom lessons and homework assignments for short courses follow, and they are also repeated in Step Three of this teacher's guide. Collect the Progress Reports that correspond to each homework assignment during class to ensure the progress of your students. For longer courses, refer to the schedules that are included on pages x to xv.

ACT • PLAN • EXPLORE SCIENCE REASONING TEACHER'S GUIDE

ACT • PLAN • EXPLORE LESSONS AND HOMEWORK

CAMBRIDGE ACT • PLAN • EXPLORE TESTPREP™ REVIEW COURSE IN-CLASS LESSONS

12-Hr. Courses	18-/21-Hr. Courses	In-Class Lesson	Homework
	Session 1	**DIAGNOSTIC TEST**	Less than 50 percent correct on ACT Diagnostic Test (Science Reasoning Test): Science Skills Review (*Cambridge ACT • PLAN • EXPLORE Science Reasoning Victory Student Textbook*, Step Two)
Sessions 1-4	Sessions 2-5	**SCIENCE REASONING** • Answer any questions on homework • Science Reasoning Lesson (*Cambridge ACT • PLAN • EXPLORE Science Reasoning Victory Student Textbook*): Review (p. 61) Problem-Solving (p. 76) Quizzes (p. 94)	Any questions from the Science Reasoning Lesson not completed in class Any quizzes from the Science Reasoning Lesson not completed in class ACT Science Reasoning Practice Tests I and II (untimed) (*Cambridge ACT • PLAN • EXPLORE Science Reasoning Victory Student Textbook*, Step Four) ACT Science Reasoning Practice Tests III and IV (timed) (*Cambridge ACT • PLAN • EXPLORE Science Reasoning Victory Student Textbook*, Step Four)
	Session 6	**FINAL PRACTICE EXAM**	
	Session 7	**POST-TEST REVIEW** (Final Practice Exam or course review) (21-hour course only)	

6. P.A.L.PREP™ TEACHING METHOD

In developing the Cambridge ACT • PLAN • EXPLORE Review Course, class length and student learning levels, as well as student attention spans, have been taken into consideration. The classroom Science Reasoning lesson is divided into three separate sections: Review, Problem-Solving, and Quizzes. The design of the Science Reasoning classroom lesson will aid in keeping the presentation of the review materials fresh and interesting.

The teaching method that you employ will greatly affect student involvement and mastery of the course materials. With basic student learning modes in mind, we have developed the Cambridge P.A.L.Prep™ (Participation and Active Learning) method to keep students interested and motivated, to reinforce the course materials, and to aid you in evaluating student comprehension.

The main objective of P.A.L.Prep™ is to call on students as much as possible and to get them actively involved in the review of the course materials. Students often learn the "foreign language" of test preparation (with all of its new terminology, question-types, and answering methods) much faster by doing, feeling, and explaining, than by simply listening and taking notes. We have found that the following teaching methods are highly effective:

- Call on students in order to involve them with review questions and exercises.

- Split classes into several small groups and assign each group specific problems or exercises that illustrate problem-solving skills and techniques.

- Have student-teams "role-play" in skits to explain problem-solving terms, strategy development, and explanatory answers to the class.

Calling on students and having them work through problem sets together will create an atmosphere of increased student/teacher and student/student interaction. These interactions provide you with feedback as to how much of the review materials students understand and actually master.

Talking about a subject and teaching it to others increases one's own understanding. Having students solve questions in small groups and explain their problem-solving techniques and answers to the entire class will provide them with the chance to reiterate what they have just learned from you and to solidify the concepts in their own minds.

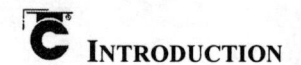

7. GRADING TESTPREP™ COURSES

If you are teaching a test preparation course that requires issuing grades, the following is a suggested formulation. Each of the four grade components is vital for assessment of student progress and improvement in student test scores.

1. Homework Assignments (HW—50 percent)
2. Attendance (A—40 percent)[*]
3. Participation (P—5 percent)
4. Quizzes (Q—5 percent)

The above percentage ratios underscore how important it is to complete homework and attend class. These ratios translate into the following formula for final grades:

$$\text{Final Grade} = 0.5(HW) + 0.4(A) + 0.05(P) + 0.05(Q)$$

For example, if a student completes 92 percent of her homework, attends 90 percent of her classes, earns a 95 percent for participation, and earns an 85 percent on her quizzes, her final grade, using the above formula, would be:

$$\text{Final Grade} = 0.5(92) + 0.4(90) + 0.05(95) + 0.05(85) = 91 \text{ percent}$$

You may want to modify this formula to suit your own needs, but do not forget to stress the importance of completing homework and attending each class.

When calculating a grade from points, convert the points to percentages and then use the formula above. For example, Russell's quiz scores are 17/20, 15/25, 10/10, and 30/40. Russell's quiz average is therefore (17 + 15 + 10 + 30) ÷ (20 + 25 + 10 + 40) = 72 ÷ 95 = 76 percent. Assuming Russell earned 8/10 points for participating, 90/95 points for homework, and 20/20 points for attendance, the four percentages for plugging into the formula are 80, 95, 100, and 76:

$$\text{Russell's Final Grade} = 0.5(95) + 0.4(100) + 0.05(80) + 0.05(76) = 95.3 \text{ percent}$$

You can modify the formula in many ways (*e.g.*, 80 percent homework and 20 percent attendance) to accommodate your class. This is only a suggested format for issuing students' grades; you can modify component percentages to best address the student population, the course format, and your teaching style. For additional ideas on how to maximize student performance, refer to "15 Key Ways to Increase Attendance and Homework Completion."

[*] If attendance is a required part of the general school curriculum, you may want to eliminate the attendance component (*e.g.*, HW—65 percent, P—25 percent, and Q—10 percent).

8. ACCOUNTABILITY

a. IN-CLASS PORTFOLIOS

If students are to succeed, they must be held accountable for their progress. Each student should have a portfolio that documents individual progress throughout the course: pre-test results; Skills Review exercises; problem-solving, concepts, and strategies problems; practice tests; and finally, post-test results. Students should only have access to their portfolios in class.

The portfolios should include Progress Reports (detailed below) that monitor homework and class work, as well as pre- and post-test score reports. For any practice tests from the student textbook that are administered in class, students should rip out the corresponding answer keys from their textbooks and keep them in their portfolios so that they are not tempted to look at the answers while completing their homework.

b. PROGRESS REPORTS

For each step, there are two sets of progress reports—one for the student and one for the instructor—located in both the student textbook and teacher's guide. For all assignments, students complete the assigned problems and correct their answers. Then, on the Student Copy of the Progress Report, they record the number of problems assigned, the number that they answered correctly, the percentage that they answered correctly, the date on which they completed the assignment, and any problems that they would like their instructor to review in class. After filling out the Student Copy, students should then transfer the information to the Instructor Copy of the Progress Report and give that report to you. For each assignment, indicate on the Instructor Copy whether the student has Mastered, Partially Mastered, or Not Mastered the material. Place the Instructor Copy in the student portfolios.

This process helps to make both students and instructors more aware of student strengths and weaknesses. In addition, you should send copies home to parents to help enlist their support and to provide them with a realistic picture of their child's knowledge and commitment.

The following chart shows how to correctly fill out the Progress Reports, using a portion of the ACT • PLAN • EXPLORE Science Reasoning Step Two Progress Report as an example.

SCIENCE SKILLS REVIEW
(Instructor Copy)

Exercise	Total # Possible	Assigned	# Correct	% Correct	Date Completed	Problem #s to Review	Mastered	Partially Mastered	Not Mastered
1. Basics of Experimental Design (p. 35)	7	7	6	86 percent	8/25	3	✓		
2. Data Organization in Controlled Experiments (p. 40)	9	9	7	78 percent	8/30	8, 9		✓	
3. Presentation of Conflicting Viewpoints (p. 43)	4	4	1	25 percent	9/3	2-4			✓

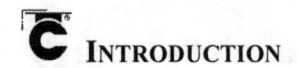

15 KEY WAYS TO INCREASE ATTENDANCE AND HOMEWORK COMPLETION

1. *Publish a brochure.* Increase course enrollments through basic advertising. Brochures demonstrate the value of Cambridge TestPrep™ Review Courses through testimonials, course synopses, and teacher qualifications.

2. *Hold admissions workshops.* Cambridge regularly assists schools in conducting college workshops entitled "How to Get Into the School of Your Choice," either in a supportive role or as an outside provider. Topics include how to get good grades and raise test scores, college applications and letters of recommendation, and the importance of extracurricular activities and job experience.

3. *Limit class size.* The ideal class size is 25 students—small enough to know the students' names and large enough to ensure an ideal cross-section of questions during the class lessons.

4. *Write a "Course Expectations" letter to parents.* Write a letter to the parents of students detailing the course expectations for students, such as class attendance and homework completion. This helps to ensure that parents support the course requirements at home and the effort necessary for improved student test scores.

5. *Sign a contract.* When parents, teachers, and students sign contracts pledging class attendance, completion of homework assignments, and in-class participation, everyone is more likely to work together.

6. *Give a Diagnostic Test Assessment.* Administer a diagnostic test at the start of each course to determine the abilities and weaknesses of each student (Step One). It can be very discouraging to a student to be placed in an ability group that is too advanced. Attendance and participation will dwindle due to such misplacements.

7. *Review basic skills.* Students in need of basic review must study the Step Two: Skills Review materials before learning the advanced concepts and test-taking strategies. Each student's Diagnostic Test Assessment will indicate if remediation is necessary.

8. *Coordinate the collection of homework.* If homework assignments are not immediately collected at the beginning of the next class, then students will assume that completing the homework is not required. At the start of each class, briefly discuss any questions on the homework and collect the ACT • PLAN • EXPLORE Science Reasoning Step Four Progress Reports for the completed homework assignment.

9. *Hold problem-solving competitions.* Healthy competition gives students concrete goals to work towards, as well as making the class lessons more fun and interesting.

10. *Make certain that parents receive accountability forms.* Keep parents informed of student progress. Many schools send copies of students' completed or blank homework accountability forms directly to the parents.

11. *Refund student tuition based on homework and attendance.* If your school does not keep 100 percent of student tuition fees, then consider issuing refunds to reward class attendance, participation, and effort on homework.

12. *Give final course letter grades.* Pass/Fail grading systems result in students putting little effort into the course other than attending classes. Therefore, reward students' effort for completing homework assignments by giving letter grades.

13. *Organize a "Show What You Know" Event.* Just before the exam testing date, organize an event at which students can showcase their course achievements. Print postcards, pencils, and banners with your slogan and invite parents to encourage the students' performance.

14. *Throw a pizza party.* Have party with food and prizes at the conclusion of the course. Give prizes for best Practice Test score, most improved course performance, perfect class attendance, most in-class participation, *etc*. Hold test preparation competitions during the party and award prizes. An end-of-course party with prizes will encourage

students' improved course performance and increased attendance at the last class, which is vital for data collection when holding your post-diagnostic test on this day.

15. *Develop personalized student study plans.* Work with students to customize their post-course study plans. These customized study plans are designed to cover the time between the last class and the actual test date. Students should focus only on those areas in which they need improvement but have a good chance of moving to the next skill level based on high, medium, low error analysis.

INTRODUCTION

THE CAMBRIDGE TOP 20 TESTPREP PLUS™ TIPS

The actual day of the test can be very stressful and hectic for students, causing even the most prepared student to forget the fundamentals of standardized test success. It is important for students to establish the proper framework for their test preparation that will carry them successfully through to the end of the test. Therefore, be sure to review with your students the following basic—but easy to forget—guidelines that we call the "Cambridge Top 20 TestPrep PLUS™ Tips." You may photocopy this sheet and distribute it to your students and their parents as an added reminder.

1. Do not minimize the importance of the ACT! Scores are used both for college admissions and for tuition scholarships; in fact, your test score will count as much as your entire four-year high school GPA. Even if you are not presently college-bound, you may later decide to go to college. Do your best on the test now, since it will only become harder as you forget many of the tested concepts and skills.

2. Even if you do not apply to college, your test score is still important. Employers oftentimes look at job applicants' test scores, as the test is a useful indicator of basic workplace skills necessary in an employee.

3. Everyone can succeed on the ACT! The test is not impossible—it is simply different from other ability indicators that you are accustomed to in school. The novelty of the standardized test is the reason for your test preparation and extensive practice. While the questions are formatted and written differently than other tests you have taken, practice using simulated and past-administered exams will provide you with the experience you need to succeed.

4. Preparation is your best weapon, so be prepared! Know your target score and what is necessary for you to reach that goal. A good test score does not entail answering every question correctly. Generally, a great test performance requires only correctly answering two or three more problems per section than on your first ACT.

5. How you decide to spend your school vacations will have a lasting influence on your future: A lot of test preparation can be done in one week or so. To ensure your success on the ACT, spend your break reviewing basic skills, solving problems, and practicing with simulated ACT Science Reasoning Practice Tests (*Cambridge ACT • PLAN • EXPLORE Science Reasoning Victory Student Textbook*, Step Four) and official past-administered exams. Pay special attention to your weakest exam subject—an entire week spent overcoming any weaknesses can dramatically increase your test score.

6. Complete your final review at least one day before the test date. By this time, you should already have completed your Customized Study Plan, so focus on the Cambridge Course Concept Outlines and Strategy Summary Sheets located at the beginning and at the end, respectively, of Step Three: Problem-Solving, Concepts, and Strategies in the *Cambridge ACT • PLAN • EXPLORE Science Reasoning Victory Student Textbook*.

7. Do not attempt any last minute cramming the night before the test. Relax, do something you enjoy, and be sure to get a full night's sleep. Gather together everything that you will need to bring to the test center, such as identification, registration verification, No. 2 pencils, calculator, *etc*. You should also get directions to the test center and plan your transportation before the day of the test.

8. Give yourself plenty of time to get ready on the day of the test. Eat a healthy, high-energy breakfast that is low in sugar. Avoid having too much, if any, caffeine the morning of the test—you do not want to "crash" in the middle of the exam.

9. On the day of the exam, report to the test center at least 10 minutes early. Furthermore, do not leave before the test proctor signals the end of the exam and collects the answer forms. If you leave early, your exam will not be scored.

10. Bring several sharpened No. 2 pencils with you to the exam. However, do not use No. 2 mechanical pencils since they are usually not dark enough. Avoid making any stray marks on your answer form. Do not forget to bring an extra eraser that will not leave smudges on your answer form. If anything besides a No. 2 pencil is used on the answer form, or if there are any interfering stray marks or eraser smudges, the scanner may score correct answers as incorrect and you will receive a lower test score.

11. Remember to bring a calculator to use during the Mathematics Test section. It is important that you bring a calculator with which you are familiar. While you should not expect to rely on your calculator—in fact, using a calculator on some problems will slow you down—it can be a useful shortcut on many questions requiring straight computations.

12. When you begin each test section, focus on that section. Do not worry about questions in previous sections that you may have answered incorrectly. You are only allowed to work on one section at a time, so focus! Furthermore, ignore your emotions during the exam. It is natural to feel anxious, frustrated, and tired during the test, but allowing these feelings to manifest has no positive benefit. Instead, focus on correctly answering every question!

13. If a particular test question is too difficult, choose an answer and immediately move on to the next item. However, do not guess blindly. First, try to eliminate one or more of the least likely answer choices; then, make an educated guess from among the remaining choices. If there is time remaining after you have attempted every problem in a section, revisit any difficult questions for which you initially guessed answers.

14. Circle your answer choices in the test booklet before darkening the answer form bubbles. Transfer your answers to the form together as a group every time you complete a group or page of problems or when the time limit for the section approaches. In addition to saving valuable test time, this method minimizes transcription errors and subsequent erasing. Of course, as the time limit approaches, transfer each answer to the form one at a time.

15. Before the time expires for a section, double-check that you have answered every question. All questions in a section count equally towards your score—you receive no more points for difficult questions than for easy questions. Therefore, try to correctly answer as many questions as possible. Since only correct answers have an effect on your ACT score, guess on the more difficult questions if necessary, but do not leave any questions unanswered.

16. Bring a watch to the exam so that you know how much time remains as you work through each section without having to rely on the test proctor.

17. Do not be tempted to copy answers from another examinee's answer form. Do not risk having your exam taken away and receiving no credit because you cheated for a few measly answers! Besides, it is likely that if you are having trouble on a particular item, then so are the other examinees. Trust your answers, not your neighbors' answers!

18. Do not be surprised or become anxious if upon first reading a question, you do not know how to answer it, or you are not even sure what the question is asking. The questions may not always be obvious, much less the answers. Read the question carefully a second time and eliminate any answers that obviously cannot be correct. Most importantly, try to remember the tested concepts and skills listed on the Strategy Summary Sheets at the end of Step Three: Problem-Solving, Concepts, and Strategies in the *Cambridge ACT • PLAN • EXPLORE Science Reasoning Victory Student Textbook*. Questions will always test one of the concepts or skills listed on the Strategy Summary Sheet.

19. It is a good idea to dress in layers. While testing rooms are notoriously cool, it is important to be able to adjust to any room conditions so that you are comfortable during the exam.

20. It is important to keep track of the remaining time and number of questions so that you record your answers as the time limit approaches and mark the last few answers one at a time. If you have worked through the entire section before the time is up, revisit any questions for which you guessed an answer.

ACT • PLAN • EXPLORE SCIENCE REASONING TEACHER'S GUIDE

CAMBRIDGE
EDUCATIONAL SERVICES®

AMERICA'S #1 STANDARDS-BASED SCHOOL IMPROVEMENT

Cambridge School Improvement Program Materials
Error Corrections, Suggestions, and Comments Form

Name/Location:_____ Day Phone:_____ E-mail Address:_____

Review Course(s): ❏ ACT ❏ CollegePrep ❏ EXPLORE ❏ GED ❏ GMAT ❏ GRE ❏ LSAT ❏ MCAT
                  ❏ PLAN ❏ PRAXIS ❏ PSAE ❏ PSAT ❏ SAT ❏ TOEFL ❏ Skills Review_____

Part of Materials: ❏ Textbook (specify step):_____ Page #:_____ Problem #:_____
                   ❏ Teacher's Guide (specify step):_____ Page #:_____ Problem #:_____
                   ❏ Test Explanations (specify year/code):_____ Page #:_____ Problem #:_____

Errors/Suggestions/Comments:_____
_____

Review Course(s): ❏ ACT ❏ CollegePrep ❏ EXPLORE ❏ GED ❏ GMAT ❏ GRE ❏ LSAT ❏ MCAT
                  ❏ PLAN ❏ PRAXIS ❏ PSAE ❏ PSAT ❏ SAT ❏ TOEFL ❏ Skills Review_____

Part of Materials: ❏ Textbook (specify step):_____ Page #:_____ Problem #:_____
                   ❏ Teacher's Guide (specify step):_____ Page #:_____ Problem #:_____
                   ❏ Test Explanations (specify year/code):_____ Page #:_____ Problem #:_____

Errors/Suggestions/Comments:_____
_____

Review Course(s): ❏ ACT ❏ CollegePrep ❏ EXPLORE ❏ GED ❏ GMAT ❏ GRE ❏ LSAT ❏ MCAT
                  ❏ PLAN ❏ PRAXIS ❏ PSAE ❏ PSAT ❏ SAT ❏ TOEFL ❏ Skills Review_____

Part of Materials: ❏ Textbook (specify step):_____ Page #:_____ Problem #:_____
                   ❏ Teacher's Guide (specify step):_____ Page #:_____ Problem #:_____
                   ❏ Test Explanations (specify year/code):_____ Page #:_____ Problem #:_____

Errors/Suggestions/Comments:_____
_____

Review Course(s): ❏ ACT ❏ CollegePrep ❏ EXPLORE ❏ GED ❏ GMAT ❏ GRE ❏ LSAT ❏ MCAT
                  ❏ PLAN ❏ PRAXIS ❏ PSAE ❏ PSAT ❏ SAT ❏ TOEFL ❏ Skills Review_____

Part of Materials: ❏ Textbook (specify step):_____ Page #:_____ Problem #:_____
                   ❏ Teacher's Guide (specify step):_____ Page #:_____ Problem #:_____
                   ❏ Test Explanations (specify year/code):_____ Page #:_____ Problem #:_____

Errors/Suggestions/Comments:_____
_____

Mail form to Cambridge Educational Services, Inc., 2720 River Road, Des Plaines, IL 60018, or fax form to 847-299-2933. For teacher's assistance, call 1-800-HIGHER-ED, or e-mail testprep@CambridgeEd.com. Visit our Web site at www.CambridgeEd.com.

Photocopying not allowed without Cambridge licensing agreement.

STEP ONE: DIAGNOSTIC TESTING AND ASSESSMENT SERVICE

CAMBRIDGE
EDUCATIONAL SERVICES

ACT • PLAN • EXPLORE
SCIENCE REASONING

STEP ONE: DIAGNOSTIC TESTING AND ASSESSMENT SERVICE

CAMBRIDGE

CERTIFICATE OF PROFICIENCY

SET OF DIAGNOSTIC TESTS AND ASSESSMENT SERVICE

CAMBRIDGE
EDUCATIONAL SERVICES®

AMERICA'S #1 STANDARDS-BASED SCHOOL IMPROVEMENT

Cambridge Course Concept Outline
STEP ONE

I. STEP ONE OVERVIEW (p. 5)

A. WHAT IS STEP ONE? (p. 5)
1. OFFICIAL ACT, PLAN, or EXPLORE TEST (p. 5)
2. ASSESSMENT REPORTS (p. 5)
   a. OFFICIAL TEST PROBLEMS MEAN VALID DATA (p. 5)
   b. CAMBRIDGE ASSESSMENT REPORTS MAKE DATA ACCESSIBLE (p. 5)
   c. STORING AND ACCESSING DATA (p. 6)

B. HOW TO USE STEP ONE AS A TEACHING TOOL (p. 6)
1. PREPARING TO TEACH STEP ONE (p. 6)
   a. KNOW THE ACT, PLAN, AND EXPLORE (p. 6)
      i. ACT TERMINOLOGY (p. 7)
      ii. WHAT IS THE STRUCTURE OF THE ACT? (p. 7)
      iii. WHAT IS THE STRUCTURE OF THE PLAN AND EXPLORE? (p. 7)
      iv. HOW IS THE ACT SCORED? (p. 8)
      v. WHAT ARE THE RULES FOR THE ACT? (p. 8)
      vi. HOW DOES THE ACT COMPARE TO THE SAT? (p. 9)
      vii. WHAT ARE THE TEST DATES AND LOCATIONS FOR THE ACT? (p. 10)
      viii. HOW DO STUDENTS REGISTER FOR THE ACT? (p. 10)
      ix. WHICH SCHOOLS REQUIRE THE ACT? (p. 10)
      x. IS THERE AN INDEX USED BY COLLEGES FOR THE ACT? (p. 10)
   b. KNOW THE TESTING AND ADMINISTRATION CONDITIONS (p. 10)
   c. ADMINISTER THE CORRECT TEST (p. 10)
2. STEP ONE CLASS SESSION: PROCTOR AN OFFICIAL ACT, PLAN OR EXPLORE (p. 11)
   a. RETURN SCANTRONS™ TO CAMBRIDGE FOR SCORING (p. 11)
   b. REVIEW LOGISTICAL TEST-TAKING TIPS (p. 11)
   c. REVIEW SCORES WITH YOUR STUDENTS (p. 12)
3. TRANSITION TO STEP TWO (p. 13)
   a. GROUP STUDENTS BY ABILITY LEVELS (p. 13)
   b. DETERMINE WHETHER SKILLS REVIEW IS NECESSARY (p. 13)
   c. HAVE STUDENTS FILL OUT PROGRESS REPORTS (p. 13)
   d. ADJUST CURRICULUM AND INSTRUCTION FOR SCHOOL IMPROVEMENT (p. 14)
   e. BUILD COMMUNITY SUPPORT: HOLD AN ADMISSIONS WORKSHOP (p. 16)

C. FAQ (p. 17)

STEP ONE

II. ACT • PLAN • EXPLORE DIAGNOSTIC PRE-TEST PROGRESS REPORTS (p. 19)

    A. ACT • PLAN EXPLORE DIAGNOSTIC PRE-TEST STUDENT PROGRESS REPORT (p. 19)

    B. ACT • PLAN EXPLORE DIAGNOSTIC PRE-TEST INSTRUCTOR PROGRESS REPORT (p. 21)

III. PROCTORING INSTRUCTIONS (p. 23)

    A. STUDENT INFORMATION NECESSARY ON ANSWER FORM (p. 23)

    B. TEST ADMINISTRATION INSTRUCTIONS AND SCRIPT (p. 24)

STEP ONE OVERVIEW

A. WHAT IS STEP ONE?

The first step of the Six-Step Approach involves gathering valid test data to diagnose student progress. Administer an official ACT, PLAN, or EXPLORE and use the results to differentiate instruction, modify curriculum, and target students' individual strengths and weaknesses.

1. OFFICIAL ACT, PLAN, or EXPLORE TEST

The pre-test is an official, retired ACT, PLAN, or EXPLORE. An official pre-test contains problems from previously administered exams. Cambridge recommends administering an official ACT, PLAN, or EXPLORE pre-test (not included with this package). If you did not order two tests (one for pre- and one for post-), you can contact your Cambridge customer service representative at 847-299-2930 to order additional official retired tests.

Each student should have his or her own copy of the test, as opposed to sharing one copy among several students. If your school cannot afford to buy an official test for every student, they can share tests at the lower grade levels only. As students get closer to the actual test date, they must experience a simulation of ALL testing conditions—including ownership of their test booklets.

2. ASSESSMENT REPORTS

a. OFFICIAL TEST PROBLEMS MEAN VALID DATA

Using unofficial problems can either make the pre-test too difficult or too simple, thereby skewing the results. Therefore, Cambridge uses only official, retired tests to generate assessment reports. If your program is using the Cambridge Assessment Service, you will have received official Cambridge Scantron™ forms that are to be submitted for machine scoring in a pre-paid overnight envelope using a pre-paid next-day air bill. The Cambridge Assessment Service scores the official tests and provides instructors with valuable data that can be used to:

- determine whether a student needs to immediately review core science skills (based on scoring less than 50 percent correct on the corresponding section of the pre-test).
- group students by ability such as high, medium, and low or low science skill sets and medium science skill sets.
- adjust curriculum and instruction according to the error analysis.

b. CAMBRIDGE ASSESSMENT REPORTS MAKE DATA ACCESSIBLE

Schools use diagnostic pre-test reports to both group students according to their ability levels in Science Reasoning and decide whether students need skills review. Teachers also use their own classroom item analyses to focus on students' strengths and weaknesses regarding particular question-types. The following is a list of the four standard assessment reports, with a brief description of what they contain and their distinct purposes.

ACT • PLAN • EXPLORE Student Summary (page one of two): The student summary indicates the number of right, wrong, and omitted problems. It gives a score and general item descriptor. This summary is used to diagnose whether a student needs to complete the Step Two: Skills Review. It also indicates a student's relative strengths and weaknesses and provides a snapshot of the level at which he or she has tested.

ACT • PLAN • EXPLORE Student Summary Item Analysis (page two of two): The item analysis report indicates the student's individual response to each question. Many times, a student will think that he or she has performed better on the exam than what has been assessed by the computer—given the coding of the answer sheet. Time spent coding problems, mental exhaustion, cheating, or a lack of sustained effort are all made evident by examining this report. We recommend that this report be mailed to each student's parents. It is an excellent communication piece for parents so that they can realistically assess their son or daughter's performance on the exam. Parents may determine the necessary additional steps that can be taken at home in order to achieve the desired score for entrance to the college of their choice and qualify for scholarships.

ACT • PLAN • EXPLORE Instructor Summary: The instructor summary shows how individual students performed on the pre-test. In addition to providing the class average, this report can also be used to compare different classes, spot overall trends, and determine what adjustments must be made in order to meet the desired goals. After the Step Five post-test, you will receive a second instructor summary report that shows how students have improved from pre- to post-test.

ACT • PLAN • EXPLORE Error Analysis: The error analysis is perhaps the most important scientific report available to test preparation. This report not only determines the specific problems with which students performed the most poorly, but it also relates the specific incorrect answer choices that were most frequently chosen by these students. Rather than simply explaining the correct answer choice to students, greater results are obtained by also showing them why their most frequently chosen incorrect answer choice ("distractor") is wrong. The report lists each test problem number and a corresponding percentage of students who chose each of the given answer choices. In order to prevent these trends from reoccurring, teachers should focus on problems (as they pertain to each ability level) that students answered incorrectly but could have answered correctly had they concentrated their efforts a little bit more.

In addition, for locations ordering more than 150 student sets, your program reports include:

ACT • PLAN • EXPLORE High, Medium, and Low Error Analysis: Data is grouped according to three levels: high, medium, and low. Students within each group tend to make the same types of errors as other students within that same group. By targeting specific problems within a specific group, school improvement can be accomplished more easily and on a more widespread and permanent basis. In addition, it makes the most sense to target frequently missed problems that skills (low) students, average (medium) students, and gifted (high) students can get right. If 90 percent of your students get a particular problem wrong, skills students will have the greatest difficulty getting this problem correct regardless of what measures are taken. These problems are targeted for gifted students who should be capable of getting all of them correct.

c. STORING AND ACCESSING DATA

Your school can store all of its site data and retrieve it twice or more per year by using Cambridge Data Warehousing (25¢ per student). This service enables programs to compare data from year to year in order to implement the proper multi-year school improvement model. All changes to curriculum and instruction must be carefully tracked on a year-to-year basis by means of individual student progress reports in all of the standards-based skill set areas. In addition, the aggregation and disaggregation of existing and new data can help your school spot trends, conduct gap analyses, and better meet state standards and NCLB requirements.

B. HOW TO USE STEP ONE AS A TEACHING TOOL

1. PREPARING TO TEACH STEP ONE

Become familiar with the actual test, testing procedures, and the administration of the ACT, PLAN, or EXPLORE. Consult your Cambridge Assessment Service instructions to determine which of the two official tests you should use as the pre-test.

a. KNOW THE ACT, PLAN, AND EXPLORE

Before you administer the diagnostic pre-test, familiarize yourself with the ACT, PLAN, or EXPLORE. If you have not done so already, self-administer the same official, retired ACT, PLAN, or EXPLORE that you will give to your students. Be sure to note passages, problems, and questions that will help indicate key skills and problem-solving techniques that are needed on the test. If you do this ahead of time, when you receive the assessment reports, you will be prepared to compare your students' test results with your own expectations of what areas need the most attention. While your actual score does not need to be disclosed, your students will feel more confident if their instructor, unlocking the "secrets" of the test, has taken the same version.

OVERVIEW

The following several pages summarize the most important things that you and your students need to know about the logistics of the ACT, PLAN, and EXPLORE. At the beginning of the course, review this material with your students.

i. ACT TERMINOLOGY

The ACT Assessment is a battery of four tests that examinees generally take on one of five dates in the spring. The four tests are English, Mathematics, Reading, and Science Reasoning. All questions are multiple-choice and the answers are entered on a special answer form. The purpose of the ACT is to allow for comparison of the preparation and ability of applicants from different backgrounds who are applying to an undergraduate program; it is generally considered indicative of an applicant's potential for academic success. The newest addition to the ACT Assessment is the ACT Writing Test, which is an optional test that will be administered beginning in the 2004–2005 school year as part of the English subtest.

The PLAN is the 10th grade version of the ACT that provides a midpoint review of students' progress toward their educational and career goals. The PLAN is a scaled-down version of the ACT (just as the PSAT is a scaled-down version of the SAT). The EXPLORE is the 8th grade version of the ACT that is designed to assess students' academic progress. In addition, the EXPLORE helps students begin to "explore" and "plan" for a wide range of available educational and career options.

The PLAN and the EXPLORE are designed to be developmentally and conceptually linked to the ACT. To reflect that continuity, the three exams include the same test sections (English, Mathematics, Reading, and Science Reasoning), though with different time restrictions and numbers of problems. Similar skills and concepts are tested by the three exams.

ii. WHAT IS THE STRUCTURE OF THE ACT?

The ACT is divided into four separately timed test sections: English, Mathematics, Reading, and Science Reasoning. All questions are presented in a format with multiple answer choices. On certain test dates, the ACT may consist of five test sections rather than four, but on these dates, the fifth test section is not scored. Instead, the extra test contains new questions that are being evaluated for possible use on future exams. The format of the ACT is detailed in the following table.

	ACT FORMAT	
Test Section	Number of Questions	Time Limit
1. English*	75 questions	45 minutes
2. Mathematics	60 questions	60 minutes
	Short Break	
3. Reading	40 questions (4 passages)	35 minutes
4. Science Reasoning	**40 questions (6-7 passages)**	**35 minutes**

*Optional 30-minute ACT Writing Test to be added to English subtest beginning in 2004–2005 school year.

iii. WHAT IS THE STRUCTURE OF THE PLAN AND EXPLORE?

The 10th grade PLAN and the 8th grade EXPLORE both have the same four test sections as the ACT. However, the time restrictions and number of questions on the PLAN and the EXPLORE are different from those on the ACT.

STEP ONE

Test Section	10th Grade PLAN		8th Grade EXPLORE	
	Number of Questions	*Time Limit*	*Number of Questions*	*Time Limit*
1. English	50 questions	30 minutes	40 questions	30 minutes
2. Mathematics	40 questions	40 minutes	30 questions	30 minutes
3. Reading	25 questions	20 minutes	30 questions	30 minutes
4. Science Reasoning	**30 questions**	**25 minutes**	**28 questions**	**30 minutes**
Additional Sections	• Interest Inventory • High School Course Information • Educational/Occupational Plan Section • Needs Assessment Profile	60-70 minutes	• Interest Inventory • Needs Assessment Profile • Plans and Background Information	45 minutes

iv. HOW IS THE ACT SCORED?

The ACT is scored on a scale of 1 (minimum) to 36 (maximum). The score is an average of the "sub-scores" for the four test sections (English, Mathematics, Reading, and Science Reasoning), each of which is scored on a 1-36 scale. The ACT score report includes the four sub-scores and the total averaged composite score.

There is not a specific "passing" ACT score. Students must contact the schools or institutions to which they are applying to determine if a minimum score is required for admission. Only the ACT score for the test date specified by the examinee will be sent to those colleges indicated on the examinee's ACT registration form.

Only correct answers affect the ACT test score—there is no penalty for incorrect answers. **Therefore, examinees should answer all questions in each test section to maximize the chances for gaining points.** However, only one answer for each question is allowed. If the scoring machine records more than one answer for a question, no credit is given for that question.

Your students' ACT scores are linked with the ACT Standards for Transition. These standards indicate what skills sets and knowledge students possess at their score level. Students scoring in the 1-12 range are at the random guessing level. Student progress is measured in the following scoring bands: 13-15; 16-19; 20-23; 24-27; 28-23; and 33-36.

Since the ACT tests curricular knowledge, it is also a good indicator of your students' knowledge of your state standards. For instance, more than 60 percent of the ACT Mathematics tests algebra and geometry, two content areas on every state standards list. So, the ACT is really measuring which state standards and skill sets are mastered and which are not.

v. WHAT ARE THE RULES FOR THE ACT?

- Work on only one test section at a time. Examinees are not allowed to work on the next section or to go back to previous sections.

- Do not cheat by looking at someone else's answer form and test booklet or by looking at notes or books. If the examiner sees an examinee doing this, the exam will be taken away. The examinee will have to leave the testing room immediately and the test score will be voided.

- Do not make any stray marks or notes on the answer form. The test booklet may be used as scratch paper—no scratch paper is provided.

- When the examiner says that time is up, stop working immediately. If an examinee continues to work, the exam will be taken away and the test score will be voided.

- Examinees are not allowed to leave the room while taking the test, except during scheduled breaks. Be prepared to sit for at least two hours at a time.

- Examinees are allowed to use a calculator only during the Mathematics Test section of the exam.

vi. HOW DOES THE ACT COMPARE TO THE SAT?

The chart on the following page provides a brief description of each test section on the ACT and SAT. It also compares the methods of scoring and the test score scales.

	ACT	SAT
English/Writing	**ACT English Test (45 Minutes)** Usage/Mechanics • 13.3 percent Punctuation • 16 percent Basic Grammar and Usage • 24 percent Sentence Structure Rhetorical Skills • 16 percent Strategies • 14.6 percent Organization • 16 percent Style **ACT Writing Test (Optional)** • Essay (30 minutes)	**SAT Writing Test (60 Minutes)** Essay (25 minutes) • 40 percent of Writing Sub-score Multiple-Choice Questions (35 minutes) • 40 percent Grammar/Usage • 20 percent Writing Process
Mathematics	**ACT Mathematics Test (60 Minutes)** Pre-Algebra (25 percent) Elementary Algebra (23.3 percent) Plane Geometry (28.3 percent) Coordinate Geometry (15 percent) Trigonometry (6.6 percent) Statistics/Probability (1.6 percent)	**SAT Mathematics Test (70 Minutes)** Algebra I (25 percent) Geometry (30 percent) Mathematical Reasoning (25 percent) Algebra II (20 percent) • Quantitative Comparison Items Eliminated • Student-Produced Responses Items Retained
Reading	**ACT Reading Test (35 Minutes)** Arts and Literature • 25 percent Prose Fiction • 25 percent Humanities (art history, music, philosophy, theater, architecture, dance, religion/ethics, literary criticism) Social Studies (25 percent) Natural Science (25 percent)	**SAT Critical Reading Test (70 Minutes)** Mixture of Long and Short Critical Reading Passages (70 percent) • Science, history, humanities, literature Sentence Completions (30 percent) • Analogy Items Eliminated
Science	**ACT Science Reasoning Test (35 Minutes)** Data Representation (37.5 percent) Research Summary (45 percent) Conflicting Viewpoints (17.5 percent)	None
Method of Scoring	The number right is scored. There is no penalty for guessing.	Scores are adjusted for guessing. Correct answers carry full weight while a chance-level penalty is applied for each incorrect answer.
Test Score Scales	ACT Composite: 1-36 (Average of 4 test scores, each worth 1-36 points)	SAT Total: 600-2400 (Sum of Writing, Mathematics, and Critical Reading test scores, each worth 200-800 points)

STEP ONE

vii. WHAT ARE THE TEST DATES AND LOCATIONS FOR THE ACT?

The ACT is administered nationally on five test dates in October, December, February, April, and June. In selected states, the ACT is also offered in late September. Visit the Cambridge Web site (**www.CambridgeEd.com**) or the official ACT Web site (**www.act.org**) for current test dates and registration deadlines.

viii. HOW DO STUDENTS REGISTER FOR THE ACT?

It is the examinee's responsibility to register for the exam by completing the registration form in the *Bulletin of Information for the ACT*. The bulletin is free and available at most high schools, colleges, universities, and public libraries. A bulletin can also be requested by mail (ACT Registration, P.O. Box 414, Iowa City, IA 52243), by phone (319-337-1270), or online (**www.act.org**). Each registration deadline is approximately four to five weeks before the test date.

ix. WHICH SCHOOLS REQUIRE THE ACT?

Colleges typically use ACT scores in making admissions decisions. In addition, college financial aid offices may use the scores to determine student eligibility for scholarships and other financial aid. Students must contact the undergraduate colleges to which they apply in order to determine whether those schools require ACT scores, have a minimum ACT score requirement, or require other tests. ACT scores are forwarded to the undergraduate colleges that the examinee selects on the ACT registration form.

x. IS THERE AN INDEX USED BY COLLEGES FOR THE ACT?

In order to ease the comparison of college applicants' GPAs and test scores, admissions committees may use an "index" that combines the GPA and test score into one number. A single index does not exist for all schools that use the ACT as part of the admissions requirements. Schools devise their own indices for combining GPAs and ACT scores.

b. KNOW THE TESTING AND ADMINISTRATION CONDITIONS

It is absolutely necessary that students take the test under actual testing conditions. An important aspect of these conditions is to administer the test in one, unbroken session. If your test prep sessions are normally scheduled for less than the required time it takes to administer the exam, arrange to hold a special long session after school or on a Saturday.

- ACT: Allow at least 3 hours (add 10-20 minutes for 1 break and proctoring time).
- PLAN: Allow at least 2 hours (add 10-20 minutes for 1 break and proctoring time).
- EXPLORE: Allow at least 2 hours (add 10-20 minutes for 1 break and proctoring time).

Be sure that you are familiar with the proctoring instructions (p. 23) and that you notify students ahead of time to bring several No. 2 pencils and an acceptable calculator. ACT defines an acceptable calculator as a four-function, scientific, or graphing calculator (see **http://www.actstudent.org/faq/answers/calculator.html** for more details on prohibited calculators).

c. ADMINISTER THE CORRECT TEST

If you are using the Cambridge Assessment Service, look at the Assessment Reports Request Form (included with your materials) to determine which of the two official tests students should take as a pre-test. It is absolutely necessary that students take the tests as they have been designated, either as a pre- or post-test. Do not administer the same test as both a pre- and post-test.

2. STEP ONE CLASS SESSION: PROCTOR AN OFFICIAL ACT, PLAN, OR EXPLORE

During the Step One class session, you will proctor an official ACT, PLAN OR EXPLORE. Use the proctoring instructions in this teacher's guide (p. 23) to administer the test. It is very important to simulate actual testing conditions as much as possible.

a. RETURN SCANTRONS™ TO CAMBRIDGE FOR SCORING

Once you have administered the test and collected the answer sheets, check to verify that all student information is correct. Missing or incomplete information will require manual inputting of data (additional charges may apply). Then, complete the Site Information page and place everything into the pre-paid FedEx envelope (or box) that has been provided. For return of your scored information within five working days, you must take this package (or arrange FedEx pickup) on the day of the test to a designated FedEx drop-off location. The package is to be shipped using overnight delivery (a pre-paid air bill is provided by Cambridge and is pre-addressed). The package will be delivered to:

Cambridge c/o Rick Hinds
3335 East Brookwood Court
Phoenix, AZ 85048

If you have any questions on testing, scoring, or scoring interpretation, please contact Cambridge at 847-299-2930 or e-mail **assessment@CambridgeEd.com**.

Before returning the completed Scantrons™ to the Cambridge Assessment Service for scoring, double-check the following items to ensure prompt processing:

- The Diagnostic Pre-Test Scantrons™ must be filled out completely by the students. Not only is it good practice, but the information is necessary to score the tests and to return assessment reports in a timely manner.

- Students often write an incorrect test administration date. Make sure that all students use the same date.

- When you ship the students' Diagnostic Pre-Test Scantrons™ to Cambridge for scoring, please include a completed Assessment Reports Request Form. If the form is either incomplete or missing, the Cambridge Assessment Service will be significantly delayed and you may incur additional charges.

b. REVIEW LOGISTICAL TEST-TAKING TIPS

A critical component of the test-taking process is filling out the answer form for machine-scored standardized tests. The test-writers report that significant points are lost strictly due to scanning errors caused by student bubbling errors. At Cambridge, we have certainly seen that this is true. For example, during an informal one-year study, we found that ACT students lost as much as three test score points due to bubbling errors.

Emphasize to your students the following points after administering the Diagnostic Pre-Test. Students should keep these points in mind during the official exam.

1. The bubble for each answer choice must be completely darkened. If the letter within the bubble can be read through the pencil mark, then it is not dark enough. Students using mechanical pencils, even with No. 2 pencil lead, often fail to press hard enough to leave a dark mark.

2. Stay within the lines.

3. When erasing pencil marks, be sure to erase the marks completely! Additional tips for marking answers:

    - Circle the answer choices in the test booklet. Towards the end of the section, or after each completed group questions, transfer the selected answers as a group to the answer form. Not only does this minimize erasing on the answer form, but it also saves time and minimizes transcription errors.

STEP ONE

✏ When changing an answer, over-darken the final answer choice after completely erasing the original mark. This extra density tends to offset the residue left from the original answer choice.

In addition, after the pre-test, review with your students the following logistical test-taking strategies:

- Code questions in the margin of the test booklet as easy or difficult before beginning to answer them. By doing so, when students are pressed for time, they can skip to questions that they are more likely to answer correctly.
- Make notes and calculations directly in the test booklet.
- Underline key words in passages.

c. REVIEW SCORES WITH YOUR STUDENTS

After you receive the results from your students' pre-test, review a few peculiarities of the ACT scaled score with them. They should be aware of the following: It is possible to answer many questions incorrectly and still get a good score. Also, answering just a few more questions correctly will raise the ACT scaled score.

On average, if students answer one additional question correctly in Science Reasoning or Reading, their total scaled score will increase by one point. If they answer two more questions correctly in Mathematics or English, their total scaled score will increase by one point. It takes only one additional correct answer in Science Reasoning or Reading because the passages in those test sections are longer and students have less time to answer the corresponding questions than they do in the Mathematics and English test sections, in which the passages/problem material is shorter.

The major difference between the ACT score and students' grades in their courses is that if they answer 50 percent of the questions correctly on the ACT, the resulting score is 18 or 19—an acceptable, although low, score. On the other hand, a score of 50 percent on a classroom test or homework is most often a failing score.

Scale	English	Math	Reading	Science	Scale
31	70	53	34	37	31
30	68 - 69	51 - 52	33	--	30
29	67	49 - 50	31 - 32	36	29
28	65 - 66	47 - 48	30	35	28
27	64	45 - 46	29	34	27
26	62 - 63	43 - 44	27 - 28	33	26
25	60 - 61	41 - 42	26	31 - 32	25
24	58 - 59	39 - 40	25	30	24
23	55 - 57	37 - 38	24	28 - 29	23
22	53 - 54	35 - 36	23	26 - 27	22
21	50 - 52	33 - 34	21 - 22	25	21
20	46 - 49	31 - 32	20	23 - 24	20
19	43 - 45	29 - 30	19	21 - 22	19
18	41 - 42	26 - 28	18	19 - 20	18
17	39 - 40	23 - 25	17	17 - 18	17
16	36 - 38	19 - 22	16	16	16
15	33 - 35	16 - 18	15	15	15
14	31 - 32	13 - 15	13 - 14	13 - 14	14
13	28 - 30	10 - 12	12	12	13
12	26 - 27	08 - 09	10 - 11	10 - 11	12
11	24 - 25	06 - 07	08 - 09	09	11
10	21 - 23	05	07	07 - 08	10

Sample ACT Scale
(Please consult the back of your test booklet for each test's specific scale.)

OVERVIEW

3. **TRANSITION TO STEP TWO**

The data from the official test will not only tell you exactly how to go about starting and completing Step Two: Skills Review, but it will also allow you to customize the entire course. Use the data to group students by ability level, determine if skills review is required, and adjust curriculum and instruction.

   a. **GROUP STUDENTS BY ABILITY LEVELS**

Grouping students by ability levels is advantageous because teachers do not have to "teach to the middle." From an administrative standpoint, this approach may not be possible and therefore only homework can be customized according to ability level. However, when at all possible, group students for science topics in either a high/low or high/medium/low format.

In an ideal world, there would be no grade levels; there would simply be high, medium, and low groups of students who have mastered various science skills. Until students had mastered certain skills, they could not advance to the next skill level. Research shows that once a student falls behind in 3rd grade reading, he or she will stay behind, and the gap will widen unless some extraordinary intervention takes place.

Although students may already be grouped according to grade level, class difficulty level, or grade point average, some of these students are placed incorrectly. Not every junior who has a grade point average that exceeds 3.5 belongs in the higher group. Many students do not perform well on multiple-choice tests that have time restrictions. They also may excel at the memorization of classroom material but struggle on a test that requires them to actually apply the knowledge that they have methodically learned. Even an honors student may be strong at math but weak in grammar, or vice-versa.

   b. **DETERMINE WHETHER SKILLS REVIEW IS NECESSARY**

As a general rule, students who answer less than 50 percent of the questions correctly on the diagnostic pre-test in Science Reasoning should be required to complete the Science Skills Review (*Cambridge ACT • PLAN • EXPLORE Science Reasoning Victory Student Textbook*, Step Two). Read the Step Two Overview for more specific instructions as to how to determine whether skills review is necessary.

   c. **HAVE STUDENTS FILL OUT PROGRESS REPORTS**

Student and instructor ACT • PLAN • EXPLORE Diagnostic Pre-Test Progress Reports are on pages 19 and 21, respectively. These progress reports are also found on pages 13 and 15 in the *Cambridge ACT • PLAN • EXPLORE Science Reasoning Victory Student Textbook*. Students should use these forms to record how many and what percentage of problems they answered correctly on the pre-test. Ask your students to transfer the information from the student copies to the instructor copies. (These directions are repeated at the top of the student progress reports.)

Collect the instructor copies from your students and indicate whether they need skills review. If they do, assign specific sections and exercises. File the reports in your students' in-class portfolios. These progress reports give students, parents, and instructors quick and accurate snapshots of students' abilities. They also help to clarify the connection between the pre-test and the rest of the course. If your school has chosen not to use the Cambridge Assessment Service, grade the diagnostic pre-tests and convert students' raw scores to scaled scores, by using the Scale Conversion Chart found on page 20 in this teacher's guide and page 14 in the student textbook.

The following portion of the ACT • PLAN • EXPLORE Diagnostic Pre-Test Progress Report demonstrates how you might complete the report for a student. **Note:** The report on the next page is only a sample. Use the reports on pages 19 and 21 in this teacher's guide.

STEP ONE

DIAGNOSTIC PRE-TEST
(Instructor Copy)

						Instructor Skill Evaluation	
Test Section	Total # Possible	# Correct	% Correct	Date Completed	Problem #s to Review	Skills Review Needed? (Y or N)	Skills Review Section and Problem Numbers Assigned
ACT, PLAN, or EXPLORE SCIENCE REASONING	40	15	38 percent	5/1/05	15, 22, 35-40	Y	Science Skills Review: Exercises 1-4

d. ADJUST CURRICULUM AND INSTRUCTION FOR SCHOOL IMPROVEMENT

Use the data from the pre-test to make important decisions about curriculum and instruction methods. Frequently, not enough time is allocated to school improvement programs. In short courses (less than 90 hours), you can treat symptoms but not solve the problem. The best way to improve overall student achievement is by lengthening the course time. This extension allows for the in-class completion of basic skills, standards-based testing points, and practice testing. The following charts show how you can use the Cambridge Six-Step Approach™ to facilitate a multi-year school improvement program.

Note: Although you are teaching an ACT • PLAN • EXPLORE program, it is still beneficial for your students to take the PSAT/NMSQT, as indicated in the chart at the end of the sophomore year, so that they have the opportunity to qualify for a National Merit Scholarship (see http://www.collegeboard.com/student/testing/psat/about.html for details about the PSAT, and http://www.nationalmerit.org/nmsp.html for details about the National Merit Scholarship Program).

OVERVIEW

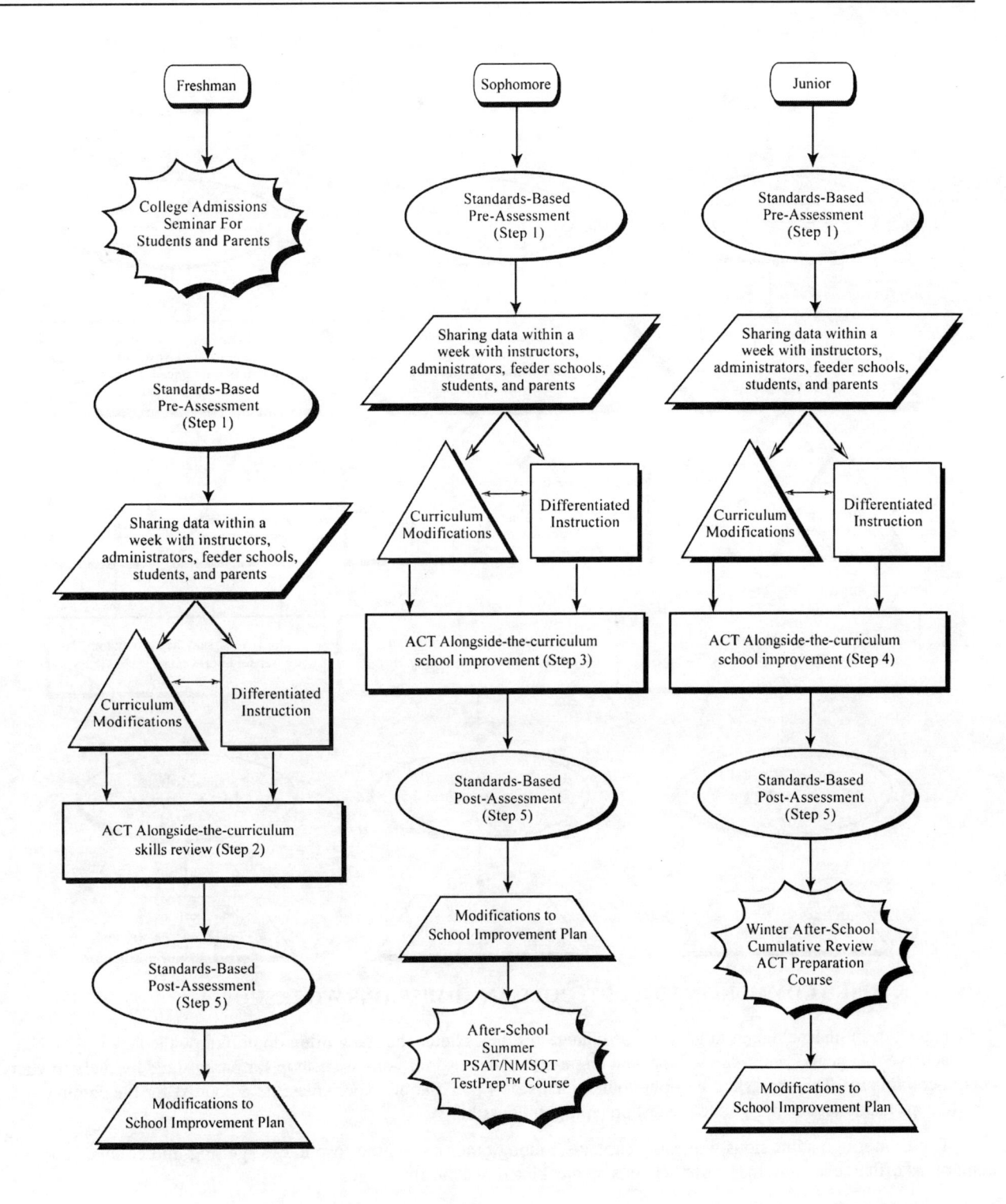

Freshman
- College Admissions Seminar For Students and Parents
- Standards-Based Pre-Assessment (Step 1)
- Sharing data within a week with instructors, administrators, feeder schools, students, and parents
- Curriculum Modifications ↔ Differentiated Instruction
- ACT Alongside-the-curriculum skills review (Step 2)
- Standards-Based Post-Assessment (Step 5)
- Modifications to School Improvement Plan

Sophomore
- Standards-Based Pre-Assessment (Step 1)
- Sharing data within a week with instructors, administrators, feeder schools, students, and parents
- Curriculum Modifications ↔ Differentiated Instruction
- ACT Alongside-the-curriculum school improvement (Step 3)
- Standards-Based Post-Assessment (Step 5)
- Modifications to School Improvement Plan
- After-School Summer PSAT/NMSQT TestPrep™ Course

Junior
- Standards-Based Pre-Assessment (Step 1)
- Sharing data within a week with instructors, administrators, feeder schools, students, and parents
- Curriculum Modifications ↔ Differentiated Instruction
- ACT Alongside-the-curriculum school improvement (Step 4)
- Standards-Based Post-Assessment (Step 5)
- Winter After-School Cumulative Review ACT Preparation Course
- Modifications to School Improvement Plan

Photocopying not allowed without Cambridge licensing agreement.

STEP ONE

```
   6th Grade              7th Grade              8th Grade
      │                      │                      │
      ▼                      ▼                      ▼
 Standards-Based       Standards-Based       Standards-Based
 Pre-Assessment        Pre-Assessment        Pre-Assessment
    (Step 1)              (Step 1)              (Step 1)
      │                      │                      │
      ▼                      ▼                      ▼
 Sharing data within a  Sharing data within a  Sharing data within a
 week with instructors, week with instructors, week with instructors,
 administrators, feeder administrators, feeder administrators, feeder
 schools, students,     schools, students,     schools, students,
 and parents            and parents            and parents
      │                      │                      │
   ┌──┴──┐                ┌──┴──┐                ┌──┴──┐
   ▼     ▼                ▼     ▼                ▼     ▼
Curriculum Differentiated Curriculum Differentiated Curriculum Differentiated
Modifications Instruction Modifications Instruction Modifications Instruction
      │     │                │     │                │     │
      ▼     ▼                ▼     ▼                ▼     ▼
 ACT Alongside-the-curriculum ACT Alongside-the-curriculum ACT Alongside-the-curriculum
 school improvement (Step 2)  school improvement (Step 3)  school improvement (Step 4)
      │                      │                      │
      ▼                      ▼                      ▼
 Standards-Based       Standards-Based       Standards-Based
 Post-Assessment       Post-Assessment       Post-Assessment
    (Step 5)              (Step 5)              (Step 5)
      │                      │                      │
      ▼                      ▼                      ▼
 Modifications to      Modifications to      Modifications to
 School Improvement    School Improvement    School Improvement
 Plan                  Plan                  Plan
```

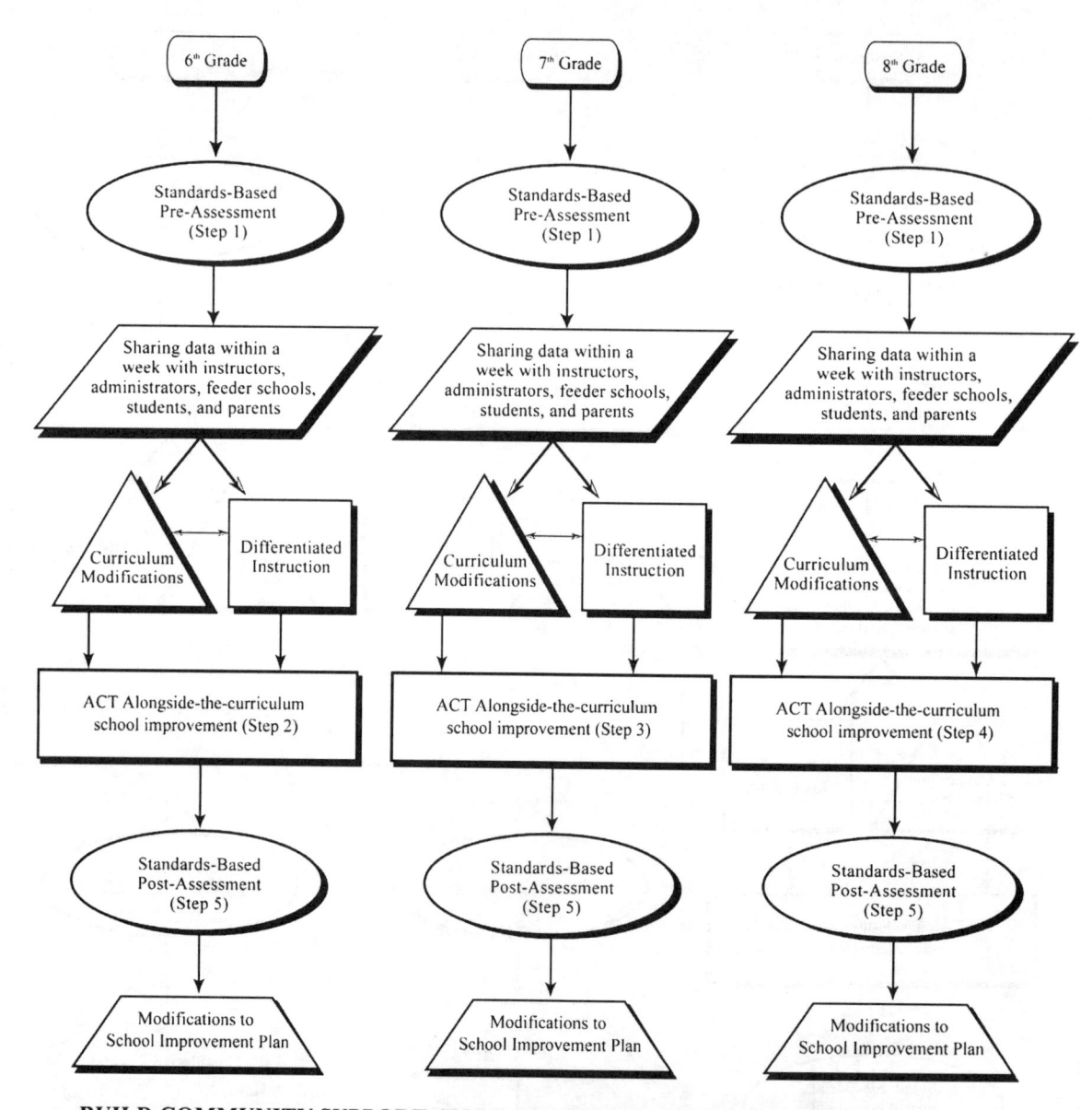

e. BUILD COMMUNITY SUPPORT: HOLD AN ADMISSIONS WORKSHOP

Parents want their children to get into the colleges of their choice, but they often do not know the best way to help them achieve this goal. Cambridge will present an on-site college admissions workshop for parents and teachers in your school community. This workshop will put your students' test preparation experience into a context for the community, which helps guarantee the most effective test prep program possible.

The Cambridge admissions workshop explains, among other issues, the formula for getting into college. College admissions offices evaluate student applications by breaking down the application:

- Grades count toward 45 percent of the evaluation.
- Test scores count toward 45 percent of the evaluation.
- Other factors (extracurricular involvement) count toward 10 percent of the evaluation.

Despite the incredible weight that is given to grades and test scores, the reality is that most students devote 90 percent of their time to other extracurricular activities. An effective test prep program makes teachers and parents aware of these circumstances so that they can all work together to create a better learning environment. Building community support is a key factor in creating a successful school improvement program.

C. FAQ

Q: *What if my program is not using the Cambridge Assessment Service?*

A: **If your program has not elected to use the Cambridge Assessment Service, it is still necessary to administer a diagnostic pre-test because it is the best way to gauge student ability levels and target differentiated instruction. Even if you are not using the assessment service, your materials should still include at least one official test. Administer the test as directed above ("Preparing to Teach Step One" and "Step One Class Session: Proctor an Official ACT, PLAN, or EXPLORE"). Students should use the Pre-Test Bubble Sheet found on page 17 of in the** *Cambridge ACT • PLAN • EXPLORE Science Reasoning Victory Student Textbook.* **After scoring the tests, use the results to group students by ability level and to allocate your in-class instruction time.**

Q: *When can I expect to receive the test results and assessment reports?*

A: **The Cambridge Assessment Service sends all results and assessment reports to instructors within one week of their receipt.**

Q: *What should I do if there appears to be a problem with the results?*

A: **Contact your Cambridge customer service representative immediately.**

Q: *Who should I contact for guidance in using the assessment data to customize my course?*

A: **For personalized advice on how to customize your course, call the Teacher Hotline at 1-800-444-4373.**

Q: *Can I receive my assessment reports electronically?*

A: **Yes. Let your customer service representative know if you would like to receive your reports electronically.**

Q: *Will Cambridge customize assessment reports?*

A: **Yes. Cambridge can generate data in a variety of customized ways, such as by gender or ethnicity. Talk to your customer service representative about getting customized reports.**

PROGRESS REPORTS

ACT • PLAN • EXPLORE
DIAGNOSTIC PRE-TEST PROGRESS REPORT
(Student Copy)

DIRECTIONS: These progress reports are designed to help you make sense of your ACT, PLAN, or EXPLORE Science Reasoning Diagnostic Pre-Test results. Complete the diagnostic pre-test and record both the number and percentage of Science Reasoning problems that you answered correctly. Refer to your Cambridge Assessment Report when recording this information if your program has elected to use the Cambridge Assessment Service. Identify the date on which you completed the Science Reasoning section of the pre-test, and list the numbers of any problems that you would like your instructor to review in class.

Transfer this information to the Instructor Copy, and then give that report to your instructor.

Name _____ Student ID _____ Date _____

DIAGNOSTIC PRE-TEST
(Student Copy)

Test Section	Total # Possible	# Correct	% Correct	Date Completed	Problem #s to Review
ACT, PLAN, or EXPLORE SCIENCE REASONING					

Photocopying not allowed without Cambridge licensing agreement.

STEP ONE

SCALE CONVERSION, DIAGNOSTIC PRE-TEST SCORE CALCULATION, AND STUDY PLAN AID
(Student Copy)

DIRECTIONS TO INSTRUCTOR: This % Correct Chart will help your students translate the number of problems that they answered correctly into an accurate representation of their abilities. Record both the number and percentage of Reading problems that your students answered correctly, circling the percentage correct in the chart below. Be sure they look under the proper column as each test section has a different number of problems. Your students will need to compare the percentage correct between each of the four ACT subject areas (assuming they took a complete, official ACT test). Help your students use this data between each subject to find the overall area on which they will need to focus more in order to improve their ACT composite performance. Students should allocate more time to the subject where they scored the lowest percentage correct and the least amount of time to the subject where they scored the highest percentage correct. Next, to determine their scaled score, have students find and record the scaled score that corresponds to the raw score that they entered below from Table 1 located in the back of the official, retired, test booklet.

Remind students to transfer this information to your instructor copy.

DIAGNOSTIC PRE-TEST SCORE CALCULATION	Total # Possible	# Correct	% Correct	Scale Score
READING Diagnostic Pre-Test				

% CORRECT CHART

Raw Score	40 Questions Total	60 Questions Total	75 Questions Total	Raw Score	40 Questions Total	60 Questions Total	75 Questions Total
1	3%	2%	1%	39	98%	65%	52%
2	5%	3%	3%	40	100%	67%	53%
3	8%	5%	4%	41		68%	55%
4	10%	7%	5%	42		70%	56%
5	13%	8%	7%	43		72%	57%
6	15%	10%	8%	44		73%	59%
7	18%	12%	9%	45		75%	60%
8	20%	13%	11%	46		77%	61%
9	23%	15%	13%	47		78%	63%
10	25%	17%	14%	48		80%	64%
11	28%	18%	15%	49		82%	65%
12	30%	20%	17%	50		83%	67%
13	33%	22%	18%	51		85%	68%
14	35%	23%	19%	52		87%	69%
15	38%	25%	20%	53		88%	71%
16	40%	27%	21%	54		90%	72%
17	43%	28%	23%	55		92%	73%
18	45%	30%	24%	56		93%	75%
19	48%	32%	25%	57		95%	76%
20	50%	33%	27%	58		97%	77%
21	53%	35%	28%	59		98%	79%
22	55%	37%	29%	60		100%	80%
23	58%	38%	31%	61			81%
24	60%	40%	32%	62			83%
25	63%	42%	33%	63			84%
26	65%	43%	35%	64			85%
27	68%	45%	36%	65			87%
28	70%	47%	37%	66			88%
29	73%	48%	39%	67			89%
30	75%	50%	40%	68			91%
31	78%	52%	41%	69			92%
32	80%	53%	43%	70			93%
33	83%	55%	44%	71			95%
34	85%	57%	45%	72			96%
35	88%	58%	47%	73			97%
36	90%	60%	48%	74			99%
37	93%	62%	49%	75			100%
38	95%	63%	51%				

ACT • PLAN • EXPLORE
DIAGNOSTIC PRE-TEST PROGRESS REPORT

(Instructor Copy)

DIRECTIONS: Transfer the information from your Student Copy to the Instructor Copy below. Leave the last two bolded columns blank. Your instructor will use them to evaluate your progress. When finished, give these reports to your instructor.

Student Name ______________________ Student ID ______________ Date ______________

DIAGNOSTIC PRE-TEST

(Instructor Copy)

						Instructor Skill Evaluation	
Test Section	*Total # Possible*	*# Correct*	*% Correct*	*Date Completed*	*Problem #s to Review*	*Skills Review Needed? (Y or N)*	*Skills Review Section and Problem Numbers Assigned*
ACT, PLAN, or EXPLORE SCIENCE REASONING							

Photocopying not allowed without Cambridge licensing agreement.

STEP ONE

SCALE CONVERSION, DIAGNOSTIC PRE-TEST SCORE CALCULATION, AND STUDY PLAN AID
(Instructor Copy)

DIAGNOSTIC PRE-TEST SCORE CALCULATION				
	Total # Possible	# Correct	% Correct	Scale Score
SCIENCE REASONING Diagnostic Pre-Test				

% CORRECT CHART

Raw Score	40 Questions Total	60 Questions Total	75 Questions Total	Raw Score	40 Questions Total	60 Questions Total	75 Questions Total
1	3%	2%	1%	39	98%	65%	52%
2	5%	3%	3%	40	100%	67%	53%
3	8%	5%	4%	41		68%	55%
4	10%	7%	5%	42		70%	56%
5	13%	8%	7%	43		72%	57%
6	15%	10%	8%	44		73%	59%
7	18%	12%	9%	45		75%	60%
8	20%	13%	11%	46		77%	61%
9	23%	15%	13%	47		78%	63%
10	25%	17%	14%	48		80%	64%
11	28%	18%	15%	49		82%	65%
12	30%	20%	17%	50		83%	67%
13	33%	22%	18%	51		85%	68%
14	35%	23%	19%	52		87%	69%
15	38%	25%	20%	53		88%	71%
16	40%	27%	21%	54		90%	72%
17	43%	28%	23%	55		92%	73%
18	45%	30%	24%	56		93%	75%
19	48%	32%	25%	57		95%	76%
20	50%	33%	27%	58		97%	77%
21	53%	35%	28%	59		98%	79%
22	55%	37%	29%	60		100%	80%
23	58%	38%	31%	61			81%
24	60%	40%	32%	62			83%
25	63%	42%	33%	63			84%
26	65%	43%	35%	64			85%
27	68%	45%	36%	65			87%
28	70%	47%	37%	66			88%
29	73%	48%	39%	67			89%
30	75%	50%	40%	68			91%
31	78%	52%	41%	69			92%
32	80%	53%	43%	70			93%
33	83%	55%	44%	71			95%
34	85%	57%	45%	72			96%
35	88%	58%	47%	73			97%
36	90%	60%	48%	74			99%
37	93%	62%	49%	75			100%
38	95%	63%	51%				

Note to Instructors: This chart has each test's student data, not just Science Reasoning, in order to show you your students' performance throughout the test and in comparison with each test subject. Ask students for a copy of all of their Step One reports to complete this chart and assign the appropriate ranking for each subject area. Assign a "1" to the subject-area that students scored the lowest percentage correct.

DIAGNOSTIC PRE-TEST SCORE CALCULATION					
	Total # Possible	# Correct	% Correct	Ranking	Scale Score
SCIENCE REASONING Diagnostic Pre-Test					
ENGLISH Diagnostic Pre-Test					
MATHEMATICS Diagnostic Pre-Test					
READING Diagnostic Pre-Test					

PROCTORING INSTRUCTIONS

Never leave the classroom during test administration. Some schools have complained that students cheat and we obviously want to prevent this from happening. The only definitive method for preventing cheating during the test is for you to never leave the room, as well as to walk up and down the rows, ensuring that students do not look ahead at the answers or work on other sections of the exam. If an examinee is caught cheating during the official exam, the test score will be voided, adversely affecting the examinee's chances of admission to college.

Marks made to Scantron™ sheets with a red pen are not recognized by the Scantron™ machine. Therefore, if you wish to omit a subject area from the pre- or post-test, you should cross it out with a red pen. Scantron™ sheets can be personalized by Cambridge ("slugging"). Teachers should never photocopy Scantron™ sheets, as they must be on a specific weight of paper. Also, no stickers or labels may be used on Scantron™ sheets.

A. STUDENT INFORMATION NECESSARY ON ANSWER FORM

After all of the students have arrived and been seated, each with several No. 2 pencils, greet the class and read the following information aloud. Everything in the following script that is in a boxed format should be read aloud to the students.

> Please clear your desk of everything except your No. 2 pencils. The answer forms will now be distributed. Do not make any marks until I give you further instructions.

Distribute the answer forms to students.

> Follow all instructions carefully. The information you provide will be used to prepare Cambridge Test Assessment Reports for you and your school's review course program. Your answer form will be scored by a computer. Fill out the answer form completely using a soft-lead No. 2 pencil. Do not use mechanical pencils, as they may not leave sufficiently dark marks to allow the computer to score accurately. Do not use ink or ballpoint pens. Fill in each block and bubble completely, making sure that all marks are dark and heavy and within the appropriate space. All errors must be thoroughly erased. Mark only one answer for each question.
>
> Now, turn to the back cover of your test booklet. Silently read these directions. Look up when you are done.

When every student has finished reading the directions, continue reading the script aloud.

> Turn your answer form to the first page, labeled *Student Information*. In the box at the top right-hand corner with three bubbles labeled *pre-test*, *mid-term*, and *post-test*, fill in the appropriate bubble. In the boxes labeled *Last Name* and *First Name*, print your last name in the blocks beneath *Last Name* and your first name in the blocks beneath *First Name*. Do not use the blocks beneath *First Name* for letters of your last name. Print as much of your name as possible, allowing one letter per block. Do not skip blocks between letters. Next, fill in the corresponding bubble below each letter of your name. If any bubbles remain after completely filling in your name, leave these bubbles empty.
>
> When you have filled in your name, take out your student ID or driver's license for confirmation of your identity.

Compare each student's identification with the class enrollment roster. After confirming the identity of each student, write your *Site ID* and *Division ID* on the chalkboard. Be sure to write these where every student can see the information. If either identification is a single number, it must be preceded by a zero.

STEP ONE

> In the box labeled *Site ID*, enter the *Site ID*: _____ (supplied by Cambridge). Fill in the corresponding bubble below each character of the *Site ID*. In the box labeled *Division ID*, enter the *Division I D*: _____ (supplied by Cambridge). Fill in the corresponding bubble below each character of the *Division ID*.
>
> In the box labeled *Zip Code*, enter the zip code of your home address. Fill in the corresponding bubble below each number of your zip code.
>
> In the box labeled *Race*, fill in the bubble that most accurately describes your cultural heritage. If you are not sure, leave this section blank.
>
> In the box labeled *Gender*, fill in the bubble that corresponds to your gender.

Next, you will ask students to record their student identification numbers. Students may use either their Social Security numbers or their academic student identification numbers. Whichever number students choose to use, they must re-enter exactly the same number on the post-test answer forms. This is important in order for accurate data-analysis and generation of the Cambridge Test Assessment Reports.

> In the box labeled *Student ID*, enter your Social Security number or your academic student identification number. Please remember the number you use for your *Student ID*, as you are required to re-enter exactly the same number on your post-test answer form. If you do not know your Social Security number or your academic student identification number, let me know and a number will be provided for you. Fill in the corresponding bubble below each number of your *Student ID*.

If you are collecting supplemental information from your students, ask them to read and respond to those questions now. Otherwise, inform students that the rest of the blocks on the first page of the answer form are to be left blank.

Proceed to the administration of the test.

B. TEST ADMINISTRATION INSTRUCTIONS AND SCRIPT

At this point, distribute the answer forms to the students if they completed the *Student Information* page before the day of the test administration. Make sure that students receive the correct forms. Additionally, every student should have several No. 2 pencils with erasers. Only No. 2 pencils are acceptable.

READ THE FOLLOWING INFORMATION ALOUD. Everything in the following script that is in a boxed format should be read aloud to the students.

> The test booklets will now be distributed. Do not open your test booklet until I tell you to do so.

Individually hand each student a test booklet—do not have students pass the test booklets back or across the desk rows. Keep an exact count of the number of test booklets distributed. After every student has received a test booklet, write the *Test & Form Code* (located at the top center portion of the test booklet cover) on the chalkboard. Make sure that every student can see the information.

> Turn your test booklet so that the front cover faces up. Find the *Test & Form Code*, which is located at the top center of the cover. Verify that it matches the code I have written on the chalkboard. In the box labeled *Test & Form Code* at the right side of the answer form cover, enter the *Test & Form Code*: _____ (located on test booklet).

Proctoring Instructions

Verify that each student has filled in the *Test & Form Code* information correctly.

> Only those responses marked on your answer form during the time allowed for that test section will be counted. I will walk around the room during the test to be sure that you are working on the correct section and are marking your answers in the correct area of the answer form. If you have a question, raise your hand for assistance rather than looking around. If you are caught looking at another student's answers, you will be expelled from the program.
>
> The use of notes, scratch paper, and foreign language or other dictionaries is not permitted.
>
> If you are wearing an alarm watch, DO NOT set the alarm, as this will cause distractions for the other students. I will keep the official time during the test administration. For each test section, I will announce when five minutes remain.
>
> Your test materials will be taken away and your test score voided if you are observed:
>
>   looking at another student's answer form or test booklet;
>   giving or receiving assistance;
>   looking back at a test section for which time has already been called; or
>   filling in answer bubbles after the time for that test section has been called.
>
> Are there any questions?

The only difference among the instructions for the ACT, the PLAN, and the EXPLORE is the length of time allowed for the Science Reasoning test section. When you read the following test instructions to your class, make sure to read the time limits that correspond to the appropriate test.

> From this time forward, there must be absolutely no talking. Listen carefully to these instructions and do not open your test booklets until I tell you to do so.
>
> Turn your answer form over and locate the section labeled **SCIENCE REASONING**. You will mark your responses to the **SCIENCE REASONING TEST** questions in this section. Mark only one answer for each question.
>
> You will have 35 (ACT), 25 (PLAN), or 30 (EXPLORE) minutes to work on the **SCIENCE REASONING TEST**. During this time, you are to work only on the **SCIENCE REASONING TEST**. If you finish before time is called, re-check your work, and then place your answer sheet inside your test booklet and close your booklet. Do not work on the previous test.

Set your timer to the appropriate time, and then say:

> You will have 35 (ACT), 25 (PLAN), or 30 (EXPLORE) minutes to work on this test. Turn to the **SCIENCE REASONING TEST**. Read the directions carefully and begin to work.

As you begin testing, record the Start, Stop, and "five minutes remaining" for the Science Reasoning Test.

Testing staff should circulate about the room and check to be sure that students are working on the correct test and marking answers appropriately. Be on the lookout for students who appear to be having difficulty with the answer sheet and/or any other directions and then intervene before too much time is lost.

REMINDER: You may post the Start and Stop times on the board; check your calculations carefully before you do so. You will read an announcement when five minutes remain on each test. Do not disturb examinees during the test session with additional verbal or written announcements of time remaining. Before you announce when five minutes remain and the Stop time, check your timer carefully against the times you have written down and verify them with the proctor (if there is one).

STEP ONE

When your watch or timer indicates that exactly 30 (ACT), 20 (PLAN), or 25 (EXPLORE) minutes have passed, and you have checked the time, say:

> You have 5 minutes remaining.

When your timer indicates that exactly 35 (ACT), 25 (PLAN), or 30 (EXPLORE) minutes have passed, and you have checked the Stop time, say:

> Please stop work. Put your pencil down and close your test booklet. I [we] will now collect your answer sheet and then your test booklet. If you put your answer sheet in your test booklet, remove it now so I [we] can collect them separately. Please remain quietly in your seats until I dismiss you.

To end the session, collect the answer sheets, test booklets, and scratch paper individually. Count the test booklets and answer sheets to verify that the number of materials distributed matches the number collected. When you are certain that all materials have been collected, dismiss the students from the testing. Depending upon your class structure, students may leave or move on to a different instructional activity. If the class session is over, remember to provide all the information that they will need for the next class—homework assignment, class meeting times, location, etc.

STEP TWO: SKILLS REVIEW

CAMBRIDGE
EDUCATIONAL SERVICES®

ACT • PLAN • EXPLORE
SCIENCE REASONING

STEP TWO: SKILLS REVIEW

CAMBRIDGE COURSE CONCEPT OUTLINE

CAMBRIDGE
EDUCATIONAL SERVICES®

AMERICA'S #1 STANDARDS-BASED SCHOOL IMPROVEMENT

Cambridge Course Concept Outline
STEP TWO

I. STEP TWO OVERVIEW (p. 33)

    A. WHAT IS STEP TWO? (p. 33)
        1. SCIENCE SKILLS REVIEW (p. 34)

    B. HOW TO USE STEP TWO AS A TEACHING TOOL (p. 34)
        1. PREPARING TO TEACH STEP TWO (p. 34)
        2. STEP TWO CLASS SESSIONS AND ASSIGNMENTS (p. 34)
            a. IN-CLASS OR AS HOMEWORK (p. 34)
            b. HAVE STUDENTS FILL OUT PROGRESS REPORTS (p. 35)
        3. TRANSITION TO STEP THREE (p. 36)

    C. FAQ (p. 36)

II. ACT • PLAN • EXPLORE SCIENCE REASONING STEP TWO PROGRESS REPORTS (p. 39)

    A. ACT • PLAN EXPLORE SCIENCE REASONING STEP TWO STUDENT PROGRESS REPORT (p. 39)

    B. ACT • PLAN EXPLORE SCIENCE REASONING STEP TWO INSTRUCTOR PROGRESS REPORT (p. 41)

III. SCIENCE REASONING SKILLS REVIEW GAMES AND ACTIVITIES (p. 43)

IV. ANSWERS AND EXPLANATIONS (p. 47)

    A. EXERCISE 1—BASICS OF EXPERIMENTAL DESIGN (p. 47)

    B. EXERCISE 2—DATA ORGANIZATION IN CONTROLLED EXPERIMENTS (p. 47)

    C. EXERCISE 3—PRESENTATION OF CONFLICTING VIEWPOINTS (p. 47)

    D. EXERCISE 4—SCIENCE REASONING PASSAGES (p. 48)

Photocopying not allowed without Cambridge licensing agreement.

STEP TWO OVERVIEW

A. WHAT IS STEP TWO?

Most students remember only a few of the standards-based skills that they have been taught over the years. In addition, due to course requirements, electives, and individual circumstances, many students either have not been exposed to such basic skills since elementary school or have not been exposed to these skills at all. For example, most students learn some grammar in early elementary school. However, 80 percent of students at the secondary level do not know how to diagram a sentence. Although part of speech is not a core skill at the secondary level, most schools realize that more than half of their students need to review basic grammar and mechanics. Even students who are taking Advanced Placement science courses may need to review certain basic science skills, and colleges are now charging tuition for remedial and basic non-credit courses.

There are vertical strands of reading, writing, mathematics, and science reasoning skills that begin in the home and continue through elementary, middle, and secondary school. Core skills, such as grammar skills, essentially never change; they only become more sophisticated. As students progress in their schooling, they learn to apply these skill sets in a variety of situations. A student in 3rd grade may read materials and understand the main idea but may not be prepared to handle implied ideas until middle school. The ACT measures core skill sets through a system called Standards for Transition.

The ACT Standards for Transition are statements that describe what students most likely possess based on their ACT score. Take some time to become familiar with these Standards for Transition and their application to your particular program of study at the following Web site: **www.act.org/standard/index.html**. The ACT Standards for Transition allows you to translate a student's score to their skill sets. Using this knowledge, you are then able to help students reach the next skill set, and a corresponding higher ACT score. The score groupings of the Standards for Transition are: 1 to 12; 13 to 15; 16 to 19; 20 to 23; 24 to 27; 28 to 32; and 33 to 36. For example, the Standards for Transition illustrate what additional skills a student in the 16 to 19 range would need to acquire in order to advance to the 20 to 23 range.

The theory behind Step Two: Skills Review is that students need to practice problems at a level in which they can get the correct answer at least 50 percent of the time. This review is a positive learning experience that builds confidence so students feel that they are able to perform at the level of the ACT, PLAN, or EXPLORE. If a student lacks competence in certain core skills, it can be extremely discouraging to his or her testing experience. In addition, advancing to the test-taking strategies that are demonstrated in Step Three: Problem-Solving, Concepts, and Strategies while some of your students are "behind before they start" is a mistake; these students are not ready to benefit from the strategies that are taught in this step.

In the *Cambridge ACT • PLAN • EXPLORE Science Reasoning Victory Student Textbook*, Step Two: Skills Review (Science Skills Review) contains problems that will enable students to do three things: 1) review material that they may have forgotten; 2) learn material that they have never learned; and 3) master specific standards-based skills that are necessary to answer the more difficult ACT, PLAN, and EXPLORE questions. Most of the problems in Step Two: Skills Review are at a skill level that is below grade level. Not only are the skills that students will learn in this step important for academic achievement, but they are also invaluable for success in the real world. In fact, these exact skills are necessary in the workplace.

The Science Skills Review lessons are designed so that you can review the material in class and have students complete the remaining exercises at home. There are explanatory answers for some of the more difficult problems. The answers and explanations appear in the back of the student textbook and in the teacher's guide at the end of Step Two: Skills Review.

The Science Skills Review contains concept lessons and corresponding review exercises. These lessons are designed to help students learn concepts and standards-based skills rather than peculiarities of the actual multiple-choice test problems. After they have mastered these core skills, students will then be able to take full advantage of the powerful test-taking strategies in Step Three of the student textbook.

Please refer to Step Two: Skills Review in the student textbook for all Skills Review lessons and exercises—they are not reproduced in this teacher's guide.

STEP TWO

1. **SCIENCE SKILLS REVIEW** (*Cambridge ACT • PLAN • EXPLORE Science Reasoning Victory Student Textbook*, Step Two)

   The Science Skills Review contains four lessons and corresponding exercises. These exercises will help students build the necessary skills to master the problem-solving, concepts, and strategies for the multiple-choice questions in the Step Three Science Reasoning lesson. Students who answer less than 50 percent of the questions correctly in the Science Reasoning section of the pre-test should complete the Science Skills Review.

   The lessons cover the following topics:
   - Basics of Experimental Design
   - Data Organization in Controlled Experiments
   - Presentation of Conflicting Viewpoints
   - Science Reasoning Passages

   Answers and explanations to the Science Skills Review are included at the end of Step Two: Skills Review in this teacher's guide.

B. HOW TO USE STEP TWO AS A TEACHING TOOL

1. PREPARING TO TEACH STEP TWO

The two most important things to consider when preparing to teach the Skills Review are:

1) student ability levels, based on the pre-test results and
2) the amount of time you have to devote to the Skills Review.

As a general rule, students who answer less than 50 percent of the questions correctly in the Science Reasoning section of their official pre-test should complete the Science Skills Review. If your program is using the Cambridge Assessment Service, simply look at the first page of the Student Summary reports, and note in which sections the students correctly answered less than one-half of the total number of possible problems. If you are not receiving individual student assessment reports, count the number of problems that students answered correctly and divide that number by the total number of problems in the Science Reasoning section in order to determine if they correctly answered less than half of the problems. The Science Reasoning test section corresponds with Step Two: Skills Review as follows:

- less than 50 percent correct in the Science Reasoning test section ⇒ Science Skills Review (*Cambridge ACT • PLAN • EXPLORE Science Reasoning Victory Student Textbook*, Step Two)

However, even if students answer more than 50 percent correct on the pre-test, they almost always need extra review in certain core skill areas (*e.g.*, line graphs). If you have students who are performing at both high and low ability levels, you may want to consider dividing up your class accordingly for at least the Step Two: Skills Review portion of the program.

It is very important that you review your students' pre-test results in detail. If you need help effectively using the pre-test results, contact your customer service representative at 847-299-2930.

2. STEP TWO CLASS SESSIONS AND ASSIGNMENTS

a. IN-CLASS OR AS HOMEWORK

Step Two: Skills Review functions properly as either in-class review tools or as homework. We recommend that you complete as much of the Skills Review as possible in class. Step Two is an important milestone in your program. All courses have unique scheduling and content concerns, but the typical class in need of skills review must spend 9-12 hours on Science Reasoning. In a shorter course, students scoring at a lower level must complete any Skills Review exercises that are not completed in class as homework. Medium- and upper-level students should complete only a portion of the necessary Skills Review exercises—for example, every other problem or every third problem in an

OVERVIEW

exercise. Sample schedules for longer courses where all steps are covered in class are located on pages x to xv in your teacher's guide.

Note: The *ACT • PLAN • EXPLORE CD-ROM* contains exercises that are especially appropriate as homework assignments, in addition to the exercises in the textbook. The Skills Review portion of the CD-ROM contains an algorithm: If students answer a question correctly, they get harder questions, and if they answer incorrectly, they get easier questions.

It is sometimes difficult to maintain a successful balance between Skills Review; Problem-Solving, Concepts, and Strategies; and Practice Test Reinforcement (Steps Two, Three, and Four, respectively). As a general rule, the lower the ability level of your students, the more important it is that you spend available time mastering Step Two, and the higher the ability level of your students, the more important it is that students complete all of Step Four. Focusing on either Step Two or Step Four in conjunction with Step Three is the best way to make sure that students reach their true potential on the ACT, PLAN, and EXPLORE.

b. HAVE STUDENTS FILL OUT PROGRESS REPORTS

Correct execution of any program is the key to its success. You should not simply assign Step Two: Skills Review exercises but also make sure that students accomplish the objective of each assigned exercise. In Step Two, it is necessary to certify that students have actually mastered particular skills. Student and instructor ACT • PLAN • EXPLORE Science Reasoning Step Two Progress Reports are on pages 39 and 41, respectively. These progress reports are also found on pages 25 and 27 in the *Cambridge ACT • PLAN • EXPLORE Science Reasoning Victory Student Textbook*. Students should use these forms to record how many and what percentage of problems they answered correctly on any Skills Review exercises that you assigned.

Ask your students to transfer the information from the student copies to the instructor copies. (These directions are repeated at the top of the student progress reports.) For each exercise that you ask your students to complete, indicate whether the students have "Mastered," "Partially Mastered," or "Not Mastered" the skill that is represented in the exercise. By checking your student's progress and evaluating their progress on the forms, you will have a clear and accurate way to:

1) hold students accountable for their progress;
2) gauge student ability levels so that you know what subject areas deserve the most attention in Step Three; and
3) monitor your own success in reviewing the material.

File these reports in your students' in-class portfolios. The progress reports give students, parents, and instructors quick and accurate snapshots of students' abilities.

The following portion of the ACT • PLAN • EXPLORE Science Reasoning Step Two Progress Report demonstrates how you might complete the report for a student. **Note:** The report below is only a sample. Use the reports on pages 39 and 41 in this teacher's guide.

STEP TWO

SCIENCE SKILLS REVIEW
(Instructor Copy)

Exercise	Total # Possible	Assigned	# Correct	% Correct	Date Completed	Problem #s to Review	Mastered	Partially Mastered	Not Mastered
1. Basics of Experimental Design (p. 35)	7	7	6	86 percent	8/25	3	✓		
2. Data Organization in Controlled Experiments (p. 40)	9	9	7	78 percent	8/30	8, 9		✓	
3. Presentation of Conflicting Viewpoints (p. 43)	4	4	1	25 percent	9/3	2-4			✓

Instructor Skill Evaluation (Check One Per Exercise)

3. TRANSITION TO STEP THREE

Step Two allows you to pinpoint your students' weakest skill areas and monitor their improvement in these specific skills. With this new information about your students, you will have a better sense of direction when you approach the heart of the course, Step Three: Problem-Solving, Concepts, and Strategies. The Science Reasoning Step Three lesson is arranged according to a list of concepts that are tested on the ACT, PLAN, and EXPLORE. When you prepare to teach Step Three, review the Cambridge Course Concept Outlines, keeping in mind which skills the students mastered and which skills they had difficulty with in Step Two. This approach will allow you to effectively and efficiently plan and schedule your Step Three lesson plans.

C. FAQ

Q: *How much time should I devote to the Skills Review?*

A: **All students and all classes perform at different levels. If time permits, you should cover the Skills Review material as long as necessary in order for your students to get up to speed with fundamental concepts. If they haven't mastered the essential skills, then they will struggle with the Step Three content lesson and not be able to take full advantage of the problem-solving strategies.**

However, if your course time is too short (less than 36 hours), Step Three is a higher priority than the Skills Review since students cannot teach themselves these question-types and strategies at home. They should, however, be able to review the core, basic skills (Skills Review) at home without the aid of a teacher. Some short courses only include a pre-test, the Step Three content lesson, and a post-test.

Q: *If my students know the material, should I skip to Step Three?*

A: **Only if all of your students correctly answered more than 50 percent of the pre-test questions in Science Reasoning.**

Q: *Should I try to teach particular skills, such as "how to interpret line graphs"?*

A: **Teach the material in the framework of broad categories. For example, if your students seem to struggle with line graphs, spend some time covering the broader topic of data organization and focus most of your time on particular points of weakness within that category. Interpreting line graphs is important but this weakness is just a symptom of an underlying curricular issue: The student has not mastered the necessary data organization skill sets.**

Q: *Should I assign and collect homework?*

A: **Yes. Simply talking about a problem in class does not imply that a student has truly learned the material. More importantly, it does not imply that they will be able to demonstrate what they know under actual testing conditions. Students should be held accountable for their progress as they work**

OVERVIEW

through Step Two: Skills Review. In addition to handing in their homework, students should complete the Step Two Progress Reports. Collect the instructor copies of the reports for the Science Skills Review and file them in your students' in-class portfolios.

PROGRESS REPORTS

ACT • PLAN • EXPLORE SCIENCE REASONING
STEP TWO PROGRESS REPORT
(Student Copy)

DIRECTIONS: These progress reports are designed to help you monitor your Science Skills Review progress. Complete the assigned problems corresponding to each Science Skills Review lesson, correct your answers, and record both the number and percentage of problems that you answered correctly. Identify the date on which you completed each exercise. List the numbers of any problems that you would like your instructor to review in class.

Transfer this information to the Instructor Copy, and then give that report to your instructor.

Name _____ Student ID _____ Date _____

SCIENCE SKILLS REVIEW
(Student Copy)

Exercise	Total # Possible	Assigned	# Correct	% Correct	Date Completed	Problem #s to Review
1. Basics of Experimental Design (p. 35)	7					
2. Data Organization in Controlled Experiments (p. 40)	9					
3. Presentation of Conflicting Viewpoints (p. 43)	4					
4. Science Reasoning Passages (p. 44)	24					

PROGRESS REPORTS

ACT • PLAN • EXPLORE SCIENCE REASONING
STEP TWO PROGRESS REPORT
(Instructor Copy)

DIRECTIONS: Transfer the information from your Student Copy to the Instructor Copy below. Leave the last three bolded columns blank. Your instructor will use them to evaluate your progress. When finished, give these reports to your instructor.

Student Name _____ Student ID _____ Date _____

SCIENCE SKILLS REVIEW
(Instructor Copy)

Exercise	Total # Possible	Assigned	# Correct	% Correct	Date Completed	Problem #s to Review	Mastered	Partially Mastered	Not Mastered
1. Basics of Experimental Design (p. 35)	7								
2. Data Organization in Controlled Experiments (p. 40)	9								
3. Presentation of Conflicting Viewpoints (p. 43)	4								
4. Science Reasoning Passages (p. 44)	24								

The last three columns are under: **Instructor Skill Evaluation (Check One Per Exercise)**

Photocopying not allowed without Cambridge licensing agreement.

SCIENCE REASONING SKILLS REVIEW GAMES AND ACTIVITIES

The following descriptions of games and activities are intended to give you ideas for supplementing the lessons and exercises in the Science Skills Review.

General Activity

The Money Game

Use this ongoing game to help students understand how important it is for them to be committed to school and the Cambridge course. Standardized test scores account for 45 percent of college application criteria (45 percent = grades, 10 percent = other factors). The more time that students dedicate to test preparation, the better they will perform on standardized tests. Moreover, an individual with a Bachelor's degree stands to earn an average income of $37,000 per year, as opposed to $21,000 per year—the average income of someone with only a high school diploma.

In order to play *The Money Game*, each student gets a certain sum of play money at the beginning of the course. As the course progresses, students earn money for their successes (*e.g.*, completing homework assignments, attending class, improvement, etc.) and lose money for lack of effort (*e.g.*, not completing homework, not attending class, etc.). At the end of the course, emphasize to students that the amount of play money they have is a kind of indication as to how successful they will be in college.

Math Games and Activities

24-Game

Reproduce the table below on a worksheet or on the board in your classroom. Students must manipulate the four numbers with mathematical operations to come up with a total of 24 in as many combinations as possible. They can use addition, subtraction, multiplication, or division. However, they must use all four numbers and use each number only once.

Examples: $5 \cdot 5 = 25$; $25 - 4 = 21$; $21 + 3 = 24$

$5 \cdot 3 = 15$; $15 + 4 = 19$; $19 + 5 = 24$

5	4
3	5

Math Baseball

Compile a list of different math problems ranging from easy to hard. Split the class into two teams. Just as in baseball, there are nine innings, with 3 outs per team, per inning. When the teams are "up to bat," one person at a time goes up to the board to answer a question. Each team picks the level of question that they would like to answer:

1 = Single (very easy), 2 = Double (easy), 3 = Triple (hard), and 4 = Home Run (very hard).

Before the game begins, set a rule whereby the batting team can only go through the batting rotation twice before it switches to the other team's turn at bat. If you do not make this type of rule, one team can stay at bat forever because they may continue to pick the easy questions.

The batting order must stay the same and once the team decides on a level of question, the person up to bat is the only one who can answer. The batter gets one chance to answer the question correctly, and if he or she answers incorrectly, it counts as an out against the team. The team with the highest score at the end of the game wins. You may decide to award a candy prize to the winning team.

Examples: Single problem: What is .015 expressed as percent?

Home run problem: If the circumference of a circle is 35 feet, what is the diameter of the circle, rounded to the nearest thousandth of a foot?

STEP TWO

Math Bingo

Create flash cards with math problems, or write problems on the chalkboard. Students must work through the problems and then cover up the spaces on their BINGO cards that contain the correct answers to the problems. In order to get BINGO, a person must have five spaces covered up in a row. The first student to get BINGO wins.

Example: 3 • 4 = 12 (cover **12** on the card)
8 • 8 = 64; (cover **64** on the card)
20 ÷ 5 = 4; (cover **4** on the card)
57 − 9 = 48 (cover **48** on the card)

B	I	N	G	O
64	14	72	9	25
18	**4**	50	36	30
56	77	**FREE**	21	20
81	144	15	**48**	49
27	16	24	6	**12**

Shopping the Sunday Circular

Have students bring in grocery store circulars from the Sunday newspaper and use them to determine price-per-unit on familiar items.

Examples: A can of corn is 16 oz. and costs 80¢. 80 ÷ 16 = 5¢ per oz.

A case of soda is $7.99; there are 24 cans in a case and 12 oz. per can. 7.99 ÷ 24 ≈ 33¢ per can, or ≈ 3¢ per oz.

Each student should create a chart with the following information:

- item
- store
- price
- volume of item
- cost per unit

Compare similar items from different stores to determine the biggest bargain.

Shopping Spree

Use department store circulars from the Sunday newspaper, or create a list of items and sales. Have students calculate the sale price of items, plus sales tax (8 percent).

Examples: Levi™ Jeans are regularly $45.00; this week they are 25 percent off. Sale price: $45.00 − (45 • .25) = $45.00 − $11.25 = $33.75.
$33.75 + (33.75 • .08) = $33.75 + $2.70 = $36.45.

Nike™ shoes are regularly $68.00; this week they are 30 percent off. Sale price: $68.00 − (68 • .30) = $68.00 − $20.40 = $47.60.
$47.60 + (47.60 • .8) = $47.60 + $3.80 = $33.32 = $51.41.

Assign a set budget and have students determine how many items they can purchase without going over the budget (*e.g.*, $150).

Online Learning Tools

FunBrain.com
- **Free** interactive math, back to school, and arcade games with cool graphics. Also includes "Diary of a Wimpy Kid," with a new entry each day—for teachers and kids

Multiplication.com
- **Free** and fun multiplication games, activities, books, resources, and worksheets

yahooligans.yahoo.com/School_Bell
- Find lots of **free** educational games
- Do a search in "just this category" for a specific subject

More Helpful Web sites

KidzOnline.org/LessonPlans

Teachnet.com

LessonPlanet.com

LessonFactory.com

ForTeachersOnly.com
- Games, activities, and teaching aides

EdHelper.com
- Worksheets and skills building

STEP TWO

ANSWERS AND EXPLANATIONS

STEP TWO: SCIENCE SKILLS REVIEW

EXERCISE 1—BASICS OF EXPERIMENTAL DESIGN (p. 35)

1. The purpose of the experiment is to <u>determine the effect of temperature on the heart rate of frogs</u>.

2. The independent variable is <u>temperature</u>. (The experimenter determined the temperature before the experiment started.)

3. The dependent variable is <u>heart rate</u>.

4. When the <u>temperature</u> is <u>increased</u>, then the <u>heart rate of the frogs</u> will <u>decrease</u>.

5. The controlled variables are <u>size, type, age, and number of frogs, as well as container size and amount of light</u>.

6. The control group is <u>Group C</u>. (Group C refers to the frogs in the container that is approximately the same temperature as the enclosure from which the frogs were removed).

7. The experimental groups are <u>Groups A, B, and D</u>.

EXERCISE 2—DATA ORGANIZATION IN CONTROLLED EXPERIMENTS (p. 40)

1. The independent variable is <u>the amount of time (in hours) over which the experiment was conducted</u>. (The experimenter determined the amount of time before the experiment was started.)

2. The dependent variable is <u>the percentage of carbohydrate digested</u>. (In the data table, the independent variable was positioned in the first column and the dependent variable in the second column. The specific variations in the amount of time and the percentage of carbohydrates digested are positioned in the rows according to the increase in time.)

3. The independent variable is on the <u>horizontal</u> axis.

4. The dependent variable is on the <u>vertical</u> axis.

5. The slope of the line indicates that generally as the amount of time <u>increases</u>, the percentage of carbohydrates digested <u>increases</u>.

6. The correct answer is (C). The slope of the graph is greatest during the four hours between the eighth hour and the twelfth hour, so the greatest amount of carbohydrate digestion occurred during this period.

7. The independent variable is <u>the source of salt</u>.

8. The dependent variable is <u>the percentage of salt</u>.

9. The mammal with a percentage of salt in its urine closest to the percentage of salt in seawater is <u>the human</u>.

EXERCISE 3—PRESENTATION OF CONFLICTING VIEWPOINTS (p. 43)

1. The dependent variable (the problem) is <u>the discovery of a dead woman</u>.

2. The conflicting viewpoint is <u>whether the death was a homicide or a suicide</u>.

3. The independent variable causing the conflict is <u>the lack of evidence indicating who shot the gun</u>.

4.

Data	More Consistent with Detective I	More Consistent with Detective II	Equally Consistent with Both Detectives I and II
Gun Owned by Woman		✓	
Bloody Pillow			✓
Bruise on Head	✓		
Firecracker-Like Noise			✓
No Forced Entry			✓
Locked Door		✓	
No Suicide Note	✓		
Divorced Victim	✓		
Despondent Victim		✓	

Photocopying not allowed without Cambridge licensing agreement.

Answers and Explanations

EXERCISE 4—SCIENCE REASONING PASSAGES (p. 44)

1. C	6. J	11. C	16. F	21. B
2. G	7. A	12. F	17. A	22. H
3. D	8. J	13. C	18. J	23. D
4. G	9. A	14. H	19. C	24. F
5. A	10. H	15. B	20. G	

STEP THREE: PROBLEM-SOLVING, CONCEPTS, AND STRATEGIES

CAMBRIDGE
EDUCATIONAL SERVICES®

ACT • PLAN • EXPLORE
SCIENCE REASONING

STEP THREE: PROBLEM-SOLVING, CONCEPTS, AND STRATEGIES

CAMBRIDGE COURSE CONCEPT OUTLINE

CAMBRIDGE EDUCATIONAL SERVICES®

AMERICA'S #1 STANDARDS-BASED SCHOOL IMPROVEMENT

Cambridge Course Concept Outline
STEP THREE

I. **STEP THREE OVERVIEW** (p. 57)

    A. **WHAT IS STEP THREE?** (p. 57)
        1. THE HEART OF THE CAMBRIDGE COURSE (p. 57)
        2. CAMBRIDGE COURSE CONCEPT OUTLINE: REVIEW, PROBLEM-SOLVING, AND QUIZZES (p. 57)

    B. **HOW TO USE STEP THREE AS A TEACHING TOOL** (p. 58)
        1. PREPARING TO TEACH STEP THREE (p. 58)
        2. STEP THREE CLASS SESSIONS AND ASSIGNMENTS (p. 58)
            a. IN-CLASS (p. 58)
            b. HOMEWORK (p. 59)
            c. HAVE STUDENTS FILL OUT PROGRESS REPORTS (p. 60)
        3. TRANSITION TO STEP FOUR (p. 61)

    C. **FAQ** (p. 61)

II. **ACT • PLAN • EXPLORE SCIENCE REASONING STEP THREE PROGRESS REPORTS** (p. 63)

    A. **ACT • PLAN EXPLORE SCIENCE REASONING STEP THREE STUDENT PROGRESS REPORT** (p. 63)

    B. **ACT • PLAN EXPLORE SCIENCE REASONING STEP THREE INSTRUCTOR PROGRESS REPORT** (p. 65)

III. **SECTION ONE—SCIENCE REASONING REVIEW** (p. 67)

    A. **SCIENCE REASONING PRELIMINARIES** (p. 67)
        1. TEACHING THE SCIENCE REASONING LESSON (p. 67)
        2. FORMATS OF THE ACT, PLAN, AND EXPLORE SCIENCE REASONING TESTS (p. 69)
        3. DIRECTIONS FOR SCIENCE REASONING PROBLEMS (p. 69)
        4. WHAT IS TESTED (p. 70)

    B. **THREE TYPES OF SCIENCE REASONING PASSAGES** (p. 70)
        1. DATA REPRESENTATION PASSAGES (p. 70)
            a. GRAPHS (p. 70)

Photocopying not allowed without Cambridge licensing agreement.

STEP THREE

             i. STRAIGHT LINES (p. 71)
             ii. PARABOLIC CURVES (p. 72)
             iii. GRAPH READING STRATEGIES (p. 72, Review Questions #1-3)
        b. TABLES (p. 73, Review Questions #4-9)
        c. TYPICAL DATA REPRESENTATION QUESTIONS
           (p. 75, Review Questions #10-14)
     2. RESEARCH SUMMARY PASSAGES (p. 76)
        a. DESIGN QUESTIONS (p. 77)
        b. PREDICTION QUESTIONS (p. 77)
        c. EVALUATION QUESTIONS (p. 77)
        d. TYPICAL RESEARCH SUMMARY QUESTIONS (p. 78, Review Questions #15-25)
     3. CONFLICTING VIEWPOINTS PASSAGES (p. 79)
        a. PREDICTION QUESTIONS (p. 79)
        b. "SPOT THE ASSUMPTIONS" QUESTIONS (p. 79)
        c. "PICK THE BEST ARGUMENT" QUESTIONS (p. 80)
        d. TYPICAL CONFLICTING VIEWPOINTS QUESTIONS
           (p. 80, Review Questions #26-36)

  C. THREE TYPES OF SCIENCE REASONING QUESTIONS (p. 82)
     1. COMPREHENSION QUESTIONS (p. 82)
     2. ANALYSIS QUESTIONS (p. 83)
     3. APPLICATION QUESTIONS (p. 83)

  D. STRATEGIES FOR THE SCIENCE REASONING TEST (p. 84)
     1. GENERAL SCIENCE REASONING STRATEGIES (p. 84)
        a. PLAN YOUR ATTACK—EASIEST PASSAGES FIRST (p. 84)
        b. DO NOT PREVIEW QUESTION STEMS BEFORE READING PASSAGE (p. 84)
        c. UNDERLINE KEY WORDS AND PHRASES (p. 84)
        d. PAY ATTENTION TO WHAT IS THERE, NOT WHAT ISN'T (p. 84)
        e. PAY ATTENTION TO DIFFERENCES (p. 85)
        f. WATCH FOR ASSUMPTIONS (p. 85)
        g. LOOK FOR TRENDS (p. 85)
        h. TRANSCRIBE ANSWERS IN GROUPS (p. 85)
     2. DATA REPRESENTATION STRATEGIES (p. 86, Review Questions #37-41)
     3. RESEARCH SUMMARY STRATEGIES (p. 86, Review Questions #42-47)
     4. CONFLICTING VIEWPOINTS STRATEGIES (p. 87, Review Questions #48-54)

IV. SECTION TWO—SCIENCE REASONING PROBLEM-SOLVING (p. 88)

  A. DATA REPRESENTATION PASSAGES (p. 88, Problem-Solving Questions #1-27)

  B. RESEARCH SUMMARY PASSAGES (p. 90, Problem-Solving Questions #28-51)

  C. CONFLICTING VIEWPOINTS PASSAGES (p. 91, Problem-Solving Questions #52-78)

V. SECTION THREE—SCIENCE REASONING QUIZZES (p. 94)

    A. **QUIZ I** (p. 94)

    B. **QUIZ II** (p. 95)

    C. **QUIZ III** (p. 95)

VI. STRATEGY SUMMARY SHEET—SCIENCE REASONING (p. 97)

OVERVIEW

STEP THREE OVERVIEW

A. WHAT IS STEP THREE?

1. THE HEART OF THE CAMBRIDGE COURSE

Problem-solving, concepts, and strategies give students ways with which to answer questions that they may not have been able to answer with their existing skill sets. Step Three: Problem-Solving, Concepts, and Strategies in the student textbook contains many problems that look like those found on the real ACT, PLAN, and EXPLORE. When compared with problems on the real tests, these problems have the same content, represent similar difficulty levels, and are solved by using the same problem-solving and alternative test-taking strategies.

Please refer to the student textbook for all Step Three: Problem-Solving, Concepts, and Strategies problems—only the corresponding Step Three lecture material and explanations appear in this teacher's guide.

2. CAMBRIDGE COURSE CONCEPT OUTLINE: REVIEW, PROBLEM-SOLVING, AND QUIZZES

The *Cambridge ACT • PLAN • EXPLORE Science Reasoning Victory Student Textbook* contains one Science Reasoning Review, Problem-Solving, and Quizzes content chapter. This chapter represents the ACT, PLAN, and/or EXPLORE Science Reasoning test section. At the beginning of the Science Reasoning content chapter, there is a Cambridge Course Concept Outline. This outline acts as a course syllabus, listing all of the concepts that are tested over a two-year testing cycle. Any single official ACT, PLAN, or EXPLORE will not necessarily test all of the given concepts in the outline. However, any of those concepts *could* appear on any given test. After each listed concept, there are references to both page numbers and accompanying student problems. There may be one or more problems used to demonstrate each concept. Difficult and/or more frequently tested concepts tend to have more accompanying student problems. If ordering more than 150 students sets, use the data on your Cambridge Assessment Service Error Analysis report or your high, medium, and low error analysis report to help determine which problems need the most coverage in class.

The Science Reasoning chapter is divided into three sections:

- Section One: Review
- Section Two: Problem-Solving
- Section Three: Quizzes

The problems in the Review section of the student textbook are organized to correspond with the course concept outline, and the outline includes cross-references to these specific corresponding problems in the student textbook. You will use the Review problems to teach content concepts, as well as to demonstrate problem-solving techniques and alternative test-taking strategies. There are various clusters of problems for each concept in the outline. A cluster will have either a fewer or greater number of problems depending on how frequently the problem-type appears on the real test. Although a single concept is not tested in consecutive questions on the real ACT, PLAN, and EXPLORE, Cambridge organizes the problems in clusters so that they are emphasized and reinforced. Some problems in the cluster are easier for students, while some problems may require more complex skill sets and a more sophisticated application of the test-taking strategies.

The problems in the Problem-Solving section of the student textbook are generally at a higher difficulty level, and they give students a chance to apply the problem-solving techniques and alternative test-taking strategies that they learned in the Review section. In this section, problems are distributed in a random order to simulate the presentation of problems on the real ACT, PLAN, and EXPLORE. These problems are in the upper-quartile of difficulty and they provide an excellent exercise for your advanced students.

Finally, the Quizzes section introduces the elements of timing, pacing, and representative difficulty levels for each problem-type. Once students have already mastered the concepts and strategies in the first two sections of the Science Reasoning chapter, they will then be ready to take on the added pressure of time restrictions and difficulty ranges. The ACT Science Reasoning Practice Tests in the student textbook (*Cambridge ACT • PLAN • EXPLORE Science Reasoning Victory Student Textbook*, Step Four) provide additional opportunities for students to practice the application of their conceptual knowledge, both with and without time restrictions.

STEP THREE

B. HOW TO USE STEP THREE AS A TEACHING TOOL

1. PREPARING TO TEACH STEP THREE

Before your first Step Three class session, be sure that you know the following:

- in what order you will be teaching the Review, Problem-Solving, and Quizzes Science Reasoning content chapter;
- how much time you have to teach the chapter; and
- which concepts will be most challenging for your students.

The course (and book) is designed to be flexible. With a shorter course (less than 36 hours), you should devote the majority of your class time to covering the Step Three lesson. Plan to spend greater amounts of time on those concepts that your students find the most challenging. These concepts are indicated by their pre-test results and their ACT • PLAN • EXPLORE Science Reasoning Step Two Progress Reports. Cambridge can customize a schedule for your program if you can provide the following information: the exact amount of time available for your classes; the number of teachers who are teaching Science Reasoning; and your students' starting pre-test scores. Contact your customer service representative for help with scheduling.

Review the Cambridge Course Concept Outline and lecture material before the first class session. Be sure that you are familiar not only with the necessary concepts but also with any peculiarities of the test for each problem-type. The lecture material in the Science Reasoning chapter covers everything that you need to know about the different problem-types, but it would still be beneficial for you to look back through the official ACT, PLAN, or EXPLORE to be sure that you are as familiar as possible with the types as they appear on the real tests. If this is your first time teaching this program, you should spend about two hours preparing for each hour of in-class instruction. The second time you teach the material, Cambridge recommends one hour of preparation for every one hour of class time. Thereafter, it is sufficient to spend about ten minutes reviewing the lesson plan. Of course, if the test has recently undergone a major change, even experienced master teachers must prepare for more time than is usually required.

2. STEP THREE CLASS SESSIONS AND ASSIGNMENTS

a. IN-CLASS

The Science Reasoning chapter lends itself to particular teaching methods, so be sure to read through the student textbook and the corresponding Step Three chapter in the teacher's guide before teaching the material in class. To ensure that the material is as effective as possible, put the following general teaching methods to practice for the Science Reasoning content chapter:

- Consistently remind students that there are almost always multiple ways (alternative strategies) to solve any given problem. Students do not need to master all of these ways in order to solve a particular type of problem; rather, they should find one method that works for them (*e.g.*, solving a Science Reasoning problem using a traditional approach or an alternative test-taking strategy). You will find detailed, alternative test-taking strategies in the teacher's guide lecture material.

- Many students will not feel comfortable using the same problem-solving approach for every given problem. Therefore, wherever applicable, demonstrate alternative methods to solving problems rather than having students rely solely on the traditionally accepted approach.

- Keep in mind that upper-level students usually prefer to use the traditionally accepted approach to solving a problem.

- Remember that both you and your students are often sources of alternative methods—ask students to share their problem-solving methods with the class.

- Remind students that although alternative test-taking strategies may prove effective, the most important factor in determining student success is knowledge of the curriculum; it is necessary to master the core, basic skills curriculum before any alternative test-taking strategies can have a positive impact.

- Tell students to use the "Notes and Strategies" pages in their textbooks to record their alternative test-taking strategies.

- Discourage students from using multiple sources of test preparation materials. Students often cannot sort out the content behind the test-taking strategies, and they find it easier to memorize problem-type labels. Each test prep publisher, however, refers to similar strategies with different names. Having multiple names for one strategy can result in needless confusion for students who are determined to memorize these problem-type labels.

- Discourage students from memorizing the correct answer to a particular problem that they may have seen on the pre-test, post-test, or any other official ACT, PLAN, or EXPLORE. Problems rarely appear on multiple exams. Rather than memorize particular problems and answers, students should memorize the types of problems that are being tested and the problem-solving strategies that will efficiently answer these types of problems. They should be taught that there is a distinction between simple memorization and conceptual memorization. The ability to grasp concepts and apply that knowledge to various situations is a much more effective way of learning.

- Remember that test preparation is not magic. It is not enough that students simply attend class in order to become a good test-taker. Marked improvement comes from within the curriculum. For example, a student should not attempt to memorize the "hit parade of words" that always seems to appear on a test. Publishers routinely mislead the public into thinking that the test is really this easy. However, the test-writers are far more sophisticated, and they would not allow this type of simple, verbatim memorization to lead to a high test score.

b. HOMEWORK

Step Three: Problem-Solving, Concepts, and Strategies contains specific homework assignments for courses that assign homework. In general, homework includes any or all of the following:

- any problems from the Review or Problem-Solving content lesson that are not completed in class
- any Quizzes from the content lesson that are not completed in class
- ACT Science Reasoning Practice Tests I and II problems (without time restrictions)
- ACT Science Reasoning Practice Tests III and IV problems (with time restrictions)

Modify homework assignments depending on the ability levels of your students and the amount of time that you have to cover the material in class. The first in-class priority should always be to complete the Review section of the Science Reasoning content chapter.

The chart on the following page summarizes the in-class lesson and corresponding homework assignment for shorter courses. For longer courses, refer to the schedules included on pages x to xv.

STEP THREE

(Note: ⌀ = not timed; ⏱ = timed.)

12-Hr. Courses	18-/21-Hr. Courses	In-Class Lesson	Homework
Sessions 1–4	Session 1	**DIAGNOSTIC PRE-TEST**	⌀ Less than 50 percent correct on ACT Diagnostic Test (Science Reasoning Test): Science Skills Review (*Cambridge ACT • PLAN • EXPLORE Science Reasoning Victory Student Textbook*, Step Two)
	Session 2–5	**SCIENCE REASONING** • Answer any questions on homework • Science Reasoning Lesson (*Cambridge ACT • PLAN • EXPLORE Science Reasoning Victory Student Textbook*): Review (p. 61) Problem-Solving (p. 76) Quizzes (p. 94)	⌀ Any questions from the Science Reasoning Lesson not completed in class ⏱ Any quizzes from the Science Reasoning Lesson not completed in class ⌀ ACT Science Reasoning Practice Tests I and II (untimed) (*Cambridge ACT • PLAN • EXPLORE Science Reasoning Victory Student Textbook*, Step Four) ⏱ ACT Science Reasoning Practice Tests III and IV (timed) (*Cambridge ACT • PLAN • EXPLORE Science Reasoning Victory Student Textbook*, Step Four)
	Session 6	**DIAGNOSTIC POST-TEST**	
	Session 7	**POST-TEST REVIEW** (Final Practice Exam or course review) (21-hour course only)	

c. HAVE STUDENTS FILL OUT PROGRESS REPORTS

In Step Three: Problem-Solving, Concepts, and Strategies, it is necessary to certify that students have actually mastered concepts and strategies. Student and instructor ACT • PLAN • EXPLORE Science Reasoning Step Three Progress Reports are on pages 63 and 65, respectively. These progress reports are also found on pages 55 and 57 in the *Cambridge ACT • PLAN • EXPLORE Science Reasoning Victory Student Textbook*. Students should use these forms to record the number of problems that they have completed and the percentage of problems that they have answered correctly. These reports will document student progress and make it easier to recognize exactly which specific problem-types deserve the most attention when they are taking the practice tests.

Ask your students to transfer the information from the student copies to the instructor copies. (These directions are repeated at the top of the student progress reports.) For each exercise that you ask your students to complete, indicate whether the students have "Mastered," "Partially Mastered," or "Not Mastered" the skill that is represented in the exercise. By checking your student's progress and evaluating their progress on the forms, you will have a clear and accurate way to:

1) hold students accountable for their progress;
2) gauge student ability levels so that you know what problem-types deserve the most attention in the practice tests; and
3) monitor your own success in reviewing the material.

File these reports in your students' in-class portfolios. The progress reports give students, parents, and instructors quick and accurate snapshots of students' abilities. They also help to clarify the connection between the pre-test and the rest of the course.

The following portion of the ACT • PLAN • EXPLORE Science Reasoning Step Three Progress Report demonstrates how you might complete the report for a student. **Note:** The report below is only a sample. Use the reports on pages 63 and 65 in this teacher's guide.

OVERVIEW C

ACT • PLAN • EXPLORE SCIENCE REASONING
(Instructor Copy)

Section	Total # Possible	Assigned	# Correct	% Correct	Date Completed	Problem #s to Review	Mastered	Partially Mastered	Not Mastered
1. Science Reasoning Review (p. 61)	54	30	25	83 percent	10/1	19, 24, 28	✓		
2. Science Reasoning Problem-Solving (p. 76)	78	50	39	78 percent	10/5	22-24, 38		✓	
3. Science Reasoning Quiz 1 (p. 94)	10	10	6	60 percent	10/10	7-10			✓

3. TRANSITION TO STEP FOUR

The transition between Steps Three and Four is not as distinct as the transition between Steps Two and Three. Depending on the length of your course, students may be completing practice test problems for homework at the same time that you are reviewing the Step Three: Problem-Solving, Concepts, and Strategies problems in class. For example, after completing the Science Reasoning Problem-Solving section, you may assign the problems in ACT Science Reasoning Practice Tests I and II without time restrictions. Steps Three and Four would overlap in this case. Alternatively, students may not begin to work through the practice test problems until they have completed all or most of the Step Three: Problem-Solving, Concepts, and Strategies problems. Regardless of how the transition is made, make sure that your students understand the difference between these two types of problems: The Step Three: Problem-Solving, Concepts, and Strategies problems help students learn concepts and strategies, and the Step Four: Practice Test Reinforcement problems simulate the real ACT in order, frequency, and difficulty level.

C. FAQ

Q: *Why are the strategies and explanations not included in the student textbook?*

A: We have found that it is much more effective for a teacher to deliver test prep instruction than for students to learn it on their own, as with a self-study model. Students are more likely to feel the immediate need to attend all classes, pay closer attention, and take good notes because none of the lecture material or explanations appear in the student textbook. Students who are able to study on their own may not even need test preparation classes. These same students (and perhaps their parents), however, may still possess "test anxiety." So, while the course may not be necessary to improve their Science Reasoning content knowledge, it may act in such a way that it builds and reinforces their test-taking confidence.

The ACT Science Reasoning Practice Tests in the student textbook (Step Four) include explanatory answers because they are often used as homework assignments and for additional review after the course has officially ended. If the students were not provided with explanatory answers for the practice test problems, then they would not be able to effectively review the material at home.

Q: *Should I stress the formally correct way to answer questions?*

A: Not necessarily. You should put the greatest stress on the most accurate and efficient problem-solving strategy for any given problem. After you have taught this program more than once, it will become natural to recommend different sets of problem-solving methods and strategies for your high (gifted), medium (average), and low (skills) groups. Also, the strategy that you recommend may depend on the question itself. Therefore, it may benefit students to use a more formal approach for some problems, while a less conventional alternative strategy may be the best method for others.

STEP THREE

Q: *How should I use the Strategy Summary Sheet?*

A: **The Strategy Summary Sheet appears in both the student textbook and teacher's guide at the end of Step Three: Problem-Solving, Concepts, and Strategies. The student textbook Science Reasoning chapter contains problems and answer keys but not lecture material or explanatory answers. As a result, the Strategy Summary Sheet is very important in the student textbook because it is the only place where students can find a succinct list of the important concepts and strategies for each problem-type. Emphasize to your students, however, that this sheet only provides a summary and that it is very important to take notes throughout your lecture. Direct them to the blank "Notes and Strategies" pages that can be found throughout Step Three in their textbooks.**

Q: *Should I assign and collect homework?*

A: **Yes. Whether attending college or building a resume for a job, students need to learn the necessity of perfecting what has been taught to them. To emphasize the importance of completing homework for their test prep course, remind them that college admissions departments use a formula to make decisions: 45 percent counts toward GPA, 45 percent counts toward test scores, and 10 percent counts toward "other" factors (extracurricular activities).**

Furthermore, students should be held accountable for their progress as they work through Step Three: Problem-Solving, Concepts, and Strategies. They should fill out the ACT • PLAN • EXPLORE Science Reasoning Step Three Progress Reports in addition to completing their homework. Collect the instructor copies of these reports for each chapter that you assign and file them in your students' in-class portfolios.

PROGRESS REPORTS

ACT • PLAN • EXPLORE SCIENCE REASONING
STEP THREE PROGRESS REPORT
(Student Copy)

DIRECTIONS: These progress reports are designed to help you monitor your ACT Science Reasoning Step Three progress. Complete the assigned problems corresponding to each lesson for Step Three, correct your answers, and record both the number and percentage of problems that you answered correctly. Identify the date on which you completed each exercise. List the numbers of any problems that you would like your instructor to review in class.

Transfer this information to the Instructor Copy, and then give that report to your instructor.

Name _____ Student ID _____ Date _____

ACT • PLAN • EXPLORE SCIENCE REASONING
(Student Copy)

Section	Total # Possible	Assigned	# Correct	% Correct	Date Completed	Problem #s to Review
1. Science Reasoning Review (p. 61)	54					
2. Science Reasoning Problem-Solving (p. 76)	78					
3. Science Reasoning Quiz 1 (p. 94)	10					
4. Science Reasoning Quiz 2 (p. 96)	10					
5. Science Reasoning Quiz 3 (p. 98)	11					

PROGRESS REPORTS

ACT • PLAN • EXPLORE SCIENCE REASONING
STEP THREE PROGRESS REPORT
(Instructor Copy)

DIRECTIONS: Transfer the information from your Student Copy to the Instructor Copy below. Leave the last three bolded columns blank. Your instructor will use them to evaluate your progress. When finished, give these reports to your instructor.

Student Name _____ Student ID _____ Date _____

ACT • PLAN • EXPLORE SCIENCE REASONING
(Instructor Copy)

Section	Total # Possible	Assigned	# Correct	% Correct	Date Completed	Problem #s to Review	Mastered	Partially Mastered	Not Mastered
1. Science Reasoning Review (p. 61)	54								
2. Science Reasoning Problem-Solving (p. 76)	78								
3. Science Reasoning Quiz 1 (p. 94)	10								
4. Science Reasoning Quiz 2 (p. 96)	10								
5. Science Reasoning Quiz 3 (p. 98)	11								

Columns grouped under "Instructor Skill Evaluation (Check One Per Section)": Mastered, Partially Mastered, Not Mastered

Photocopying not allowed without Cambridge licensing agreement.

SCIENCE REASONING

SECTION ONE—SCIENCE REASONING REVIEW
(*Cambridge ACT • PLAN • EXPLORE Science Reasoning Victory Student Textbook*, Step Three, p. 61)

A. SCIENCE REASONING PRELIMINARIES

1. TEACHING THE SCIENCE REASONING LESSON

This lesson plan is built on the "accordion" principle—it can expand or contract according to the time demands of your review course schedule and the learning level of your class. The most common time allocation is three hours.

Step Three of the *Cambridge ACT • PLAN • EXPLORE Science Reasoning Victory Student Textbook* includes three sections. Section One—Science Reasoning Review contains passages and questions corresponding to Section One in this Science Reasoning teacher's guide. (Students who are not familiar with the necessary basic science skills should review the Science Skills Review [*Cambridge ACT • PLAN • EXPLORE Science Reasoning Victory Student Textbook*, Step Two] before the Science Reasoning class.) Since these passages and questions are designed to illustrate and reinforce specific Science Reasoning skills and concepts, the passages and questions are not necessarily reflective of the distribution and difficulty range of questions on the Science Reasoning Test. Assign any Science Reasoning Review questions skipped in class as additional homework.

Section Two—Science Reasoning contains questions to be done after the Science Reasoning Review is completed. These questions are representative of the distribution, format, and difficulty range of questions on the ACT Science Reasoning Test. Generally, these questions will be more difficult than those on the PLAN and the EXPLORE, as these are 10th grade and 8th grade versions of the ACT, respectively. Clearly, students able to solve the ACT problems will be prepared for both the PLAN and the EXPLORE.

Both the progress of your students and the remaining class time will have an impact on how many, if any, Science Reasoning Problem-Solving questions you choose to cover in class. The explanations to the Science Reasoning Problem-Solving questions are in Section Two of this Science Reasoning teacher's guide. When deciding on how many Science Reasoning Problem-Solving questions to work through with your students, do not forget to reserve enough time to administer at least one 9-minute Science Reasoning Quiz from Section Three—Science Reasoning Quizzes.

Section Three—Science Reasoning Quizzes contains three quizzes. These quizzes are accurately timed simulations reflective of the distribution, format, and difficulty range of the passages and questions on the ACT Science Reasoning Test. The explanations to the quizzes are in Section Three of this Science Reasoning teacher's guide. Review with your students the explanations to any quiz completed in class.

Blank "Notes and Strategies" pages are provided in the *Cambridge ACT • PLAN • EXPLORE Science Reasoning Victory Student Textbook* for students to take notes. Important testing information, review concepts, and test preparation strategies are set apart in boxed format throughout the *Cambridge ACT • PLAN • EXPLORE Science Reasoning Victory Teacher's Guide*. It is vital that you review each of these important points with your students and remind them to keep their own notes, as most of the information contained in the *Cambridge ACT • PLAN • EXPLORE Science Reasoning Victory Teacher's Guide* is not included in the student textbook.

STEP THREE

🎓 ACT • PLAN • EXPLORE SCIENCE REASONING LESSON

Science Reasoning Review: Work through Section One—Science Reasoning Review (*Cambridge ACT • PLAN • EXPLORE Science Reasoning Victory Teacher's Guide*, Step Three, p. 67) and the corresponding review passages and questions (*Cambridge ACT • PLAN • EXPLORE Science Reasoning Victory Student Textbook*, Step Three, p. 61).

Science Reasoning Problem-Solving: Solve the Section Two—Science Reasoning Problem-Solving questions (*Cambridge ACT • PLAN • EXPLORE Science Reasoning Victory Student Textbook*, Step Three, p. 76) and review the answers (*Cambridge ACT • PLAN • EXPLORE Science Reasoning Victory Teacher's Guide*, Step Three, p. 88), as the remaining class time allows.

Science Reasoning Quizzes: Administer at least one 9-minute quiz from Section Three—Science Reasoning Quizzes (*Cambridge ACT • PLAN • EXPLORE Science Reasoning Victory Student Textbook*, Step Three, p. 94) and review the answers (*Cambridge ACT • PLAN • EXPLORE Science Reasoning Victory Teacher's Guide*, Step Three, p. 94).

Strategy Summary Sheet—Science Reasoning: If time allows at the end of class, discuss the Strategy Summary Sheet—Science Reasoning (*Cambridge ACT • PLAN • EXPLORE Science Reasoning Victory Student Textbook*, Step Three, p. 102 and *Cambridge ACT • PLAN • EXPLORE Science Reasoning Victory Teacher's Guide*, Step Three, p. 97).

It is important to keep track of the time while teaching the Science Reasoning lesson. Each class will have its own learning curve, so you may have to adjust in-class coverage to save time for at least one Science Reasoning Quiz. Assign any problems not completed in class as additional homework.

📬 ACT • PLAN • EXPLORE SCIENCE REASONING HOMEWORK

⏱ Any Section One—Science Reasoning Review or Section Two—Science Reasoning Problem-Solving questions not completed in class (*Cambridge ACT • PLAN • EXPLORE Science Reasoning Victory Student Textbook*, Step Three, pp. 61 and 76)

⏱ Any Skills Review exercises not completed in class (*Cambridge ACT • PLAN • EXPLORE Science Reasoning Victory Student Textbook*, Step Two, p. 31)

⏱ ACT Science Reasoning Practice Tests I and II (*Cambridge ACT • PLAN • EXPLORE Science Reasoning Victory Student Textbook*, Step Four, pp. 125 and 135)

🕒 Any quiz from Section Three—Science Reasoning Quizzes not completed in class (9 minutes each) (*Cambridge ACT • PLAN • EXPLORE Science Reasoning Victory Student Textbook*, Step Three, p. 94)

🕒 ACT Science Reasoning Practice Tests III and IV (35 minutes each) (*Cambridge ACT • PLAN • EXPLORE Science Reasoning Victory Student Textbook*, Step Four, pp. 145 and 157)

SCIENCE REASONING

2. FORMATS OF THE ACT, PLAN, AND EXPLORE SCIENCE REASONING TESTS

The ACT, the PLAN, and the EXPLORE each have four test sections: English, Mathematics, Reading, and **Science Reasoning**. All questions are multiple-choice. The ACT Science Reasoning Test typically has seven scientific discussions including diagrams, charts, tables, graphs, equations, or figures; each discussion is three to five paragraphs long and accompanied by 5-7 questions, totaling 40 questions with a 35-minute time limit. The PLAN Science Reasoning Test is 30 questions in 25 minutes; the EXPLORE Science Reasoning Test is 28 questions in 30 minutes.

TEST FORMATS

	ACT	PLAN	EXPLORE
➤ Test 1: English	75 questions 45 minutes	50 questions 30 minutes	40 questions 30 minutes
➤ Test 2: Mathematics	60 questions 60 minutes	40 questions 40 minutes	30 questions 30 minutes
➤ Test 3: Reading	40 questions 35 minutes	25 questions 20 minutes	30 questions 30 minutes
➤ **Test 4: Science Reasoning**	**40 questions 35 minutes**	**30 questions 25 minutes**	**28 questions 30 minutes**

The Science Reasoning Test is the last section of the ACT, the PLAN, and the EXPLORE, and often it is erroneously viewed as the most difficult test section. This test section will seem easier to students when they understand that most Science Reasoning questions can be directly answered based on the passage's written text, diagrams, charts, tables, graphs, equations, and/or figures. Practice with Science Reasoning questions and passages and a review of the explanations will provide students with the background necessary to conquer the Science Reasoning Test.

SCIENCE REASONING QUESTIONS TEST REASONING

Remember, the title of this test section is Science Reasoning, not Science Knowledge or Science Trivia. The importance of this is that examinees will be given all the information necessary to answer the questions in the text of the accompanying passage. Examinees must be able to reason the correct answers from the available information.

3. DIRECTIONS FOR SCIENCE REASONING PROBLEMS

Students should be familiar with the test directions so that they do not waste valuable time during the test reading directions. The following instructions for the ACT Science Reasoning Test were taken directly from the most recently administered official ACT exam. Whereas calculators are allowed for the ACT Mathematics Test, examinees are NOT permitted to use a calculator during the ACT Science Reasoning Test.

SCIENCE REASONING DIRECTIONS

There are seven passages in this test. Each passage is followed by several questions. After reading a passage, choose the best answer to each question and blacken the corresponding oval on your answer document. You may refer to the passages as often as necessary.

STEP THREE

4. WHAT IS TESTED

Science Reasoning selections include material from physics, chemistry, biology, and the physical sciences likely to be encountered in introductory college courses. The questions are answerable based on information provided in the passage; however, the questions do require a certain amount of "science reasoning" skills. While it might be beneficial for students to review past science course experiences and knowledge, it is NOT necessary.

The four subject areas from which Science Reasoning passages and questions are drawn are biology, physics, chemistry, and earth sciences. Generally, the Science Reasoning Test questions are based on three types of passages, or scientific discussions. The following is a summary of the distribution of the Science Reasoning problems.

NUMBER OF QUESTIONS PER TYPE OF PASSAGE	ACT (40 questions)	PLAN (30 questions)	EXPLORE (28 questions)
Data Representation	15	17	12
Research Summary	18	6	10
Conflicting Viewpoints	7	7	6

B. THREE TYPES OF SCIENCE REASONING PASSAGES

Each group of Science Reasoning questions asks about scientific information presented in one of three forms: 1) Data Representation, 2) Research Summary, and 3) Conflicting Viewpoints. These three types of Science Reasoning passages and the accompanying questions test an examinee's ability to understand and to draw further conclusions based on the scientific discussion.

Note to Teacher

Due to the nature of the Science Reasoning passages, you may wish to use an overhead projector with transparencies to highlight key components of the scientific discussions, diagrams, charts, tables, graphs, equations, and/or figures. This will help students to easily follow your discussion.

1. DATA REPRESENTATION PASSAGES

Graphs, charts, and tables are used in Data Representation passages. Knowledge of the general characteristics of the Data Representation type of passage helps in the analysis of these passages.

> **DATA REPRESENTATION PASSAGE FORMAT**
>
> Data Representation passages require examinees to interpret information presented in graphs, charts, and tables.

a. GRAPHS

A graph or chart is as important for what it says as for what it does not say: "a picture is worth a thousand words." A graph or chart consists not just of lines, bars, or other similar devices; it also includes a main title, categories, units, clarifying notes, and other information. These words and numbers are as important for understanding the presented information as the picture itself.

Graphs and charts are always drawn to scale. The function of a graph or chart is to present data in pictorial form, and that function cannot be fulfilled unless the picture is accurately drawn. Students should review the graphs and charts visually, without reading the actual numbers—this will save considerable time. For example, in most cases, a taller column will correspond to a greater amount than a shorter column.

IMPORTANT POINTS FOR READING GRAPHS AND CHARTS

1. Everything on a graph or chart is important. Pay attention to the titles of graphs and charts, categories, units, and other information.
2. Graphs and charts are drawn to scale. Therefore, it is possible to directly compare pictures (column sizes, pie slices, *etc.*) without actually reading the numbers.

---

i. STRAIGHT LINES

A graph with two axes represents the relationship between two variables. There may exist a direct, inverse, or constant relationship. The slope of the line, or the direction of the curve, determines the relationship. A straight line indicates a simple (linear) relationship between two variables as described by the slope-intercept form of the equation:

$$y = mx + b$$

The slope of the line is m; the y-intercept, or the y-value when x is equal to zero, is b.

If the y-intercept equals zero, then the line crosses through the origin of the coordinate system. Thus, in this case, the only difference between the y-value and the x-value is the slope of the line. Slope can be positive, negative, or zero.

A direct relationship exists when there is an increase in both variables—the slope of the line is positive:

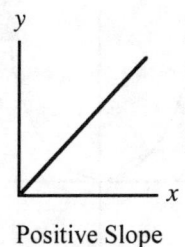

Positive Slope

An inverse relationship exists when there is an increase in one variable and a decrease in the other—the slope of the line is negative:

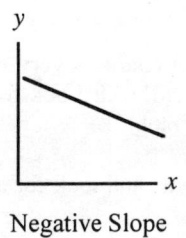

Negative Slope

A constant relationship exists when there is an increase in one variable and the other remains constant—that is, the y variable does not change no matter what the x value is. This is represented by a horizontal line and has a slope of zero.

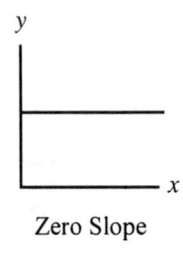

Zero Slope

SUMMARY OF STRAIGHT GRAPH LINES

1. Positive sloped lines represent direct relationships between the two variables represented on the x- and y-axes.

2. Negative sloped lines represent inverse relationships between the two variables represented on the x- and y-axes.

3. Horizontal lines have no slope and represent the relationship in which one variable remains constant, while the other increases.

---

ii. PARABOLIC CURVES

A parabola is a curve representing an equation in which one variable is equal to the square of the second variable multiplied by some constant. For example, the graph of kinetic energy as a function of velocity is plotted by setting the x-axis equal to the velocity, v, and the y-axis equal to the kinetic energy, or $K.E. = \frac{1}{2}(mv^2)$.

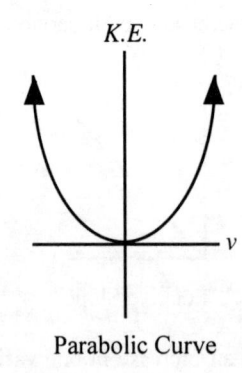

Parabolic Curve

iii. GRAPH READING STRATEGIES

The strategy for correctly reading graphs and charts is very much like the strategy for reading passages on the Reading Test. Start at the most basic comprehension level: Look for the main point of the graph, which is sometimes summarized by the main heading or title above the graph.

Next, glance over the general content of graphs, and look for answers to questions such as: "What do the various categories mean?" and "What units are used?".

SCIENCE REASONING

Do NOT try to memorize the presented data—rather, take note of the locations of the represented items. Just as when reading for the third level of comprehension, bracket any material of which the significance may not be initially clear. Remember that the accompanying questions will indicate the necessary relevant information.

> **STRATEGY FOR READING GRAPHS AND CHARTS**
>
> 1. Summarize the main point of the graph or chart—read the main title or description.
>
> 2. Preview the graph or chart—read the description of the axes and note the units used.
>
> 3. Quickly summarize and preview—the questions will lead back to the actual relevant information.

The above strategy is just as relevant to pie charts as it is to bar graphs or charts. Pie charts are simply another way to portray numerical information in pictorial form.

Passage I

1. **(B)** The slope-intercept form of a linear equation is: $y = mx + b$; m is the slope and b is the y-value when x is equal to zero. The graphed line intercepts the origin of the coordinate axis; thus, $b = 0$, and the y-values are equal to the x-values multiplied by the slope. The question states that the y-axis, or kinetic energy, is plotted in units of $g \cdot cm^2/s^2$: $K.E. = m \cdot$ height (cm) $= g \cdot cm^2/s^2 \Rightarrow m = g \cdot cm/s^2$, (B). Alternatively, recognize that the slope is "rise-over-run," or a plotted change in y-value divided by the corresponding change in x-value. Therefore, the units of measurement for the slope would be the units for the "rise" divided by the units for the "run": $\frac{g \cdot cm^2/s^2}{cm} = g \cdot cm/s^2$.

2. **(F)** If the heights ("run") used in the new set of experiments are the same as those used in the original experiment, but the kinetic energy values ("rise") are double the original values, then the denominator of the new slope ("run") is unchanged, while the numerator of the new slope ("rise") is multiplied by two. Therefore, the new slope is equal to twice the original slope, (F).

3. **(C)** The passage text states that the plotted measurements are for an object of mass m, and the y-variable is in units of $g \cdot cm^2/s^2$. Therefore, the kinetic energy of an object of mass m dropped from 4.5 cm is found directly from the graph. (If the question asked about an object of mass $2m$, it would be necessary to double the y-axis values). Locate 4.5 on the x-axis and the corresponding coordinate pair on the line. The y-value of this coordinate pair is the kinetic energy for the object of mass m dropped from 4.5 cm: 45, (C).

On a graph, given a value for one of the plotted variables, it is possible to find the value of the other variable. Draw a straight line from the known value to the plotted line and then from the plotted line straight to the other axis. Thus, in the previous question, if the kinetic energy of the object of mass m were given (45 $g \cdot cm^2/s^2$) instead of the height from which it was dropped, then the height would be determined by tracing along those same lines.

b. TABLES

A table is another way to summarize information. Tables present numerical information in matrix form. Rows indicate various occurrences (*e.g.*, experiment number, atomic number, altitude, beaker contents, *etc.*); columns contain specific attributes pertaining to each row (*e.g.*, age, temperature, atmospheric layer, pH level, *etc.*). Questions may ask specifically about data within a particular row or column, similar to Specific Detail questions on the Reading Test; questions may also refer to an entire table, asking for identification of a trend or for application of the given data to a new situation, similar to Evaluation questions on the Reading Test.

STEP THREE

The three types of questions about data in tables correspond to the three levels of reading comprehension: 1) Understanding Nature of Data, 2) Recognizing Trends, and 3) Drawing Conclusions. The first level of comprehension—understanding what is presented—is necessary to answer any of the three types of questions.

The first level of comprehension is achieved simply by reading the column headings—these will be the variables in the experiments. Then, check the rows to see what variables were changed in each trial. To achieve the second level of comprehension, read each column, noting the trend as the row variable changes. Finally, advanced comprehension requires use of the headings and any explanations in the text above or below the table to picture how the experiment was done.

Passage II

The first thing to notice about this Data Representation passage is that it is about the effect of two variables (temperature and food) on the sexual maturity of an animal. If interested in the effect of food, refer to the "age" column and compare Experiments 1, 2, and 3, or compare Experiments 4, 5, and 6. In each of those groups, temperature remains constant so that a change in age can only be related (as far as is indicated) to a change in amount of food intake. If interested in the effect of temperature, compare rows in which the only changing factor is temperature.

FIRST LEVEL OF COMPREHENSION FOR DATA REPRESENTATION

The first type of Data Representation question asks about the nature of the experiment, how it should be set up or studied, or how the data is arranged.

The following two questions test the first level of comprehension needed for Data Representation passages.

4. **(G)** A male at any age, (H) and (J), cannot be used to determine the age at which a female gives birth. Furthermore, if the experiment is begun with adults, (F), then there is no way of knowing how big a role the current control of the animals' environment has compared to their past, and unknown, environment. Therefore, newborn females, (G), are the best test subjects for the experiment.

5. **(C)** To study the effect of temperature on sexual maturity, experiments in which only temperature is varied must be compared. Of the answer choices, only Experiments 1 and 4, (C), have the same food intake (15 g.) at two different temperatures (25° C and 35° C).

The second level of comprehension necessary for this Data Representation passage requires identification of the data trends; specifically, the effects of increasing food and increasing temperature on the age of sexual maturity.

SECOND LEVEL OF COMPREHENSION FOR DATA REPRESENTATION

The second type of Data Representation question requires identification of the data trends. Typical questions ask for predictions of what will happen if particular variables are changed in the experiment or for comparisons of the results of two or more trials.

The next three questions test the second level of comprehension necessary for interpreting the graphs.

6. **(H)** Both an increase in temperature, (F) and (J), and an increase in food, (G), cause a decrease in the birthing age. Rather, the question asks for the factor that will cause an increase in the birthing age. If all other variables are kept constant, either a decrease in food, (H), or temperature will result in an increased age of first birth.

SCIENCE REASONING

> **ALWAYS ANSWER THE ACTUAL QUESTION!**
>
> ☞ Examinees must answer the question that was actually asked, rather than a question assumed to have been asked. If examinees are not careful, they can easily lose points on questions that they can answer!

7. **(D)** A controlled experiment for Experiment 5 would have to be identical except for the variable of interest. Only Experiment 6, (D), is identical to Experiment 5 except for the average food intake.

8. **(H)** Compare the variables of the suggested experiment with Experiments 1 through 6. The proposed experiment has the same food intake as Experiments 2 and 5, while the temperature of the proposed experiment is in between those of Experiments 2 and 5. Thus, food intake is held constant, and the temperature is varied. Changing the temperature from 25° C to 35° C causes the birthing age to decrease from 6 to 3 months. It is inferable that at 30° C, the birthing age would be between 6 and 3 months, or 4.5 months, (H).

Finally, take a moment to imagine how the experiments might have been performed. This is an evaluation of the presented information that goes beyond what is specifically stated and is the third level of comprehension required for understanding graphs and tables. The third type of Data Representation question tests this level of comprehension.

> **THIRD LEVEL OF COMPREHENSION FOR DATA REPRESENTATION**
>
> ✎ The third type of Data Representation question involves evaluating conclusions drawn from the data presented. The major pitfall with this type of question is to make conclusions that are not supported by the data.

The next question illustrates the third type of Data Representation question.

9. **(C)** In the presented set of experiments, only the effects of temperature and food intake on the mother are known; nothing is known about the offspring at all. Even though it might be reasonable to suppose that some of the extra food goes to the infant, there is no information provided that would back that idea. Therefore, neither (A) nor (B) is correct. In order to decide between (C) and (D), look for a data trend in the table that relates the mother's birthing age to food intake: The age of the mother decreases with increasing food intake, (C).

c. TYPICAL DATA REPRESENTATION QUESTIONS

Data Representation questions require application of the presented data to a new situation. The following is a list of typical questions based on Data Representation passages, graphs, and tables.

> **? EXAMPLES OF DATA REPRESENTATION QUESTIONS**
>
> *Select a conclusion that can be supported by Figure 1.*
> *Determine what the slope of a given line represents in Figure 2.*
> *Predict the results given an assumption or a new situation.*
> *Select a statement that is best supported by the data represented in Graph 1.*
> *Determine the results based on the difference of time or location.*
> *Determine the relationship between the two variables.*
> *Determine which conclusion is NOT consistent with the information given in Graph 2.*
> *Select an explanation for a given outcome.*
> *Identify the LEAST significant assumption made when determining a particular outcome.*

STEP THREE

The top half of the graph accompanying questions #10-14 illustrates an inverse relationship between two variables. As *Average Blood Pressure* decreases, the *Distance from the Left Ventricle of the Heart* increases, although this is represented only from the left ventricle aorta to the capillaries.

The bottom half of the graph illustrates a direct relationship between two variables. As *Relative Total Surface Area* increases, the *Distance from the Left Ventricle of the Heart* increases; however, this is represented only from the left ventricle aorta to the capillaries.

Passage III

10. **(H)** The "*" indicates that the pulse pressure is the difference between systolic and diastolic pressures. Therefore, to measure pulse pressure it is necessary to know systolic and diastolic pressures. The only region on the chart where both average systolic and diastolic pressures are shown is between the aorta and the capillaries, (H).

11. **(A)** Average blood pressure decreases from left to right across the top graph. This decrease in pressure corresponds to an increase in the distance of vessels from the left ventricle, (A).

12. **(H)** In the bottom graph, the relative total surface area peaks in the center (capillaries) and decreases to either side of the peak. In the top graph, vessels to the left of capillaries have higher average blood pressures, while vessels to the right of capillaries have lower average blood pressures. Thus, as surface area decreases, blood pressure may increase or decrease, (H).

13. **(D)** In the bottom graph, vessels with the smallest relative total surface area are to the extreme left and extreme right of the center (capillaries). The arrow underneath the graph indicates that the extreme left and right represent vessels with distances that are closest to and farthest from the left ventricle of the heart, (D).

14. **(F)** Since capillaries have the largest relative total surface area of any vessels (bottom graph), as well as the lowest blood velocity (3 cm/sec), it is inferable that an even larger surface area (as in the newly discovered people of the Amazon) should result in slower blood velocity, (F).

2. RESEARCH SUMMARY PASSAGES

Typically, Research Summary selections summarize two or three experimental studies. Occasionally, one or four experiments are presented. This passage type is used for data not easily translated into numbers and thus unsuitable for presentation in tables or graphs (for example, color changes or changes in the pitch of a sound).

Often, experiments are carried out using a model. Models provide simplified pictures of the processes occurring in real life. The actual values of model measurements are meaningless; however, if the model is valid, then the general trends indicated by the data are useful. For example, a model of an eardrum is made by stretching a thin rubber sheet across a round metal hoop. A set of experiments using this model determines how changes in the frequency or loudness of a sound affect the vibration of the rubber sheet. Even though the actual vibration measurements of the model are irrelevant, the pattern of the measured responses suggests why humans hear shriller noises better than lower pitched ones and why humans cannot hear dog whistles.

Research Summary selections describe the methods used for a given set of experiments and the results of those experiments. If any special information is needed, such as the meaning of a particular chemical test result, that information will be detailed in the experiment description. Additionally, before describing any experiments, a Research Summary passage may review the hypothesis that the experiments are intended to test.

SCIENCE REASONING

There are three basic types of questions based on Research Summary passages. As with the Data Representation questions, these three types serve to test the three levels of comprehension required for Research Summary passages.

THREE TYPES OF RESEARCH SUMMARY QUESTIONS

Design questions require an understanding of the information stated in the passage about the design and implementation of the various experiments, as well as any results.

Prediction questions require the examinee to make inferences or predictions based on the presented experimental results and data trends.

Evaluation questions require assessment of the experimental data and determination of whether the hypothesis is supported or not.

---

a. DESIGN QUESTIONS

Design questions ask about what is represented by a particular part of an experiment. In the ear model example, a typical question would ask what the metal hoop represents (the supporting bone for the eardrum). Another question might focus on the controlled variables in the experiment (the rubber sheet and the metal hoop).

b. PREDICTION QUESTIONS

Prediction questions ask for conjecture based on the trends observed in the experiments. These questions are similar to the second type of Data Representation question, except that the answers to Research Summary questions are qualitative rather than quantitative. Therefore, it is important to understand not only the experiment, but also any special results, such as the significance of a certain color or the forming of a solid.

c. EVALUATION QUESTIONS

Evaluation questions involve relating the experimental results to proposed hypotheses. These questions might ask how the experiments can be altered to test a new hypothesis or for identification of the hypothesis best supported by a particular experiment.

If redesigning an experiment to test a new hypothesis, identify which variable is to be investigated and which ones should be held constant. For the correct description of the new experiment methods, only the investigated factor will vary in value. If identifying which hypothesis is best supported by the experiment's data, compare each choice to determine the hypothesis most specifically described by the actual experiment methods and reported data trends.

A hypothesis for the ear model example that says something about flexible membranes on round frames would be better than one that discusses flexible membranes on frames in general. Since the experiment is specific to round frames, the first hypothesis more closely describes the actual experiment and is therefore the better choice.

C STEP THREE

GENERAL STRATEGY FOR RESEARCH SUMMARY QUESTIONS

It may help to work out the answer to Research Summary questions before looking at the answer choices. This is because some of the answer choices will be bizarre, suggesting that not everything was taken into account.

---

d. TYPICAL RESEARCH SUMMARY QUESTIONS

? EXAMPLES OF RESEARCH SUMMARY QUESTIONS

Identify the difference in the experimental design of the two experiments.
Predict an outcome based on the results of Experiment 2.
Predict the outcome of Experiment 1 when one of the variables is altered.
Identify an assumption of Experiment 2 based on the results.
Identify a conclusion supported by the given results of Experiment 1.
Select an experiment that should be conducted in order to test another hypothesis.
Identify a hypothesis that was investigated in Experiment 1.

Passage IV

15. **(C)** The description of Experiment 1 states that when bacteria reproduce successfully, colonies form on the agar, giving it a cloudy appearance. Therefore, it is inferable that if bacterial reproduction or growth does not occur, the agar will remain clear, (C).

16. **(F)** The plates with water-soaked paper disks are the experiment controls. A clear 2"-area around the water-soaked disks, (F), similar to that found around the antibiotic-soaked disks indicates that the inhibition of bacteria growth was not due to the presence of the antibiotic.

17. **(D)** In Experiment 1, Plate A (Antibiotic I) and Plate B (Antibiotic II) both prevent bacterial growth, as indicated by the clear 2"-region around the soaked paper disks, (D). The water disk did not prevent growth at all since Plate C was entirely cloudy.

18. **(J)** In Experiment 2, the normal concentration of Antibiotic II (Plate B) had no effect on bacterial growth; therefore, both Plate B (Antibiotic II) and Plate C (water) were completely cloudy with bacterial growth. In Experiment 3, the concentration of Antibiotic II was doubled and Plate B then had a clear 2"-area around the antibiotic-soaked disk, indicating the inhibition of bacterial growth. Therefore, the effectiveness of Antibiotic II depends on its concentration, (J).

19. **(B)** Both (A) and (D) are incorrect because neither statement is true with respect to the paper disks soaked in water. (C) is incorrect because the antibiotics cannot interfere with each other if they are not on the same plate of agar. Since the clear area never extends beyond 2" from the antibiotics, the degree to which substances can diffuse through a thick medium such as agar is limited, (B).

20. **(F)** Since the antibiotics would be prescribed for internal use, their effects at body temperature (37° C) are most important to consider. Experiment 1 showed that both Antibiotics I and II work equally well in the same concentrations at 37° C (body temperature). Thus, the result is the same, regardless of which one is used, (F).

SCIENCE REASONING

Passage V

21. **(C)** In order to test the hypothesis, the only variable factor should be the coarseness of the plaster, so that by comparing the cast imprints, any differences can be easily seen. Thus, all other factors, including the type of leaf, should be controlled variables, (C).

22. **(F)** Compression by tons of earth, as indicated by the question itself, applies pressure to the fossil. The correct answer will be the part of the experiment that supplies only pressure. While the glass, (G), supplies some pressure to the plaster, it really serves to distribute the weight of the 5-lb weight evenly over the plaster. Therefore, it is the force of the 5-lb weight, (F), that simulates the pressure by tons of earth.

23. **(D)** Results from the three experiments demonstrate that the larger the size of the particles in the plaster, the fewer visible details there are in the imprint. Therefore, mixing the plaster with a coarser grain would result in a worse imprint than the one from Experiment 1, (D).

24. **(G)** None of the experiments includes making an imprint without baking, so it is unknown if baking is a requirement, (H). There were no imprints made of anything besides leaves, so there is no support for the claim that only organic material will leave an imprint, (J). While Experiment 1 demonstrates that very fine plaster produces detailed imprints, there is no way of knowing that the imprint is superior to those produced by coarser grades of plaster until the results of Experiments 2 and 3 are examined; (F) is not supported solely by Experiment 1. However, Experiment 1 is enough to show that hardened sediment preserves imprints, (G).

25. **(B)** Allowing both the pressure and the plaster to vary, (A), prevents the determination of the effect of pressure on imprint quality. Removing the glass, (C), would simply result in poorer quality imprints as the weight would be directly in the plaster. While changing the depth of the leaf in each experiment, (D), would cause a slight change in pressure, it would be very difficult to distinguish among the samples. Only (B) provides the one factor that should be varied: variable weight simulates varying pressure.

3. CONFLICTING VIEWPOINTS PASSAGES

The third type of Science Reasoning selection is the Conflicting Viewpoints passage. These selections present the hypotheses, arguments, or viewpoints of two individuals (*e.g.*, Scientist 1 and Scientist 2) addressing a given question or topic. Scientist 1 presents an argument that includes both facts and an interpretation of the facts; Scientist 2 counters Scientist 1's argument with an alternative explanation.

a. PREDICTION QUESTIONS

Some questions that follow Conflicting Viewpoints passages ask for a prediction of results based on one of the presented viewpoints. This type of question is no different from similar Data Representation and Research Summary questions—each requires using the demonstrated trends to predict additional results. In fact, for the Conflicting Viewpoints selections, the arguments for each presented hypothesis are made using the data trends; therefore, part of the work necessary to answer Prediction questions is already done.

b. "SPOT THE ASSUMPTIONS" QUESTIONS

Other questions ask for identification of any assumptions regarding the data that were used to support either viewpoint. These assumptions may or may not be justified—the key point is that they were not proven true. Sometimes an assumption is easy to spot because it includes a weak phrase such as "may be," "it is likely that," or "this could indicate."

STEP THREE

c. "PICK THE BEST ARGUMENT" QUESTIONS

The third type of question based on Conflicting Viewpoints passages asks which argument best supports or undermines the hypothesis. Concentrate on the central point of the hypothesis and any assumptions that were made regarding the data. Since an assumption is the weakest part of a hypothesis, it will have the greatest impact on the hypothesis whether the argument supports or undermines it.

> **MAKE NOTES TO CLARIFY VIEWPOINTS**
>
> Be sure to understand each scientist's viewpoint. It may help to make notes in the test booklet that summarize the viewpoints as you read them.

d. TYPICAL CONFLICTING VIEWPOINTS QUESTIONS

> **EXAMPLES OF CONFLICTING VIEWPOINTS QUESTIONS**
>
> *Predict results based on Scientist 1's argument.*
> *Select a generalization that is most accurate given that Scientist 1's argument is correct.*
> *Select the findings upon which Scientist 1 and Scientist 2 would NOT agree.*
> *Predict which observations support Scientist 1's argument.*
> *Select the weakest link in one of the arguments.*
> *Select the findings that support the interpretations of both scientists.*
> *Select a criticism that Scientist 2 would make about Scientist 1's conclusion.*

Passage VI

26. **(F)** The basic idea of the octet rule is that the central atom, in this case carbon, has eight shared electrons, (F).

27. **(B)** Theory 1 is based on the octet rule: stable compounds form when the central atom is surrounded by eight valence electrons. However, as stated in Theory 2, xenon has eight electrons in its atomic state, so "that xenon could form compounds such as XeF_4 forced consideration of a new theory." This implies that according to Theory 1 and the octet rule, XeF_4 should not exist as a stable compound since it would have more than eight shared electrons, (B): eight electrons from the central xenon atom and four more electrons from the surrounding fluorine atoms.

28. **(J)** Since the BF_3 molecule has six electrons, it violates Theory 1—eliminate (F) and (G). According to Theory 2, "the shapes of compounds were such as to keep the pairs of electrons as far from each other as possible." The compound's structure in (J) has the fluorine atoms, and thus the shared electrons, farther apart than the arrangement in (H); (J) must be the correct answer.

29. **(B)** This question is simply asking for a restatement of the argument in favor of Theory 2. At first glance, (C) seems correct; however, it incorrectly implies variability within the same atom rather than among different ones. (B) correctly states that the variability in the number of electrons is between different atoms.

30. **(G)** Theory 2 allows for no more than 12 valence electrons in a stable compound; it would be weakened by the existence of any stable compound having more than 12 valence electrons. Since XeF_4 has 12 valence electrons, XeF_5 has 13 valence electrons. Thus, the existence of XeF_5 would be a threat to Theory 2.

Passage VII

31. **(C)** Scientist 1 maintains that the early atmosphere of Earth had little oxygen, so creatures that required oxygen must have arrived relatively later. The only answer choice that requires oxygen is (C), insects.

32. **(H)** If Scientist 1 is right about volcanoes providing extra oxygen to the atmosphere, then the total amount of oxygen will increase, (H). Since Scientist 1 does not provide a mechanism to tie up oxygen, a decrease in atmospheric oxygen contradicts Scientist 1's hypothesis.

33. **(D)** It is inferable that Scientist 2 assumes a link between the oxygen in the rock and the oxygen in the air; otherwise, there is no point in bringing up the oxides at all; eliminate (A). Scientist 2's argument is based on the idea that there was once oxygen in the atmosphere, though it does not require that all the oxygen in the rock be free, (C)—amounts of oxygen in the rocks proportional to that in the atmosphere, (D), are sufficient.

34. **(F)** Scientist 1 holds that the behavior of the anaerobic bacteria is based on the environment in which it developed, which lacked oxygen. This is significant for early Earth only if the anaerobes were among the oldest living things. Scientist 1 assumes that since the anaerobes have short DNA, they indeed must be among the oldest, (F).

35. **(C)** (A) has an assumption as its argument, which is circular reasoning and incorrect. (B) is an argument without support in the selection. (D) is a weak argument since it is based on probability—a simple "it only had to happen once" refutes the argument. (C) is the strongest argument for countering Scientist 2 because if it were true, there might be no freezing lake at all.

36. **(G)** The key point of Scientist 1's argument is that life could begin only if ultraviolet light filtered through the atmosphere. This argument is destroyed by eliminating the biological molecules' need for ultraviolet light, (G). (F) could be used as an argument for either side—Scientist 1 could claim that the fact that the amount of oxide does not change demonstrates that it is not relevant to what is going on in the atmosphere; Scientist 2 could claim that it indicates that the atmosphere has also held a constant amount of oxygen. (H) is a weak retort to Scientist 1's second point—Scientist 1 could respond that the complex anaerobe evolved later under special circumstances. (J) says nothing about composition since the pressure can remain unchanged while the relative amounts of the gases change.

STEP THREE

> **THERE IS NOT NECESSARILY A CORRECT VIEWPOINT**
>
> Do not waste time trying to decide which position in a Conflicting Viewpoints selection is the valid argument. Questions ask for identification of data trends and assumptions underlying the different arguments, not for judgments of the viewpoints.

C. THREE TYPES OF SCIENCE REASONING QUESTIONS

From the previous sections reviewing the various types of Science Reasoning selections and their associated question types, it should be evident that the Science Reasoning Test is comprised of three general types of questions.

> **THREE TYPES OF SCIENCE REASONING QUESTIONS**
>
> *Comprehension* questions are the easiest type of question and test the most basic level of science reasoning skills and reading comprehension.
>
> *Analysis* questions require a more in-depth reading of the selection and test the second level of science reasoning skills and reading comprehension.
>
> *Application* questions are the most difficult type and test the highest level of science reasoning skills and reading comprehension.

1. COMPREHENSION QUESTIONS

A passage about a strange topic is more difficult to read and understand than one about familiar material. Thus, the test-writers intentionally select material that will test reading comprehension rather than knowledge of a particular subject. Since this is NOT a science knowledge test, the passages contain everything needed to answer the question.

The Comprehension question type based on Science Reasoning selections tests an examinee's ability to recognize and understand the basic ideas presented in the passage. When answering Comprehension questions, read the question stem carefully. Double-check that answers have the appropriate scales and units.

The following are examples of Comprehension questions for the three types of Science Reasoning passages.

> **COMPREHENSION QUESTION EXAMPLES**
>
> *Data Representation*:
> - According to this figure, the salt content of the ice above the ocean water is:
> - Based on the information in the table, the atmospheric layer with the narrowest range of altitude is:
>
> *Research Summary*:
> - In Experiment 1, the data indicate that after the reaction has proceeded:
> - Under which conditions does salivary amylase appear to work best?
>
> *Conflicting Viewpoints*:
> - Which of the following examples clearly provides support for Viewpoint 1?
> - Which viewpoint would support the idea that present-day species are descended from earlier forms?

2. ANALYSIS QUESTIONS

Analysis questions ask for identification of the relationships and trends presented in the passage. Pay particular attention to direct (factors change in the same direction) and inverse (factors change in opposite directions) relationships.

> **? EXAMPLES OF ANALYSIS QUESTIONS**
>
> *Data Representation*:
> - If the chart were continued to the element having atomic number 20, its value for E would be expected to be closest to ——.
> - The best explanation for biomass being measured as dry weight is:
>
> *Research Summary*:
> - The results of Experiment 2 and Experiment 3 lead to which of the following conclusions?
> - Which of the following hypotheses is supported by the results of Experiment 1?
>
> *Conflicting Viewpoints*:
> - Which factor is vital to Darwin's ideas, but not to those of Lamarck?
> - Theory 2 could be threatened by evidence of ——.
> - A food-seeking blue jay captured a distinctively colored butterfly that had a bad-tasting substance in its tissues. After spitting out the butterfly, the blue jay never again tried to capture a similarly colored butterfly. This supports which viewpoint?

3. APPLICATION QUESTIONS

Application questions ask an examinee to draw conclusions, predict outcomes, and synthesize new information related to the information provided in the passage. Generally, this requires application of the presented information to a new situation. Look for words that indicate absolute positions or theories, such as "all," "none," "always," and "never." A single case of contradictory evidence is all that is necessary to disprove an absolute theory.

> **? EXAMPLES OF APPLICATION QUESTIONS**
>
> *Data Representation*:
> - If there were an additional trophic level of carnivores, its relative biomass at any given time would be approximately:
>
> *Research Summary*:
> - Based on the results of Experiment 1, what would probably occur if Experiment 2 were carried out at a pH level of 5?
> - Six moles of a gas at 1 atm. pressure and 273 K occupy a volume of 13.4 liters. The temperature is then changed to 300 K and the volume changed to 10.0 liters. To predict the final pressure on the six moles of gas, use the results of Experiment(s):
> - Which of these changes to Experiment 2 would produce a current of 0.004 amp.?
>
> *Conflicting Viewpoints*:
> - To refute the strict "genetic blueprint" of Viewpoint 1, a scientist could show that:
> - A scientist seeking to explain why Theory 2 has more predictive power than Theory 1 might argue:
> - Which of the following observations would provide evidence to support Scientist 1's theory but NOT Scientist 2's theory?

STEP THREE

D. STRATEGIES FOR THE SCIENCE REASONING TEST

The ACT Science Reasoning Test examines reasoning skills, NOT scientific knowledge. The passages include the information necessary to answer the questions. Several general strategies, as well as specific strategies for attacking the different types of Science Reasoning passages and questions, are outlined below.

1. GENERAL SCIENCE REASONING STRATEGIES

a. PLAN YOUR ATTACK—EASIEST PASSAGES FIRST

Before reading any of the Science Reasoning passages, quickly glance over the passages and code them according to passage type: Data Representation (DR), Research Summary (RS), or Conflicting Viewpoints (CV). Coding the passages helps to determine the order in which to attack the passages. Additionally, a passage's subject matter may influence the assigned difficulty level. With a little practice, coding the passages should take no more than five seconds.

Once the coding is done, plan the order of attack—which passages to read first, second, third, *etc.* Complete the easier selections first and save the difficult passages for last. This will increase the number of correct answers and ensure that the easier passages are completed. The type of passage that is the most difficult will differ with each student. Through practice, students must determine the type of passage with which they are most comfortable. On the actual exam, they should answer these easiest passages first.

> **CODE PASSAGES FROM EASIEST TO HARDEST**
>
> Before reading any particular passage, quickly scan all of the passages and determine each type. This helps when deciding which passages to answer first (easiest) and which passages to save for last (hardest). Additionally, glance at the first sentence of each passage to determine its subject matter—this will affect the perceived difficulty level.

b. DO NOT PREVIEW QUESTION STEMS BEFORE READING PASSAGE

Contrary to the strategy for the Reading Test passages, do NOT preview the Science Reasoning question stems before reading the passage. The question stems can be difficult to understand without first having read the information provided in the passage! Therefore, after coding the passages and determining the order for completion, begin reading the selected passage and any associated graphs, charts, and tables.

c. UNDERLINE KEY WORDS AND PHRASES

When students read the passages, they should bracket or underline key words and phrases, thus creating quick and easy reference points. Additionally, some students may find it helpful to read the first sentence in each paragraph before reading the entire selection, depending on the passage's difficulty level. This preview strategy refers primarily to Conflicting Viewpoints passages, but it may also help when reading Data Representation and Research Summary passages with a lot of written text.

d. PAY ATTENTION TO WHAT IS THERE, NOT WHAT ISN'T

Since each question is based on the information provided in the passage, rather than on any outside knowledge, pay meticulous attention to the given information, especially any information noted with an asterisk. On the other hand, be as alert to what is not stated as to what is: do NOT infer additional facts or information. Avoid confusing prior science course knowledge with what is presented in the passage; answer questions based only on the given facts. Finally, do not dwell on technical or difficult material—simply refer to the passage as often as necessary.

> **KEEP IT SIMPLE!**
>
> All of the information needed to answer the questions is provided in the passage. Pay attention to material noted with an asterisk—this is important information. Do NOT infer any additional information or confuse previous experience with the passage.

e. PAY ATTENTION TO DIFFERENCES

Pay attention to the differences in the presented information rather than the similarities. Identify how each table is different from the others, the different experimental methods and results, or how two viewpoints diverge from one another.

f. WATCH FOR ASSUMPTIONS

Watch for assumptions made in the presented experimental results, arguments, or hypotheses. Identify any assumptions that are not supported by the given information—whether an assumption is in the passage, the question stems, or the answer choices.

g. LOOK FOR TRENDS

Analyze the tables and graphs, looking for data trends and how those trends vary for each data set. Determine how the investigated factor changes as a function of the controlled parameters. Do the data demonstrate proportional or inverse relationships?

h. TRANSCRIBE ANSWERS IN GROUPS

> **ANSWER ALL QUESTIONS FOR A SELECTION BEFORE MOVING ON**
>
> Do not read a selection, or even part of one, more than once! Guess if needed, but answer all of the questions for a selection before moving on. If time remains after completing the last group of questions, revisit problems for which an answer was guessed and double-check the answer.

Circle the answers to the Science Reasoning Test questions in the test booklet. For each selection, transcribe the answers to the answer sheet together as a group. Only when the time limit approaches should examinees transcribe the answers individually to the answer sheet.

> **ANSWER BY GROUPS TO SAVE TIME AND ELIMINATE MISTAKES**
>
> To save time and eliminate mistakes, transcribe the answers for each selection from the test booklet to the answer sheet as a group. Record the answers individually as the time limit approaches.

STEP THREE

2. DATA REPRESENTATION STRATEGIES

STRATEGIES FOR DATA REPRESENTATION SELECTIONS

1. First, get an overview of the represented data, then read the question(s) carefully and return to the tables, charts, or graphs to find the necessary information.

2. Underline or circle key words and points of information. This makes referencing them easier and quicker when actually answering the questions.

3. If data is represented in the form of a graph or chart, then pay particular attention to the scale, the units of measure, the legend, and any noted information.

4. Pay attention to the labeled axes when reviewing data presented in graphs. Determine what the presented information is and the units of measurement used.

5. Pay attention to data trends; identify the relationships as proportional or inverse.

Passage VIII

37. **(D)** For all depths below 1-2 cm, the salt content of the ice increases until it reaches approximately 4% at 10 cm.

38. **(F)** The arrow and the dashed line indicate that the seawater salinity is about 3.5%, which is greater than the salinity throughout almost the entire ice layer.

39. **(B)** The graph shows that the ice is salty at its surface (~3%), falls off rapidly in the first couple of centimeters below the ice surface, and gradually increases again to about 3% at a depth of 7 cm.

40. **(H)** A salinity of 1.75% occurs twice: at approximately 0.4 cm and 3.6 cm below the ice surface.

41. **(C)** The ice 1.3 cm below the surface is about one-fourth as salty as that at 10 cm. Therefore, the shallow sample must be about four times as large as the sample from 10cm.

3. RESEARCH SUMMARY STRATEGIES

STRATEGIES FOR RESEARCH SUMMARY SELECTIONS

1. Identify the controls and the variables. For a given experiment, the controls are constant—only the investigated factor for that particular experiment is varied.

2. Anticipate how to alter experimental variables to support alternative hypotheses and predict the results of these new experiments.

3. For depicted data trends, determine any proportional or inverse relationships between the investigated factor and the experimental results.

4. If an assumption is faulty because it is not supported by the given information, the experiment may fail to prove the hypothesis, and conclusions based on the assumption might be invalid. Question the validity of any assumptions.

SCIENCE REASONING

Passage IX

42. **(G)** In all three experimental sandboxes, the side with plants growing had smaller and fewer channels or ruts.

43. **(A)** Light winds cause erosion—Sandbox 1 has channels in the soil with 5 mph winds, but no rain or steep slopes.

44. **(J)** If the "normal" volume of a light, 15-minute shower were to fall in 5 minutes, it would simulate a cloudburst.

45. **(D)** By using the same soils in each sandbox, the investigator can relate any differences in experimental results to the one factor that did change between experiments (water vs. no water, steep slope vs. level area, *etc.*).

46. **(H)** The changing slope simulates the increasing force of gravity, which causes the "rain water" to flow faster.

47. **(D)** The experiments demonstrate the effects of gravity, (I), water, (II), and plants, (III), on soil erosion.

4. CONFLICTING VIEWPOINTS STRATEGIES

> **STRATEGIES FOR CONFLICTING VIEWPOINTS SELECTIONS**
>
> 1. Be prepared to predict results based on each of the presented viewpoints.
> 2. Watch for assumptions in each viewpoint—they may or may NOT be justified.
> 3. Be prepared to identify which argument best addresses the issue. Pay attention to any stated assumptions since they may be the weakest part of the argument.
> 4. Identify the viewpoints' main point(s) and logical value; identify the differences.
> 5. Read the viewpoints, but do NOT dwell on the details—the test is "open-book."
> 6. Read the answer choices carefully. Preparing choices that are workable distracters is more difficult for test-writers than writing the correct response—no more than two or three out of five choices will have any real merit. Distracters, while related to the general topic of the initial statement, ignore the logical structure of the argument.

Passage X

48. **(H)** A mother gull's red spot is the appropriate stimulus, or releaser, that leads to baby gulls' pecking behavior.

49. **(D)** If practice improves the accuracy of the baby gulls' pecking, there is a learned component to the behavior.

50. **(G)** The bad taste serves as a deterrent so that in the future, the blue jay avoids eating that type of butterfly.

51. **(C)** The stickleback's aggressive behavior is a "Fixed Action Pattern," which is stimulated at the sight of anything that is the appropriate size and red.

52. **(F)** The baby chickens' experience of eating, which results in decreasing their hunger, clearly influences their "Fixed Action Pattern." Therefore, this example supports Viewpoint 1.

53. **(D)** According to Viewpoint 1, the nestlings need not first practice flapping and fluttering their wings while in the nest in order for them to do so when they reach the age of flight.

54. **(F)** There is a learned component to the bird's singing, since it will only do so after first hearing other birds of the same species sing. However, this also indicates a genetic component because the bird is not stimulated to sing if it hears the song of any other bird species.

STEP THREE

SECTION TWO—SCIENCE REASONING PROBLEM-SOLVING
(*Cambridge ACT • PLAN • EXPLORE Science Reasoning Victory Student Textbook*, Step Three, p. 76)

The problems in this section are representative of the format and difficulty range of ACT Science Reasoning questions. Remember to save enough time for at least one Science Reasoning Quiz from Section Three of the Step Three Science Reasoning lesson. Assign any uncompleted problems as homework.

When taking the ACT, it is common for examinees to become tired and worn out by the time the Science Reasoning Test starts. It is important for students to understand that they have all they need to answer the Science Reasoning questions successfully—the only difficult thing is the time limit. Therefore, students should build confidence in their Science Reasoning skills by working through questions both with and without timing.

A. DATA REPRESENTATION PASSAGES

Passage I

1. **(D)** The graph with the thin line indicates that female moths can hear sounds especially well at frequencies between 35 and 50 Hertz, even if the intensity level of the sound is 1. That is, the minimum relative sound intensity needed to stimulate a female moth's hearing is between 35 and 50 Hertz.

2. **(F)** It would be appropriate for the female moths to approach only males issuing the mating song (peak intensity = 5-15 Hertz) and to avoid the wing-buzzing sounds of the predatory wasp (peak intensity = 35-50 Hertz).

3. **(B)** The male moth mating song (medium line) includes frequencies between 0 and 25 Hertz; the wasp wing-buzzing sound (thick line) includes frequencies between 10 and 60 Hertz. Thus, the male moth mating song has a narrower range of frequencies than the wasp wing-buzzing sound.

4. **(G)** Although female moths are the most sensitive at 35-50 Hertz, they are still very sensitive between 5 and 15 Hertz. Because the male mating song is so intense, as indicated by extending to a level of 12, the female moth does not require the maximum hearing sensitivity.

5. **(C)** Above a relative frequency of 60 Hertz, female moths can only hear sounds at intensity levels of 11 or higher (thin-thickness line). A wasp emitting low-intensity sounds at these frequencies would not be heard; therefore, such a wasp would make a highly successful predator.

6. **(G)** For the female moth to hear anything at 20-25 Hertz, the sound must have an intensity level of 7 or higher. Therefore, since the male moth's mating song intensity is only at level 4, he is unlikely to find a mate.

Passage II

7. **(B)** Enzyme A's effectiveness, or rate of action, is described by the graphs of the two A curves in the two graphs. Therefore, the values of the variables where the A curves are maximized indicate the conditions for which it is most effective: 45° C and a pH level of 5.

8. **(G)** The plot of curve B in Graph II indicates that its maximum effectiveness occurs for a high, or basic, pH.

9. **(C)** The point where curves A and B intersect in Graph I equals the temperature for which the two enzymes have the same rate of action: 37° C.

10. **(F)** The point where curves A and B intersect in Graph II equals the pH for which the two enzymes have the same rate of action: 6.9.

11. **(B)** The temperature at which enzyme A's rate of action is one-half that of enzyme B is indicated on Graph I at the point where the A curve is one-half the height of the B curve: 25° C.

12. **(H)** The temperature at which enzyme B's rate of action is one-half that of enzyme A is indicated on Graph I at the point where the B curve is one-half the height of the A curve: 42° C.

13. **(C)** Both enzymes are active when the two curves in Graph I overlap as a function of pH: the pH range is 6 to 8.

14. **(J)** The maximum enzyme activity is indicated by the highest point on the curve. Clearly, the activities of the two enzymes peak at different pH levels.

Passage III

15. **(C)** A seismic station can determine if an earthquake epicenter occurs on the circumference of a circle with the station at its center. Therefore, the station at the center of the smallest circle was closest to the earthquake epicenter, (C).

16. **(H)** The earthquake epicenter must be located on both A's circle and B's circle. This is true where the circles intersect: II and III.

17. **(D)** The earthquake epicenter must be located on both A's circle and C's circle: I and III.

18. **(G)** All three circles intersect at only one point: III.

19. **(C)** If a fourth station is added, then its circle must intersect the other three circles at the same point as when there were only three stations. Therefore, the fourth circle intersects A's circle at III.

20. **(H)** Again, the intersection point is unchanged: III.

21. **(A)** The minimum number of points where the circumferences of two circles can meet is one. The answer cannot be zero because then the two circles would not be touching.

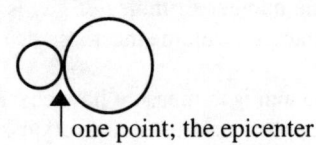

one point; the epicenter

Passage IV

22. **(F)** If the site were above water during formation, then the fossils would be from land animals rather than fish. This corresponds to the formation of Layers 1 and 2.

23. **(A)** Since the uppermost layer is the most recent layer, and it includes land animal fossils but no fish fossils, the site was most recently above water.

24. **(H)** If it is not assumed that the plants and animals lived at the site where they were found, then there is no information to be gained from their presence there.

25. **(D)** It is possible that no trilobite in the region was fossilized.

26. **(F)** The nautilus must have been present while Layer 3 formed; otherwise, its shell would not be in Layer 3.

27. **(B)** Again, the most recent layer is the top layer. Therefore, a new layer will form over Layer 1.

C STEP THREE

B. RESEARCH SUMMARY PASSAGES

Passage V

28. **(H)** Since the entry under "NaBr" in the "Final Wt." row is 0, the NaBr must have been completely used up. Additionally, NaBr does not appear to the right of the equation arrow.

29. **(B)** Mass is conserved; the total initial mass is 273 grams, which is equal to the total final mass. The atoms are conserved; the number of atoms on the left side of the balanced equation is equal to the number on the right.

30. **(G)** In Experiment 2, the total mass of the products (117 g. + 18 g. = 135 g.) is less than the total mass of the reactants (106 g. + 72 g. = 178 g.).

31. **(D)** The evolution of gas is the only answer choice that represents a difference between Experiments 1 and 2. Since all of the products were "measurable" in Experiment 1, they were not gases.

32. **(F)** Mass must be consumed since the apparent, but incorrect, final weight is less than the initial weight.

33. **(B)** If a method for measuring the mass of the CO_2 gas were known, then Experiment 2 would demonstrate conservation of mass, similar to Experiment 1.

Passage VI

34. **(H)** Experiment 1 tests the effect of temperature change on pressure. The data trend indicates a directly proportional relationship: if the temperature is doubled, then the pressure doubles.

35. **(B)** In Experiment 2, if the gas volume at a constant temperature doubles, the gas pressure decreases by half.

36. **(G)** In Experiment 3, the number of moles of the gas at a constant temperature and pressure was tripled; the resulting volume tripled as well. Hence, the volume of the gas varied directly with the number of moles.

37. **(C)** In the proposed experiment, the number of moles of gas is to be reduced by one-fourth; if the pressure and temperature are to be held constant, the volume must also be reduced by one-fourth.

38. **(H)** In the proposed experiment, the aim is to measure how changes in the temperature or volume of the gas affect its pressure. Experiments 1 and 2 demonstrate these relationships.

39. **(C)** This question asks for the relationship between the variations in temperature and volume and the resulting change in pressure. Each variation tends to increase pressure, so the overall effect is an increase in pressure.

Passage VII

40. **(J)** Experiment 1 indicates that the digestion of starch is the fastest (after 3 minutes, some starch is gone and sugar is already present) and the most thorough (after 15 minutes, all of the starch has become sugar) at a pH level of 7. Experiment 2 shows similar results when the temperature is 37° C.

41. **(B)** The experiments investigate enzyme activity. By comparing experimental groups (enzyme present) with control groups (only water present) under otherwise identical conditions, any differences in the experimental results are attributable to the presence of the enzyme in the experimental groups.

42. **(H)** Although salivary amylase is most effective when the pH level is 7, the enzyme begins to convert starch to sugar at pH levels of 5 and 9—after 15 minutes, low levels of sugar appear, suggesting the onset of starch digestion; after 60 minutes, moderate levels of starch remain and moderate levels of sugar have accumulated.

43. **(C)** To investigate the effects of enzyme concentration on digestion, all variables must be kept the same for each beaker except for the amount of enzyme.

44. **(G)** Since salivary amylase works less efficiently at 45° C than at 37° C, higher temperatures would tend to make the enzyme even less functional (enzyme denaturation probably occurs well before 70° C). Furthermore, the other answer choices cannot be correct since high levels of starch were detected.

45. **(B)** Originally, Experiment 2 was carried out at an "optimal pH" (probably close to 7). Since a pH level of 5 is less than optimal, as indicated by Experiment 1, the action of salivary amylase in the proposed experiment would probably be less efficient regardless of temperature.

Passage VIII

46. **(F)** The experiments show that each of the two resistors measure one-half of the battery voltage.

47. **(B)** A directly proportional relationship between voltage and resistance is shown in all three experiments: $R_1/R_2 = 1{,}000$ ohms$/1{,}000$ ohms $\Rightarrow V_1/V_2 = 3$ volts$/3$ volts, $R_1/R_2 = 1{,}000$ ohms$/1{,}000$ ohms $\Rightarrow V_1/V_2 = 6$ volts$/6$ volts, and $R_1/R_2 = 2{,}000$ ohms$/1{,}000$ ohms $\Rightarrow V_1/V_2 = 4$ volts$/2$ volts.

48. **(G)** Experiments 1 and 3 demonstrate that if the resistance is increased, then the current decreases (2,000 ohms/0.003 amp.; 3,000 ohms/0.002 amp.).

49. **(C)** Current and resistance are inversely proportional; resistance and voltage are directly proportional. Therefore, the formula relating the three variables is: $\text{current} = \frac{\text{voltage}}{\text{resistance}} = \frac{V_b}{R}$.

50. **(H)** Again, increasing the voltage or decreasing resistance will cause an increase in current.

51. **(D)** The current in Experiment 2 is 0.006 amp. (12 volts/2,000 ohms). To decrease the current to 0.004 amp., use either an 8-volt battery (8 volts/2,000 ohms) or resistors totaling 3,000 ohms (12 volts/3,000 ohms).

C. CONFLICTING VIEWPOINTS PASSAGES

Passage IX

52. **(J)** Lamarckians believe in the inheritance of acquired characteristics. Darwinists believe that chance differences among individuals can have reproductive advantages and lead to more offspring in the next generation.

53. **(C)** Both Lamarck and Darwin recognized similarities between fossils and the modern species living at that time.

54. **(F)** In the last sentence of the Darwinism argument, it states that adaptations "advantageous 'today' may not be advantageous 'tomorrow' under different conditions."

55. **(B)** Following the Lamarckian argument of adaptive changes being passed on genetically, a giraffe who had lost a leg and learned to walk without it would give birth to three-legged offspring.

56. **(H)** Lamarckians would claim that because the moles lived in the dark and no longer used their eyes, the eyes deteriorated and this characteristic was passed on genetically to offspring.

57. **(D)** Both scientists use the fossil record, observations of modern species, and inheritance of adaptations in the formulation of their ideas. Only Darwin felt that individuals in a population could have important chance differences in their characteristics, leading to reproductive advantages under the appropriate conditions.

Step Three

58. **(F)** Unless the adaptation provides a reproductive advantage, there will be no increase or decrease in the number of offspring with that adaptation. If the temperature never drops low enough, these individuals will not have the opportunity to express their advantageous trait.

Passage X

59. **(C)** Scientist 1 assumes that since meteors were hitting Earth at the time life began, they brought life to Earth.

60. **(H)** Scientist 2's assumption that Earth could produce life would be best supported if complex biomolecules spontaneously formed in a model of early Earth chemistry.

61. **(D)** Finding meteors with amoebas bolsters the claim of Scientist 1 that life on Earth came from meteors.

62. **(G)** Scientist 1 would say that all life has similar biochemistry because it all had the same source: meteors.

63. **(B)** Scientist 2 would say that all life has similar biochemistry because it all had the same source: Earth.

64. **(J)** Neither argument requires that life be the same at all places in the universe.

65. **(B)** To explain why other meteors have not brought life with different biochemistry to Earth, Scientist 1 would either say it was coincidence or claim that all life is identical throughout the universe—a claim with no proof.

66. **(G)** (F) is too strong—as long as the life did not come here, its biochemistry is irrelevant. (G) is the best choice.

Passage XI

67. **(B)** The viewpoint of Scientist 1 specifically states, "there is only so much energy in the universe."

68. **(F)** If the galaxies are moving away from each other with a constant speed, then there is no force pulling them back.

69. **(D)** Scientist 1 argues that the universe will spread out forever, so he would claim that it does not have sufficient mass to collapse. (B) is wrong—if the mass is equal to m, then the universe will collapse.

70. **(F)** Scientist 2 would claim that the average temperature of the universe would be higher in ten billion years than it is now, since the energy will be more concentrated.

71. **(C)** Again, Scientist 1 says, "there is only so much energy in the universe."

72. **(G)** The net force would be zero, which would mean no acceleration. An object in motion moves in a straight line with a constant speed under the conditions of zero acceleration.

Passage XII

73. **(C)** Scientist 1 assumes that the radioactive material was formed at the same time as the Earth; otherwise, there is no connection between the radioactive "clock" and the age of the Earth.

74. **(F)** For the landing of the meteorites to upset the "clock," they would have to contain the radioactive material or its disintegration products. Since Scientist 2 claims that the estimate of the Earth's age is too low, the meteorites must contain radioactive material and have landed since the formation of Earth, thus upsetting the "clock."

75. **(D)** Since Scientist 2's theory is based on the assumption that meteorites landing on Earth contain radioactive material, finding no meteorites containing radioactive material undermines the theory.

76. **(G)** According to Scientist 2, the amount of radioactive material and its disintegration products would increase over time because meteorites would bring more material, while the Earth has no way of getting rid of it.

77. (C) Since there is no additional source for new radioactive material, the amount of radioactive material as it decays through the various disintegration products is constant.

78. (J) If all of the radioactive material were gone, there would be no indication of when the "clock" ran out.

STEP THREE

SECTION THREE—SCIENCE REASONING QUIZZES
(*Cambridge ACT • PLAN • EXPLORE Science Reasoning Victory Student Textbook*, Step Three, p. 94)

Note to Teacher

Before administering the Science Reasoning Quizzes, write the homework assignment (p. 68 of this Science Reasoning teacher's guide) on the chalkboard. Remind your students of the importance of completing the homework assignment and practicing both with and without timing. It is essential for students to solve problems successfully and efficiently.

Allow your students 9 minutes for each quiz. After each quiz, review the answers with your class. Assign any quizzes not completed in class as additional homework.

QUIZ I (10 questions; 9 minutes)

Passage I

1. (D) The trophic level with the largest biomass is at the base of the pyramid (100,000 kg.).

2. (J) The relative dry weight of the organisms in each trophic level decreases from bottom to top. That is, the relative weight of each level's organisms is smaller than the relative weight of the food it eats in the next lower level.

3. (D) Light is always needed by the photosynthetic organisms of any ecosystem. Since light does not penetrate into the deeper waters, producers must remain near the water surface.

4. (H) Each trophic level supports 10% of the biomass found in the previous trophic level. Therefore, since the 4° consumer trophic level has a relative biomass totaling 10 kg, it will support 1/10 of 10 kg = 1 kg of relative biomass in the next trophic level.

5. (C) The definition of biomass, as indicated by the "*," states that dry weight reflects the usable chemical energy stored at each trophic level. Since water weight represents no additional usable energy, it is not included in measures of biomass.

Passage II

6. (J) At sea level (0 km), the temperature is 18° C. As the altitude increases, the temperature decreases to -50° C, increases to -3° C, decreases to -90° C, and finally increases beyond 1,200° C.

7. (B) Although the troposphere occupies a large space in the table itself, the altitude only ranges from 0 to 12 km.

8. (H) Both cirrus and cirrostratus clouds are located below the 0° C freezing point (between -50°C to -3°C and near -50° C, respectively).

9. (A) The greater the amount of solar heat absorbed by an atmospheric layer, the hotter that layer will become. The hottest layer is the thermosphere.

10. (G) The mesosphere decreases from -3° C to -90° C, which is a decrease of 87° C. It increases in altitude from 50 km to 80 km, which is an increase of 30 km. This averages to a temperature decrease of 2.9° C for every kilometer increase in altitude.

SCIENCE REASONING

QUIZ II (10 questions; 9 minutes)

Passage I

1. (A) The chart shows that if the sample contains Ag^+, it precipitates as AgCl.

2. (F) The experimental scheme as diagrammed tests first for silver and then for cupric ions. The other answer choices involve ions not present in the original sample—these ions could not be in the precipitates.

3. (A) One test is enough for identification of either cupric or zinc in a sample. For example, if the Cu^{+2} test is positive, then cupric is confirmed in one step, while if it is negative, then zinc is confirmed.

4. (J) H_2S is used in both steps, but with 0.3M H^+ in the first step and NH_4OH in the second step.

5. (C) The first reaction in the diagram is that of silver reacting with chloride. Since the solution was clear, the sample could not have had solid silver chloride in it and thus Ag^+ could not have been present.

Passage II

6. (H) At three months of age, the white-tailed deer drink equal amounts of water, 0.2M salt-flavored fluid, and 0.6M salt-flavored fluid—2 ml. In the other age groups, at least one of three fluids is preferred.

7. (D) At both six months of age and nine months of age, the white-tailed deer have a preference between the two salty fluids and the two sweet fluids. This demonstrates that they can detect the different concentrations of salt and sugar in each pair.

8. (F) The amount of 0.2M salty fluid that the deer consumed increases to 2 ml at 3 months, increases again to 7 ml at 6 months, and decreases to 4 ml at 9 months. The quantities consumed of the other flavors steadily increase (0.2M sweet; 0.6M salty), steadily decrease (0.6M sweet), or remain constant (water).

9. (C) The chart shows that preference for the 0.2M sweet fluid steadily increases with age, while preference for the 0.6M sweet fluid decreases. Similarly, preference for the 0.6M salty fluid steadily increases with age, while preference for the 0.2M salty fluid decreases.

10. (G) Although there is no difference in the quantity swallowed between water and the two salty fluids at three months, white-tailed deer do prefer either of the sweet fluids (7 ml) to water (2 ml) at this age. Therefore, the conclusion that the deer cannot taste such differences before six months of age is incorrect.

QUIZ III (11 questions; 9 minutes)

Passage I

1. (C) For each element in the table, the ionization energy increases with increasing energy level: $E_1 < E_2 < E_3$.

2. (G) Of the four answer choices, only carbon, C, doubles in ionization energy with each successive energy level.

3. (C) The data trend for the ionization energy of the second energy level as a function of increasing atomic number is to increase for a few values, then to suddenly decrease, followed by another increase, *etc*. This question confirms that ionization energies, like other chemical properties, are periodic properties.

4. (H) The values of E_1 make a sudden drop between atomic numbers 18 and 19, 2 and 3, and 10 and 11. E_1 is 40% higher for atomic number 12 than it is for 11, so it is likely that the same is true for atomic number 20.

5. (A) There are seven elements with values of E_1 below 200: Li, B, Na, Mg, Al, Si, and K.

STEP THREE

Passage II

6. **(F)** Air resistance slows the stone relative to its speed in a vacuum chamber, causing it to take a longer time to reach the ground.

7. **(A)** Less acceleration means less speed at comparable times, so the lunar photos will show images of the stone that are more bunched up.

8. **(H)** In a vacuum, objects of equal mass fall at the same rate, regardless of size, shape, or density. On the other hand, the resistance of air on a falling object will cause a decrease in its acceleration. Cork has a much lower density than stone—a piece of cork with the same mass as the stone will be much larger. The larger the surface area of an object, the more air resistance it encounters when falling in air, and thus the slower it will fall in air when compared to a denser object of equal mass.

9. **(B)** Since the stone moves faster as it drops due to acceleration, it will fall farther in each 1-second interval.

10. **(G)** At the 2-second point, the stone's speed becomes constant, covering equal distances in equal times. It does not stop, as in (F), since it needs no gravitational acceleration to help it continue with the speed that it already has.

11. **(C)** Since the moon's gravity is one-sixth of the Earth's gravity, the cork will accelerate more slowly on the moon than on Earth. Yet, the moon has no atmosphere, so the cork will fall at the same rate as a stone of equal mass when dropped on the moon.

SCIENCE REASONING

CAMBRIDGE EDUCATIONAL SERVICES

AMERICA'S #1 STANDARDS-BASED SCHOOL IMPROVEMENT

Strategy Summary Sheet
ACT • PLAN • EXPLORE—SCIENCE REASONING

STRUCTURE OF THE ACT, PLAN, AND EXPLORE SCIENCE REASONING TESTS: The ACT Science Reasoning Test is 35 minutes long with 40 multiple-choice questions. (The PLAN is 30 items in 25 minutes; the EXPLORE is 28 items in 30 minutes). There will be about seven reading passages divided among biology, Earth/space sciences, chemistry, and physics. While there is no general ladder of difficulty (increasing difficulty with increasing problem number), the questions within a question group tend to get harder towards the end of the group of questions. There will be six to eight groups with five to seven questions each, preceded by a scientific discussion. The approximate distribution of the Science Reasoning problems is as follows:

	ACT (40 questions)	PLAN (30 questions)	EXPLORE (28 questions)
Data Representation	15	17	12
Research Summary	18	6	10
Conflicting Viewpoints	7	7	6

SCIENCE REASONING GENERAL STRATEGIES: This section tests your reasoning skills, not your scientific knowledge. Most of the passages have all of the information you will need to answer the questions. In some cases, background information at the level of your high school general science courses is required, but do not assume data that is not given. The following are basic general Science Reasoning strategies:

- *Pacing is important.* Remember that within the 35-minute limit, you will have to read and think about seven reading passages and the accompanying question sets. In other words, you will have an average of just five minutes per passage. You will need to work quickly to answer every question.

- Before reading any passage, quickly *glance over each passage and code each according to the type of passage* in order to determine the order in which you will attack the passages. Identifying and coding each passage should take no more than five seconds.

- *Do not preview the question stems.* Previewing the Science Reasoning question stems will only confuse you and slow you down, since they tend to be confusing without having first read the passage.

- It is important to only *read the passage thoroughly once,* rather than skimming it several times. The material can be difficult to understand; thus it is important to read thoughtfully and carefully. *Be an active reader.* Use your pencil to underline key words and points of information. That way, you will be able to locate them easily when answering the questions.

- When a reading passage includes tables or graphs, make sure you *read and understand the labels* on axes, columns, and rows. You need to know what information is being presented and what units of measure are being used.

- Tables and graphs present results, often of observations or experiments. Questions will usually ask you to spot patterns in the data, so *look for trends* such as upward movement, downward movement, inverse variation, and the like.

STEP THREE

- Many passages will contain much more information than you need to answer a particular question. In your search for a logical conclusion, *do not be misled by data that do not relate to the question at hand.*

- The experiments described in Research Summary questions are based on scientific assumptions. However, if an assumption is faulty, the experiment may not prove what it claims to prove, and conclusions drawn from it may be invalid. Therefore, for questions that ask about the validity of a scientific conclusion, *consider the validity of underlying assumptions.*

- The arguments presented in Conflicting Viewpoint questions are also based on scientific assumptions. Again, *if the assumption is wrong, the entire argument is open to challenge.* Assumptions that are based on scientific fact add strength to an argument; faulty assumptions weaken it.

- Offering the assumptions that you started with as proof of your argument is called circular reasoning, and this is not acceptable proof. For that reason, any conclusions discussed in Science Reasoning passages or offered as answer choices must be based on additional evidence (*e.g.*, experiments) to be valid. *Beware of any conclusions that are nothing more than a restatement of an underlying premise.*

- All the information you need to answer the questions is provided in the passage—do not imply any information not given or relate previous experience to the passage. *Pay attention to material noted with an asterisk.*

- *Transcribe your answers from the test booklet to the answer sheet in groups* (by passage). However, when you get to the last passage, transcribe each answer as it is determined.

STRATEGIES FOR EACH TYPE OF PASSAGE:

1. *Data Representation*: When given data in the form of a graph or a chart, pay particular attention to the scale, units, legend, and other noted information.

2. *Research Summary*: When given multiple experiments, identify the controls and variables. Note that the controls must remain the same and that variables can only change one at a time in all experiments.

3. *Conflicting Viewpoints*: When given two points of view on a topic, identify the main points of difference and the logical value of each argument. After you understand the nature of the passage, attack the questions.

STRATEGIES FOR EACH TYPE OF QUESTION:

1. *Comprehension*: Recognize basic concepts. Read carefully. Make sure your answers consider appropriate scales and units. Also, note the difference between absolute and percentage changes.

2. *Analysis*: Identify relationships and trends. Pay particular attention to direct and inverse relationships.

3. *Application*: Draw conclusions, predict outcomes, and synthesize new information. In answering application questions, beware of "all, none, always, never." Remember that a single case of contradictory evidence is all that is necessary to disprove an absolute theory.

ADDITIONAL NOTES AND STRATEGIES FROM IN-CLASS DISCUSSION: _____

_____

_____

_____

STEP FOUR: PRACTICE TEST REINFORCEMENT

CAMBRIDGE
EDUCATIONAL SERVICES

ACT • PLAN • EXPLORE
SCIENCE REASONING

STEP FOUR: PRACTICE TEST REINFORCEMENT

CAMBRIDGE COURSE CONCEPT OUTLINE

CAMBRIDGE
EDUCATIONAL SERVICES®

AMERICA'S #1 STANDARDS-BASED SCHOOL IMPROVEMENT

Cambridge Course Concept Outline
STEP FOUR

I. STEP FOUR OVERVIEW (p. 105)

    A. WHAT IS STEP FOUR? (p. 105)
        1. APPLYING NEW AND IMPROVED SKILLS (p. 105)

    B. HOW TO USE STEP FOUR AS A TEACHING TOOL (p. 105)
        1. PREPARING TO TEACH STEP FOUR (p. 105)
        2. STEP FOUR CLASS SESSIONS AND ASSIGNMENTS (p. 106)
            a. IN-CLASS (p. 106)
            b. HOMEWORK (p. 106)
            c. HAVE STUDENTS FILL OUT PROGRESS REPORTS (p. 107)
        3. TRANSITION TO STEP FIVE (p. 108)

    C. FAQ (p. 108)

II. ACT SCIENCE REASONING STEP FOUR PROGRESS REPORTS (p. 109)

    A. ACT • PLAN EXPLORE SCIENCE REASONING STEP FOUR STUDENT PROGRESS REPORT (p. 109)

    B. ACT • PLAN EXPLORE SCIENCE REASONING STEP FOUR INSTRUCTOR PROGRESS REPORT (p. 111)

III. ANSWERS AND EXPLANATIONS (p. 113)

    A. ACT SCIENCE REASONING PRACTICE TEST I (p. 113)

    B. ACT SCIENCE REASONING PRACTICE TEST II (p. 116)

    C. ACT SCIENCE REASONING PRACTICE TEST III (p. 119)

    D. ACT SCIENCE REASONING PRACTICE TEST IV (p. 122)

Photocopying not allowed without Cambridge licensing agreement.

STEP FOUR OVERVIEW

A. WHAT IS STEP FOUR?

1. APPLYING NEW AND IMPROVED SKILLS

Practice makes perfect. Students who complete all of the practice tests typically show 30 percent more growth than those students who do not complete the practice tests. Students achieve this level of growth because the practice tests:

1) reinforce test content;

2) help students become more comfortable with timing and pacing;

3) reduce test anxiety through test familiarity; and

4) give students the chance to practice alternative test-taking strategies.

The practice tests give students a chance to apply everything that they have learned throughout the Cambridge course. In the *Cambridge ACT • PLAN • EXPLORE Science Reasoning Victory Student Textbook*, Step Four: Practice Test Reinforcement contains four ACT Science Reasoning Practice Tests with corresponding explanations for all four of these tests. The problems on the practice tests mimic the real test in content and difficulty level. They are also arranged in an order and with a frequency that approximates the real ACT.

We have made an effort to ensure that each practice test section reflects the broadest distribution of question-types possible. On the actual, official test, students will not encounter as many different question-types on a single exam as they would encounter in the entire pool of tested question-types. In fact, many students who do not do well the first time they take the test will make the mistake of studying only those exact question-types. As a result, they will not be prepared for the additional question-types that they are certain to encounter on their second, official test. For this reason, Cambridge's practice test section exposes students to all of the possible question-types that are eligible to be tested on the ACT, PLAN, and EXPLORE.

If you do not have time to complete the practice tests in class, assign them as homework assignments. You may also choose to assign corresponding practice test sections alongside Step Three: Problem-Solving, Concepts, and Strategies problems that are not completed in class. We recommend that you assign the first and second practice tests without time restrictions and the third and fourth practice tests with time restrictions. Answers and explanations to ACT Science Reasoning Practice Tests I-IV appear in the back of the student textbook and in the teacher's guide at the end of Step Four: Practice Test Reinforcement.

B. HOW TO USE STEP FOUR AS A TEACHING TOOL

1. PREPARING TO TEACH STEP FOUR

Before your first Step Four: Practice Test Reinforcement class session, know the following:

- how much time you have to teach each chapter and
- which concepts will be most challenging for your students.

Administer ACT Science Reasoning Practice Tests I-IV in class. If you do not have available class time, students should complete all of the practice tests as homework. In either case, you should be prepared to review all of the assigned problems in class.

Refer to the ACT • PLAN • EXPLORE Science Reasoning Step Three Progress Reports in order to anticipate which test sections will be the most challenging for your students. Review your lessons and notes in Steps Two and Three so that you are prepared to review these most challenging concepts or problem-types at a more comprehensive level.

Whether in class or at home, students should complete the first two practice tests without time restrictions and the second two practice tests with time restrictions. With time restrictions, students get a chance to reinforce their understanding of the Step Three: Problem-Solving, Concepts, and Strategies lesson under simulated testing conditions.

STEP FOUR

Without time restrictions, students are able to get a sense of how long it would take for them to comfortably and accurately solve a problem. If students cannot solve a problem in less than five minutes, they will not be able to solve the problem on an actual timed test in less than one minute. By first assigning practice tests without time restrictions, you allow your students to gradually develop their test-taking skills. By then assigning practice tests with time restrictions, students are forced to pace themselves as they would on a real test, which helps reduce anxiety about time constraints.

2. **STEP FOUR CLASS SESSIONS AND ASSIGNMENTS**

    a. **IN-CLASS**

    Unlike the Step Three: Problem-Solving, Concepts, and Strategies lesson, the practice tests are intended to be an extended exercise. Therefore, if you are using the practice tests as in-class material, do not cover one problem at a time. Instead, your students should work through an entire test before you review the material. When reviewing the test, allow for at least twice the amount of time that it takes to administer the test.

    b. **HOMEWORK**

    If students complete some or all of the practice tests as homework, they should then take advantage of the explanatory answers that are located at the back of the *Cambridge ACT • PLAN • EXPLORE Science Reasoning Victory Student Textbook*. It is important to provide explanations so that they can review anything that you may not have had the time to go over in class. The explanatory answers are especially valuable tools to review after the course has officially ended. If you do not want your students to have access to the explanatory answers or answer keys, have them rip out those sections and keep them in the students' in-class portfolios.

The chart below summarizes the in-class lesson and corresponding homework assignment for shorter courses. For longer courses, refer to the schedules included on pages x to xv.

(Note: ∅ = not timed; ⊙ = timed.)

12-Hr. Courses	18-/21-Hr. Courses	In-Class Lesson	Homework
	Session 1	**DIAGNOSTIC PRE-TEST**	∅ Less than 50 percent correct on ACT Diagnostic Test (Science Reasoning Test): Science Skills Review (*Cambridge ACT • PLAN • EXPLORE Science Reasoning Victory Student Textbook*, Step Two)
Sessions 1–4	Sessions 2–5	**SCIENCE REASONING** • Answer any questions on homework • Science Reasoning Lesson (*Cambridge ACT • PLAN • EXPLORE Science Reasoning Victory Student Textbook*): Review (p. 61) Problem-Solving (p. 76) Quizzes (p. 94)	∅ Any questions from the Science Reasoning Lesson not completed in class ⊙ Any quizzes from the Science Reasoning Lesson not completed in class ∅ ACT Science Reasoning Practice Tests I and II (untimed) (*Cambridge ACT • PLAN • EXPLORE Science Reasoning Victory Student Textbook*, Step Four) ⊙ ACT Science Reasoning Practice Tests III and IV (timed) (*Cambridge ACT • PLAN • EXPLORE Science Reasoning Victory Student Textbook*, Step Four)
	Session 6	**DIAGNOSTIC POST-TEST**	
	Session 7	**POST-TEST REVIEW** (Final Practice Exam or course review) (21-hour course only)	

CAMBRIDGE ACT • PLAN • EXPLORE TESTPREP™ REVIEW COURSE IN-CLASS LESSONS

OVERVIEW

c. HAVE STUDENTS FILL OUT PROGRESS REPORTS

In order to ensure Step Four: Practice Test Reinforcement accountability, use the student and instructor ACT • PLAN • EXPLORE Science Reasoning Step Four Progress Reports on pages 109 and 111, respectively. These progress reports are also found on pages 111 and 113 in the *Cambridge ACT • PLAN • EXPLORE Science Reasoning Victory Student Textbook*. Students should use these forms to record the percentage of problems that they have answered correctly. These reports will document student progress and will become especially helpful at the end of the course. At that point, you will help students develop a study plan for reviewing any areas in which they are still exhibiting a deficiency.

Ask your students to transfer the information from the student copies to the instructor copies. (These directions are repeated at the top of the student progress reports.) After collecting the completed instructor copies from your students, photocopy the reports in this teacher's guide and for each test section that you ask your students to complete, indicate whether the students have "Mastered," "Partially Mastered," or "Not Mastered" that test section. By checking your student's progress and evaluating their progress on the forms, you will have a clear and accurate way to:

1) hold students accountable for their progress;
2) gauge student ability levels so that you know what problem-types they need to focus on the most after the course has officially ended; and
3) monitor your own success in reviewing the material.

File these reports in your students' in-class portfolios. The progress reports give students, parents, and instructors quick and accurate snapshots of students' abilities. They also help to clarify the connection between the pre-test and the rest of the course.

The following portion of the ACT • PLAN • EXPLORE Science Reasoning Step Four Progress Report demonstrates how you might complete the report for a student. **Note:** The report below is only a sample. Use the reports on pages 109 and 111 in this teacher's guide.

ACT SCIENCE REASONING PRACTICE TESTS
(Instructor Copy)

ACT Science Reasoning Practice Test	Total # Possible	Total # Assigned	# Correct	% Correct	Date Completed	Problem #s to Review	Mastered	Partially Mastered	Not Mastered
1. Practice Test I (p. 125)	40	40	36	90 percent	10/20	11, 22, 25	✓		

Instructor Skill Evaluation (Check One Per Section)

STEP FOUR

3. TRANSITION TO STEP FIVE

The practice tests are a valuable and necessary tool for student improvement. Completing all of the tests before the post-test will improve scores and reduce stress. Even if your course does not allow for the completion of the practice tests before the post-test, students should complete all of these tests before they take the actual ACT, PLAN, or EXPLORE.

C. FAQ

Q: *Should I collect homework?*

A: **Yes. Students should be held accountable for their progress as they go through the ACT Science Reasoning Practice Tests. In addition to handing in their homework, students should complete the ACT • PLAN • EXPLORE Science Reasoning Step Four Progress Reports. Collect the instructor copies of the reports for each test section that you assign.**

Q: *What if I do not have time to review the tests in class?*

A: **If possible, try to expand the allotted time so that you can review at least one of the practice tests with your students in class. If it is not possible to expand your time, refer students to the explanatory answers that appear at the back of the** *Cambridge ACT • PLAN • EXPLORE Science Reasoning Victory Student Textbook.*

Q: *Are the practice tests real tests?*

A: **No. The practice tests are simulated exams that are specifically designed to reinforce the concepts and strategies that students learned in the Step Three: Problem-Solving, Concepts, and Strategies lesson. However, we have confidence in our ability to reproduce authentic ACT questions, which is why we use real, retired ACT, PLAN, and EXPLORE tests to assess the effectiveness of our material in Steps One and Five and allow you to look at the retired tests alongside our problems.**

PROGRESS REPORTS

ACT SCIENCE REASONING
STEP FOUR PROGRESS REPORT
(Student Copy)

DIRECTIONS: These progress reports are designed to help you monitor your ACT Science Reasoning Practice Test progress. Complete the assigned problems, correct your answers, and record both the number and percentage of problems that you answered correctly. Identify the date on which you completed each section of the tests. List the numbers of any problems that you would like your instructor to review in class.

Transfer this information to the Instructor Copy, and then give that report to your instructor.

Name _____ Student ID _____ Date _____

ACT SCIENCE REASONING PRACTICE TESTS
(Student Copy)

ACT Science Reasoning Practice Test	Total # Possible	Assigned	# Correct	% Correct	Date Completed	Problem #s to Review
1. Practice Test I (p. 125)	40					
2. Practice Test II (p. 135)	40					
3. Practice Test III (p. 145)	40					
4. Practice Test IV (p. 157)	40					

Photocopying not allowed without Cambridge licensing agreement.

ACT SCIENCE REASONING
STEP FOUR PROGRESS REPORT

(Instructor Copy)

DIRECTIONS: Transfer the information from your Student Copy to the Instructor Copy below. Leave the last three bolded columns blank. Your instructor will use them to evaluate your progress. When finished, give these reports to your instructor.

Name ______________________ Student ID ______________ Date ______________

ACT SCIENCE REASONING PRACTICE TESTS

(Instructor Copy)

	Total #						**Instructor Skill Evaluation (Check One Per Exercise)**		
ACT Science Reasoning Practice Test	*Possible*	*Assigned*	*# Correct*	*% Correct*	*Date Completed*	*Problem #s to Review*	*Mastered*	*Partially Mastered*	*Not Mastered*
1. Practice Test I (p. 125)	40								
2. Practice Test II (p. 135)	40								
3. Practice Test III (p. 145)	40								
4. Practice Test IV (p. 157)	40								

Photocopying not allowed without Cambridge licensing agreement.

ANSWERS AND EXPLANATIONS

STEP FOUR: PRACTICE TEST REINFORCEMENT

PRACTICE TEST I ANSWER KEY (p. 125)

DIRECTIONS: The following grid is used to score the practice test by question type. For each *correct* answer, check the corresponding unshaded box. Then, total the number of checkmarks for each of the two subject categories (UM, RH), and add these two totals in order to determine the raw score for each test.

TEST 4: SCIENCE REASONING

	B C P ES		B C P ES		B C P ES
1. A		16. J		28. G	
2. F		17. B		29. C	
3. B		18. J		30. G	
4. H		19. D		31. D	
5. C		20. F		32. F	
6. J		21. C		33. A	
7. B		22. F		34. H	
8. H		23. B		35. B	
9. D		24. J		36. J	
10. F		25. C		37. C	
11. C		26. F		38. G	
12. H		27. D		39. D	
13. D				40. F	
14. G					
15. C					

Biology (B): ___/17

Chemistry (C): ___/12

Physics (P): ___/6

Earth Science (ES): ___/5

Science Reasoning Raw Score (B + C + P + ES): ___/40

PRACTICE TEST I EXPLANATORY ANSWERS (p. 125)

1. **(A)** All three of the tabulated properties generally increase with the number of carbons.

2. **(F)** The change from methane (-162° C) to ethane (-89° C) is greatest (73° C increase).

3. **(B)** This property can be seen by looking at propane (3 carbons: -188° C) to butane (4 carbons: -138° C), pentane (5 carbons: -130° C) to hexane (6 carbons: -95° C), *etc*.

4. **(H)** Only boiling points and number of carbons increase without exception.

5. **(C)** Pentane (0.56) to hexane (0.66) is an increase of 0.10 ($\frac{0.10}{0.56} = 18\%$).

6. **(J)** Momentum equals mass multiplied by velocity. Therefore, the momentum is:

   2 kilograms • 4 $\frac{m}{sec}$.

7. **(B)** The momentums of the two masses are initially 8 and 0; afterward, the momentum of the combined mass is 7.98.

8. **(H)** Notice the negative sign on the final velocity for Object 1, as well as the note in the text about the meaning of negative velocity.

9. **(D)** Since no actual value is given in the phrase "far more massive," it is unlikely that an explicit calculation is needed. To be successful, a reader needs to visualize a collision of a very light object with a massive one; the large one will not budge.

Answers and Explanations

10. **(F)** The lighter object would recoil even faster than the observed -1.71 m/sec.

11. **(C)** Using the formula given, initial kinetic energy is found to be 16.0; the final kinetic energy has decreased to about 4.5.

12. **(H)** An increase in temperature influences flowering, while a decrease in temperature is one factor that causes leaf drop-off.

13. **(D)** The table shows that plant growth occurs when Hormones 1 and 3 increase. Yet, even if these two hormones increase, a similar increase in either H_4 or H_5 will lead to no plant growth—H_4 and H_5 inhibit growth.

14. **(G)** The table shows various factors that influence each plant activity. Seed germination is influenced by only one factor (H_3), while flowering is influenced by four different factors (H_3 and H_5, day length, and temperature).

15. **(C)** Changing a houseplant's growing conditions from 12 hours of light per 12 hours of dark to constant light is an example of altering day length, which only affects flowering.

16. **(J)** H_2 only affects flower drop-off, fruit drop-off, and leaf drop-off. For each of these activities, H_1 must also play a role (as H_2 increases, H_1 decreases).

17. **(B)** The only way the bag can gain weight between weighings is if additional fluid has moved inside. In this case, water moved inside (by osmosis) faster than it moved out.

18. **(J)** The fluid compartment (bag or beaker) that initially has only water (no red dye) never gets red. This indicates that the red dye is not free to pass across the bag's "membrane."

19. **(D)** In Experiment 2, the bag has gained 10 grams after only 10 minutes (water has entered the bag faster than in Experiment 1). By 20 minutes, more water will have entered and the bag should be even heavier.

20. **(F)** The experiments show that water will flow toward the compartment containing red dye. The more concentrated the red dye, the faster the flow of water.

21. **(C)** Water is free to flow into or out of the bag. Since there is no dye in the bag or the beaker, water will flow at an equal rate in both directions and the bag's weight should remain the same.

22. **(F)** Since salts are not able to enter or leave the cell, only water will move—in a direction that tends towards balanced concentrations. The water will flow toward the greater concentration of salt (from red blood cell to sea water), causing shrinkage of the cells.

23. **(B)** Magnesium is a positively charged mineral (Mg^{+2}). The soil that has the worst relative ability to hold such minerals is coarse sand.

24. **(J)** As particles get larger (from less than 2 micrometers to 200-2,000 micrometers), their relative ability to retain water decreases (from 1 to 4).

25. **(C)** Soils that are neither best nor worst at any ability cannot be ranked 1 or 4. The only soils that are never ranked 1 or 4 are silt (2-20 micrometers) and sand (20-200 micrometers). The total size range, therefore, is between 2-200 micrometers.

26. **(F)** Since loam is mostly clay, it primarily has small particles that hold minerals and water well. The larger silt and sand particles in loam are adequate at maintaining air spaces containing oxygen. None of the other predictions fit the data in the chart.

27. **(D)** Clay is best (relative ability: 1) at both holding positively charged minerals and retaining water.

28. **(G)** Concentrations of reactants, not products, determine rate in both theories.

29. **(C)** This question tests critical comprehension of the passage, and it requires an understanding of the relationship between the two theories.

30. **(G)** This question tests understanding of the relation of numbers of reactants in the overall equation to exponents in the rate law.

31. **(D)** The coefficients of the reactants determine their exponents in the rate law.

32. **(F)** This question tests comprehension of the differences between the theories.

33. **(A)** If the first stage is very slow and the second stage is much quicker, the overall rate is essentially that of the first stage.

34. **(H)** If the sum of the rates of each stage always equaled the rate of the reaction taken as a whole, there would be no need to analyze each sub-reaction.

35. **(B)** Temperature range for a life function is the high temperature minus the low temperature. For both species and both humidity conditions, oviposition always has the narrowest range.

36. **(J)** For each life function, Species M achieved 90% success at the same low temperatures in moist or dry air. At high temperatures, however, dry air was detrimental (Under dry conditions, 90% success was not achieved at the same high temperatures as when conditions were moist!).

37. **(C)** Since dry conditions had no effect on Species D for mating, oviposition, or pupation, it is likely that dry conditions will have little effect on caterpillar survival in Species D as well. The temperature range would, therefore, be the same as observed at 100% relative humidity.

38. **(G)** Mating success in the light and in the dark should be compared at the same temperature. It should be a temperature at which both species can successfully mate. Otherwise, additional variables confuse the issue.

39. **(D)** Species M and Species D are both equally successful at low temperatures for pupation.

40. **(F)** (G) and (H) are not relevant to the question. (J) only refers to light conditions. (F) is a hypothesis supported by the results.

ANSWERS AND EXPLANATIONS

PRACTICE TEST II ANSWER KEY (p. 135)

DIRECTIONS: The following grid is used to score the practice test by question type. For each *correct* answer, check the corresponding unshaded box. Then, total the number of checkmarks for each of the two subject categories (UM, RH), and add these two totals in order to determine the raw score for each test.

TEST 4: SCIENCE REASONING

	B	C	P	ES			B	C	P	ES			B	C	P	ES
1. D					13. B						30. H					
2. F					14. J						31. D					
3. C					15. A						32. G					
4. J					16. G						33. C					
5. D					17. C						34. G					
6. H					18. J						35. D					
7. A					19. C						36. J					
8. G					20. F						37. B					
9. D					21. D						38. F					
10. F					22. H						39. B					
11. B					23. A						40. H					
12. H					24. G											
					25. C											
					26. H											
					27. B											
					28. G											
					29. B											

Biology (B): ___/11
Chemistry (C): ___/12
Physics (P): ___/11
Earth Science (ES): ___/6
Science Reasoning Raw Score (B + C + P + ES): ___/40

PRACTICE TEST II EXPLANATORY ANSWERS (p. 135)

1. **(D)** The radii increase (0.37, 1.35, 1.54, *etc.*) and the electronegativities decrease (2.20, 0.98, 0.93, *etc.*) as one goes down each column.

2. **(F)** It is essential to remember that the second number means electronegativity. For fluorine (F), it is 3.98.

3. **(C)** The bond length is the sum of the radii for each of the bonded atoms (1.10 + 0.99).

4. **(J)** Carbon and nitrogen have the smallest electronegativity difference, 0.49.

5. **(D)** Electronegativities increase steadily across each row and decrease steadily along each column, so the most widely separated elements have the most ionic bonds, or greatest ionic character.

6. **(H)** Several choices include the value 3.16, which is the electronegativity difference in RbF. Since Cs is below Rb, it may be expected to have an electronegativity below the value of 0.82, which is found for Rb, a prediction that leads to an electronegativity difference for CsF that is greater than 3.16.

7. **(A)** Venus is only 0.05 units smaller in diameter than Earth (0.95 Earth diameters).

8. **(G)** 1 A.U. equals 0.5 inches in the scale used in Experiment 2. The paper is only 14 inches long. Neptune's distance is 30 A.U. (30 • 0.5 = 15 inches) and would not fit on the paper (nor would Pluto, which is even farther away).

9. **(D)** As planets get farther from the Sun (A.U. column), some are larger than the Earth (Jupiter and Saturn have larger diameters), while others

—116—

STEP FOUR

are smaller than the Earth (Mars and Pluto have smaller diameters).

10. **(F)** If the asteroids are 2.8 A.U. away from the Sun, they would be found between Mars and Jupiter. Thus, an asteroid year is longer than that on Mars but shorter than that on Jupiter.

11. **(B)** If the Sun's diameter is 110 times greater than that of the Earth, its diameter would be 110 • 5 inches = 550 inches (Experiment 1 uses a scale where 1 Earth diameter = 5 inches).

12. **(H)** The relative mass information given in the question is very similar to the order of planets based on their relative diameters (Table 1: Earth diameters column).

13. **(B)** If carbon dioxide (CO_2) is the variable in question, all factors except carbon dioxide should remain fixed. Only then can the effects of various carbon dioxide levels be evaluated.

14. **(J)** The only difference between Experiments 1 and 2 is that the concentration of leaf extract (containing a mixture of pigments) was reduced in Experiment 2. Using the lower concentration of pigments, the rate of photosynthesis leveled off, suggesting that the amount was inadequate to maintain the previously observed increase in rate.

15. **(A)** The description of Experiment 3 states that wavelengths must be absorbed to maintain photosynthesis (which is measured by counting oxygen bubbles). The bubble counts (and therefore peak absorption) for Pigment A are at 450 and 650 nanometers. For Pigment B, peak count is between 500-575 nanometers.

16. **(G)** Since the reduced concentration of pigments in Experiment 2 led to a leveling off in bubble count, an increase in pigment concentration should lead to an increase in the rate of photosynthesis and an associated increase in bubbles.

17. **(C)** Proper interpretation of the graphs in Figures 1 and 2 reveals that at light intensity level of 4, 40-50 bubbles/minute are produced.

18. **(J)** Figure 3 shows that at 600 nm. (orange light), both Pigments A and B show very little absorption, as measured by the low oxygen bubble count. Since light must be absorbed to provide energy for photosynthesis, orange light would be least effective.

19. **(C)** The meters/minute scale increases from bottom to top. The highest point on the chart shows the fastest speed to be approximately 590-600 meters/minute.

20. **(F)** The lines represent the best-fitting slopes of points, which show how running speed has increased.

21. **(D)** In 1960, the ratio is based on 4 minutes/mile (1-mile run) to approximately 3.1 minutes/mile (440-yard dash).

22. **(H)** The speeds for the 2-mile run are all between 340-380 meters/minute. The gain in speed must be closest to the "30 meters/minute" choice.

23. **(A)** This problem, requiring the right-hand scale, asks for an extrapolation beyond the given data. The 880-yard line crosses the 1980 axis at approximately 3.5 minutes/mile.

24. **(G)** Temperature rises at an even rate during the time that the sample is heated.

25. **(C)** Experiment 1 starts above 0° C, whereas Experiment 2 starts below 0° C. In addition, the temperature in Experiment 2 stabilizes along the "x-axis" for a while.

26. **(H)** The passage states that "constant" amounts of heat were added "continuously" to samples over a "defined" period of time. Assuming that all of these given conditions remain unchanged, (F), (G), and (J) can be eliminated. Therefore, a process such as heat absorption is the best explanation for the flat part of the graph since it is not a given condition.

27. **(B)** Ice melts at 0° C. This is the temperature at which the graph temporarily levels off.

28. **(G)** The experiment utilized constant heating. Yet, temperature change was not constant.

29. **(B)** At the boiling point of water (100° C), there should be another flat section corresponding to the heat absorbed by the liquid in order to convert it to vapor.

ANSWERS AND EXPLANATIONS

30. **(H)** An examination of the diagram reveals that primary tissue layers and primary germ layers are names for the same developing parts. This information is part of the description of the gastrula stage.

31. **(D)** The diagram arrows show the changes that occur as each developmental stage follows the previous one. The greatest amount of differentiation in structure and function occurs during organogenesis as the primary germ layers in the gastrula become the many specialized systems, organs, and related structures of the organism.

32. **(G)** The arrows show that during organogenesis, the body's bones develop from the middle primary germ layer (mesoderm), not the innermost layer (endoderm).

33. **(C)** Structures (receptor cells) that contribute to visual abilities in the monkey would develop as parts of the eye, "a special sense organ." The arrows show that parts of the special sense organs arise from the ectoderm.

34. **(G)** The asterisk indicates that during cleavage the many new cells that form from the zygote and its materials do not grow. Thus, as the zygote's material is simply subdivided, the resulting cells must be extremely small.

35. **(D)** Theory 1 allows for all proportions of reactants.

36. **(J)** Theory 1 simply states that any proportion of reactants may mix. It does not explain the relation of the amounts of reactants to the amounts of product produced by the reaction.

37. **(B)** Theory 2 states that a certain proportion of reactants will react; if otherwise, one or another reactant will fail to react completely.

38. **(F)** Both reactants must be in the appropriate proportions to be used in the process of forming more product.

39. **(B)** This is the only response that provides a ratio of Fe to O that is different from the two ratios that proved successful in the problem.

40. **(H)** Theory 1 only states that products contain the original elements.

STEP FOUR

PRACTICE TEST III ANSWER KEY (p. 145)

DIRECTIONS: The following grid is used to score the practice test by question type. For each *correct* answer, check the corresponding unshaded box. Then, total the number of checkmarks for each of the two subject categories (UM, RH), and add these two totals in order to determine the raw score for each test.

TEST 4: SCIENCE REASONING

	B C P ES			B C P ES			B C P ES
1. C			12. G			25. A	
2. H			13. D			26. J	
3. A			14. H			27. D	
4. H			15. A			28. J	
5. C			16. F			29. C	
6. J			17. C			30. J	
7. A			18. G			31. C	
8. H			19. D			32. J	
9. C			20. G			33. A	
10. G			21. C			34. H	
11. A			22. J			35. C	
			23. A			36. H	
			24. F			37. D	
						38. G	
						39. B	
						40. G	

Biology (B): ___/17   Earth Science (ES): ___/7
Chemistry (C): ___/6   Science Reasoning Raw Score (B + C + P + ES): ___/40
Physics (P): ___/10

PRACTICE TEST III EXPLANATORY ANSWERS (p. 145)

1. **(C)** Generally, the Wright data show lower lift at a given angle than the Lilienthal data.

2. **(H)** The highest point on the graph is at 16 degrees (approximately 5.5 pounds/sq. ft.).

3. **(A)** By extending both lines to the 50° mark, the difference between them is clearly observed to be less than 1 pound/sq. ft.

4. **(H)** Count the crossing points of the two curves.

5. **(C)** The widest region is between 18° and 43°.

6. **(J)** Since plastic beads are not alive, they cannot possibly carry out cellular respiration. This control is designed to detect any atmospheric changes (in the laboratory) that may cause a change in gas volume inside the tubes.

7. **(A)** Oxygen in the air of the tube is consumed by the peas during cellular respiration (see summary equation).

8. **(H)** Without KOH to remove the carbon dioxide produced during cellular respiration, the same number of gas molecules ($6CO_2$) would always be added to the tube as gas molecules were being consumed in the tube ($6O_2$).

9. **(C)** Experiment 2 was conducted at a higher temperature than Experiment 1. The greater decrease in gas in the same time period (15 minutes) demonstrates a faster consumption of oxygen.

10. **(G)** If results are identical in light and dark (Experiments 1 and 2), then light/dark conditions are irrelevant to cellular respiration rates in the

Photocopying not allowed without Cambridge licensing agreement.

–119–

ANSWERS AND EXPLANATIONS

experiment; only temperature conditions are important.

11. **(A)** Glucose must be consumed in order for cellular respiration to occur. Since cellular respiration did not occur at equal rates in Experiments 1 and 2, (A) is the only possible answer. Peas are seeds containing a supply of glucose.

12. **(G)** Scientist 1 believes that processes associated with sudden events in the past shaped the Earth, whereas Scientist 2 believes that the processes are continuing in the present.

13. **(D)** Mountains could not have formed only when land masses were raised at the beginnings of the Earth if recent fossils of sea creatures are found at mountain tops. This evidence suggests that the rocks were underwater relatively recently.

14. **(H)** Scientist 1 never refers to time or how old the Earth may be. Scientist 2 refers to "long" or "vast" periods of time.

15. **(A)** If the worldwide ocean precipitated granite first, it must be the lowest layer, with other precipitated materials covering it later.

16. **(F)** If the major rock types (three) formed when the worldwide ocean precipitated different materials on three occasions, no further types can be expected since this ocean no longer exists (possibly due to evaporation).

17. **(C)** Processes cannot be uniform from the beginning. Processes that formed the Earth at its origin must have differed from those that maintain and mold the Earth as an existing planet.

18. **(G)** Scientist 1 refers to three rock types forming during three separate precipitations. Regions of lava (with no present volcanoes), rivers presently continuing to cut their channels, and "related" fossils that could not have immigrated from other geographic areas are factors that support the views of Scientist 2.

19. **(D)** Ten individuals had their heart rates recorded every 10 minutes during a 30-minute experiment (three times). Therefore, 30 values were used to calculate the average heart rate for each of the experiments.

20. **(G)** Since Species B had an increase in heart rate when environmental temperature increased, it is the likely species to be poikilothermic (Species A's heart rate stayed about the same).

21. **(C)** Just by chance alone, any one individual might have an extremely high or extremely low heart rate. The larger the sample of individuals tested, the lower the chances of getting extreme average values.

22. **(J)** Since Species B (poikilothermic) had an increase in average heart rate when environmental temperature increased, a decrease in average heart rate is likely when temperatures drop. Species A should have approximately the same average heart rate at all three temperatures.

23. **(A)** At 22° C, Species A had an average heart rate of 150 beats/minute, while Species B averaged 100 beats/minute.

24. **(F)** The poikilothermic Species B should have an increase in body temperature in Experiment 2 (35° C conditions in the incubator compared to 22° C in Experiment 1). The homeothermic Species A should have no significant change in body temperature during the experiments.

25. **(A)** Each photon can promote an electron from level 1 to level 2 since the difference in energies is 0.60. (Note that the actual value of level 1 alone, which happens to be 0.60 also, does not determine the answer. Differences in energy are what matter.)

26. **(J)** There is no way to distinguish between the two emissions since each releases a photon of equal energy.

27. **(D)** Only the level 3 to level 1 emission has an energy difference of 0.92.

28. **(J)** Each electron can go from level 1 to any of 4 other levels, with each of the four transitions requiring a photon of a different energy.

29. **(C)** Since absorption of photons occurs first, then emission, electrons must be promoted (gaining the necessary energy from the absorbed photons), then emitted. Transitions between levels 3 and 4 have the necessary energies, namely 0.23.

30. **(J)** Although 2.07 is the absolute energy of level 5, there is no difference of energy levels anywhere

on the diagram that equals 2.07; hence, the photons will not be absorbed.

31. **(C)** Note how θ_1 and θ_2 are defined on the original drawing, then imagine how the diagram will change as the angles become smaller. (B) would be correct if the angles were defined as those between the ray and the horizontal, not vertical, axis.

32. **(J)** Only the last choice fits both experiments.

33. **(A)** This question simply requires interpretation of the meaning of the diagram.

34. **(H)** The beam of light only passes into the air for observation in Experiment 2.

35. **(C)** This response covers all elements of the three diagrams.

36. **(H)** The number of butterflies captured for marking is found under the heading: "# marked." Reading across the table for each size group, the "dark brown" category always has the fewest butterflies marked.

37. **(D)** By comparing the number of butterflies recaptured to the number marked, students can derive a proportion that represents how easy it is to recapture each type of butterfly. The proportion for small, white butterflies (30:35) is much higher than that for any of the other choices.

38. **(G)** An examination of the table shows that for all colors, as size increases the number of butterflies marked gets larger.

39. **(B)** A poisonous chemical will have adverse effects on the butterfly after marking (perhaps by killing or by preventing flight). The group with the lowest number (and proportion) of individuals recaptured in flight (10:40 = 1:4 = $\frac{1}{4}$ recaptured) is the group consisting of small, tan butterflies.

40. **(G)** For medium-sized butterflies, the proportion of individuals recaptured in each color is as follows: white (15:30 = 1:2), tan (20:40 = 1:2), and dark brown (10:20 = 1:2).

ANSWERS AND EXPLANATIONS

PRACTICE TEST IV ANSWER KEY (p. 157)

DIRECTIONS: The following grid is used to score the practice test by question type. For each *correct* answer, check the corresponding unshaded box. Then, total the number of checkmarks for each of the two subject categories (UM, RH), and add these two totals in order to determine the raw score for each test.

TEST 4: SCIENCE REASONING

	B	C	P	ES
1. B				
2. H				
3. D				
4. J				
5. B				
6. G				
7. A				
8. J				
9. B				
10. H				
11. B				
12. F				
13. D				
14. J				
15. C				
16. G				

	B	C	P	ES
17. C				
18. G				
19. A				
20. J				
21. C				
22. J				
23. D				
24. F				
25. C				
26. H				
27. B				

	B	C	P	ES
28. G				
29. A				
30. H				
31. B				
32. H				
33. B				
34. H				
35. D				
36. J				
37. C				
38. H				
39. A				
40. G				

Biology (B): ____/13   Earth Science (ES): ____/6
Chemistry (C): ____/10   Science Reasoning Raw Score (B + C + P + ES): ____/40
Physics (P): ____/11

PRACTICE TEST IV EXPLANATORY ANSWERS (p. 157)

1. **(B)** The sharpest sloping curve is for potassium nitrate (KNO_3).

2. **(H)** The sodium salts, NaCl and $NaNO_3$, have different solubilities, indicating that solubility depends on more than the nature of sodium. Thus, (F) and (G) must be incorrect. (J) is incorrect because it is not known whether the solubility curves for all sodium compounds have been given. (H) is correct because it takes into account the differences in solubilities of different sodium salts.

3. **(D)** The table gives data only for aqueous solutions, not alcoholic.

4. **(J)** Since the solubility curves intersect (at 71°C), the first material to leave solution depends on whether the maximum solubility is exceeded above or below the point of intersection.

5. **(B)** Soda goes flat as gas (carbon dioxide) leaves the liquid. The warmer the soda, the faster it goes flat. (A) shows the effect of pressure, not temperature, on solubility. (C) shows the solubility of a solid (sugar), which has nothing to do with the solubility characteristics of a gas. (D) deals with relative densities of gases and not with solubilities.

6. **(G)** Mercury's period of revolution equals 0.25 • period of Earth's revolution = 0.25 • 365.3 days ≈ 90 days. Mercury's period of rotation equals 60 • period of Earth's rotation = 60 • 1 day = 60 days. The ratio of revolution to rotation = $\frac{90}{60} = \frac{3}{2}$.

7. **(A)** Mercury's density equals that of the Earth. Density is mass divided by volume. Mercury's density = $\frac{\text{Mercury's mass}}{\text{Mercury's volume}} = \frac{0.58 \cdot \text{Earth's mass}}{0.58 \cdot \text{Earth's volume}} = \frac{\text{Earth's mass}}{\text{Earth's volume}}$ = Earth's density.

STEP FOUR

8. **(J)** Rate is distance divided by time. Divide the average distance to the sun by the period of revolution to get the relative rate. The smallest relative rate is the slowest. In this specific case, the planet with the greatest relative period of revolution orbits the sun at the slowest rate.

9. **(B)** Gravity depends on both the distance between the centers of objects (and thereby the volume—assuming the planets are roughly spherical in shape) and on the mass of the objects. Compare Mars and Mercury to see the effect of volume (by considering their diameters). Mars is more massive, but the smaller size of Mercury gives it an equivalent surface gravity. Density, a ratio of mass and volume, is not enough because gravity depends on the amount of mass and the amount of distance, not their ratio.

10. **(H)** $\frac{\text{Pluto's volume}}{\text{Earth's volume}} = 0.729 \Rightarrow \frac{\frac{4}{3}\pi r^3_{\text{Pluto}}}{\frac{4}{3}\pi r^3_{\text{Earth}}} = 0.729 \Rightarrow$

    $\frac{r^3_{\text{Pluto}}}{r^3_{\text{Earth}}} = 0.729 \Rightarrow \frac{r_{\text{Pluto}}}{r_{\text{Earth}}} = \sqrt[3]{0.729} = 0.9$. Pluto's diameter $= 2 \cdot (0.9 \cdot \text{Earth's radius}) = 1.8$ times the Earth's radius.

11. **(B)** The neighbors that are farthest from each other are Uranus and Neptune. Relative distances to the sun are as follows:

    $\frac{\text{Mercury}}{0.4} < \frac{\text{Venus}}{0.7} < \frac{\text{Earth}}{1} < \frac{\text{Mars}}{1.5} < \frac{\text{Jupiter}}{5.3} < \frac{\text{Saturn}}{10} < \frac{\text{Uranus}}{19} < \frac{\text{Neptune}}{30} < \frac{\text{Pluto}}{40}$

    The largest difference $(30 - 19) = 11$.

12. **(F)** The death rate for the 6-20 gram/day cholesterol eater from prostate cancer is 1.03, while that for a non-cholesterol eater is 2.02. Thus, (F) is correct. (G) contradicts the data for colon cancer; (H) ignores the direct relationship between coronary deaths and cholesterol intake; and cardiac arrest is a more common form of death than cerebral clots for the 20+ eaters.

13. **(D)** The death rate for all three groups of cholesterol-eaters from depression is 0.30. This number is lower than for non-cholesterol-eaters, so (A) and (B) are both wrong. According to the data, large amounts of cholesterol are just as effective in combating depression as small amounts, so (C) is incorrect.

14. **(J)** Although the 20+ diet increases coronary arrest to the highest absolute death rate, the percentage increase is less than 100% (from 6.00 to 11.00). The percentage increase for coronary thrombosis is greater than 100% (from 5.02 to 10.05).

15. **(C)** (C) is the only group in which low intake of cholesterol decreases the death rate from all three diseases. Intake of 0 to 5 grams raises the probability of death for lung and colon cancer only. This question is probably best answered by recognizing that fact and eliminating those choices that include either lung or colon cancer.

16. **(G)** Standardizing the death rate involves correcting for variables inherent in the subject groups but not involved in the experiment. Age, weight, genetic histories, and accidental deaths are just some of the variables that the scientist must consider. However, (F) does not correct for intrinsic variables; rather, it ignores results that might not conform to a "neat" result. This does not standardize the death rate so much as "fudge" it. (H) involves an arbitrary assumption that is in fact incorrect. Assuming a zero death rate in the male population distorts the result of this experiment and does not correct for variations within the subject groups. (J) is incorrect because this experiment does not consider women at all. It might be valid to compare results with a different experiment involving women, but the actual death rates for men and women for different diseases are not necessarily similar (*e.g.*, the gender-related differences for breast cancer).

17. **(C)** Since voltage is directly related to current, voltage increases by the same factor as current if other variables are held constant. The same applies for resistance; therefore, the only correct formula is (C).

18. **(G)** $V = IR$, so the circuit with the greater resistance would have the greater voltage. Since resistance is directly proportional to resistivity, the germanium circuit would have the greater resistance and voltage.

19. **(A)** The total resistance R_s of the series resistors is $R_1 + R_2 = 2 + 2 = 4$. This resistance is double that of the circuit where $R = 2$. If R doubles, then the voltage doubles as long as the current remains the same.

ANSWERS AND EXPLANATIONS

20. **(J)** According to the formula for resistors in parallel: $\frac{1}{R_p} = \frac{1}{4} + \frac{1}{4} = \frac{2}{4} = \frac{1}{2} \Rightarrow R_p = 2$.

21. **(C)** If R is constant, then P increases with I^2; this is the definition of exponential growth.

22. **(J)** $V = IR \Rightarrow I = \frac{V}{R}$. To keep I constant if V increases, R must be increased.

23. **(D)** Compare Trials 2 and 3 to see what changing concentration of only one component has on rate. In this case, there is no change in rate with change in concentration of A, so rate is independent of concentration.

24. **(F)** Compare Trials 2 and 4, or Trials 1 and 3.

25. **(C)** Compare Trials 1 and 4, or Trials 2 and 3.

26. **(H)** Averaging or intermediate mechanisms do not work because one mechanism has no dependence on A with regard to rate. (G) is unlikely because a well-mixed solution should be homogeneous and have no pockets for mechanisms 1 and 2.

27. **(B)** This is a subtle question. (C) and (D) are incorrect because they over-generalize from a single case. It cannot be said that mechanisms can always be changed, (C), or that in every case the mechanism depends on solvent effects, (D). (A) is a special case of (D), where the claim is made that all reactions are solvent dependent. (B) alone allows for the possibility that solvents need not have an effect (note the word "may").

28. **(G)** acceleration $= \frac{D_v}{D_t} = \frac{\text{change in velocity}}{\text{change in time}}$.

    Experiment 1 (steel ball): The acceleration is constant at 3.50 m/sec^2. This can be demonstrated by choosing a time interval and dividing the corresponding velocity change during the time interval by the length of the time interval. For example, between 1 and 2 seconds, the velocity changes from 3.5 m/sec to 7 m/sec; therefore, acceleration equals $\frac{\Delta v}{\Delta t} = \frac{7 - 3.5}{2 - 1} = \frac{3.5}{1} = 3.5$ m/sec^2.

    For a time interval from 0.5 seconds to 1 second, the corresponding velocity would change from 1.75 m/sec to 3.5 m/sec; thus, the acceleration equals $\frac{\Delta v}{\Delta t} = \frac{3.5 - 1.75}{1 - 0.5} = \frac{1.75}{0.5} = 3.5$ m/sec^2.

    Experiment 2 (sled): The acceleration is a constant 4.9 m/sec^2. For example, the change in velocity corresponding to the time interval from 0.5 seconds to 1 second is 4.90 m/sec − 2.45 m/sec = 2.45 m/sec. The acceleration $= \frac{\Delta v}{\Delta t} = \frac{4.90 - 2.45}{1 - 0.5} = \frac{2.45}{0.5} = 4.9$ m/sec^2.

    Experiment 3 (box): The acceleration is constant at 0.66 m/sec^2.

29. **(A)** When friction is reduced in Experiment 4, the sled and the ball still travel at about the same accelerations as in the previous experiments. This can be demonstrated by using the equation $d = 0.5at^2$, which relates the distance that an object travels starting from rest to the time (traveling at constant acceleration) it takes to travel the indicated distance. Since the board is 10 meters in length, the distance that each travels is 10 meters.

    For the sled: $d = \frac{1}{2}at^2$
    $10 = \frac{1}{2}at(2.02)^2 \approx \frac{1}{2}(a)(4)$
    $a = 5$ m/sec^2

    For the ball: $d = \frac{1}{2}at^2$
    $10 = \frac{1}{2}a(2.39)^2 \approx \frac{1}{2}a(5.7)$
    $a = 3.50$ m/sec^2

    The ball and sled travel at about the same accelerations before and after oiling, so the differences in their relative accelerations must be due to something other than friction. The difference is the rolling of the ball.

30. **(H)** Experiment 4 shows that friction affects the relative acceleration between the box and either the sled or ball. Calculate the acceleration for the box: $d = \frac{1}{2}at^2 \Rightarrow 10 = \frac{1}{2}a(4.08)^2 \approx \frac{1}{2}a(16) \Rightarrow a = 1.25$ m/sec^2.

    Because the oiling in Experiment 4 caused a change in the box's acceleration, friction is a factor. Rolling must also be a factor as per the answer explanation to item #29.

31. **(B)** The acceleration of the ball is constant at 3.50 m/sec^2 (either Experiment 1 or 4). The acceleration of the sled is constant at 4.90 m/sec^2 (Experiment 2 or 4). Ratio $= \frac{3.50}{4.90} = \frac{5}{7}$.

32. **(H)** Although the acceleration of the ball is relatively insensitive to the amount of friction, the

acceleration of the box is very sensitive to friction. Therefore, in a ratio, the effect of changing the amount of friction will change the numerator (ball acceleration) only slightly, whereas the denominator (box acceleration) will change significantly depending on friction. (J) is not correct because the acceleration remains constant within each experiment.

33. **(B)** Two genetically distant species cannot breed.

34. **(H)** For early modern humans to completely replace Neanderthals, there could not have been a region containing Neanderthals that did not also contain early modern humans.

35. **(D)** Neither hypothesis necessarily rules out isolated communities. Both are concerned about areas where contact occurred.

36. **(J)** This information suggests that early modern humans killed Neanderthals, which supports Scientist 2.

37. **(C)** This fact shows that even if two species can breed, they may not do so voluntarily. Scientist 2 can therefore use this case as an example of the fact that two genetically compatible but dissimilar-looking animals choose not to interbreed. (D) is not readily relevant because lions and tigers are brought together artificially. No one disputed the notion that animals can interbreed, so (A) does not enter the argument. (B) is incorrect because lions and tigers do not share the same niche (tigers are solitary forest hunters while lions are group-hunting plains dwellers), and their ranges rarely overlap.

38. **(H)** The mixing of traits is part of Scientist 2's objections to Scientist 1's hypothesis.

39. **(A)** Both hypotheses attribute the disappearance of Neanderthals to early modern humans.

40. **(G)** (F) is a perfectly logical argument but it does not strengthen the position of Scientist 1. (J) does not strengthen the position of Scientist 1 since there is no way to prove from the given information whether others also died violently (clubs may have been used, or spearpoints that were used may have been valuable and were taken by the victors). Even if (J) is acceptable, it does not strengthen the position of Scientist 1. It only casts doubt on the position of Scientist 2. (H) is true in general. The only possible answer that strengthens a scientist's argument is (G).

STEP FIVE: FINAL EXAM, ASSESSMENT REPORT, AND REVIEW

CAMBRIDGE
EDUCATIONAL SERVICES®

ACT • PLAN • EXPLORE
SCIENCE REASONING

STEP FIVE: FINAL EXAM, ASSESSMENT REPORT, AND REVIEW

CAMBRIDGE
EDUCATIONAL SERVICES®

AMERICA'S #1 STANDARDS-BASED SCHOOL IMPROVEMENT

Cambridge Course Concept Outline
STEP FIVE

I. STEP FIVE OVERVIEW (p. 133)

    A. WHAT IS STEP FIVE? (p. 133)
        1. OFFICIAL ACT, PLAN, OR, EXPLORE (p. 133)
        2. ASSESSMENT REPORTS (p. 133)

    B. HOW TO USE STEP FIVE AS A TEACHING TOOL (p. 134)
        1. PREPARING TO TEACH STEP FIVE (p. 134)
            a. KEEP STUDENTS MOTIVATED (p. 134)
            b. KNOW THE TESTING AND ADMINISTRATION CONDITIONS (p. 134)
            c. ADMINISTER THE CORRECT TEST (p. 135)
        2. STEP FIVE CLASS SESSION: PROCTOR AN OFFICIAL ACT, PLAN, OR EXPLORE (p. 135)
        3. TRANSITION TO STEP SIX (p. 135)
            a. STUDENT PROGRESS REPORTS AND STUDY PLANS—AN INDIVIDUAL APPORACH (LEVEL ONE) (p. 136)
            b. EVALUATE YOUR CURRENT TEST PREP PROGRAM—A GROUP APPROACH (LEVEL TWO) (p. 136)
            c. SCHOOL IMPROVEMENT PROGRAM: MODIFYING CURRICULUM (LEVEL THREE) (p. 136)
            d. BUILDING COMMUNITY SUPPORT: HOLD ADMISSIONS AND MOTIVATIONAL WORKSHOPS (p. 137)

    C. FAQ (p. 138)

II. ACT • PLAN • EXPLORE DIAGNOSTIC POST-TEST PROGRESS REPORTS (p. 139)

    A. ACT • PLAN EXPLORE DIAGNOSTIC POST-TEST STUDENT PROGRESS REPORT (p. 139)

    B. ACT • PLAN EXPLORE DIAGNOSTIC POST-TEST INSTRUCTOR PROGRESS REPORT (p. 141)

STEP FIVE OVERVIEW

A. WHAT IS STEP FIVE?

Step Five: Final Exam, Assessment, and Review reflects what was accomplished in Step One: Diagnostic Testing and Assessment Service. It measures the true impact of your Cambridge test preparation program. Students are given the opportunity to apply everything that they have learned up until this point by completing another official, retired test. The second test enables an official pre- and post-test comparison that measures both student and teacher progress. Teachers and administrators use this valuable pre- and post-test comparison data to fine-tune existing instruction, help students formulate personal study plans, and plan the following year's program changes to allow for even greater growth.

1. OFFICIAL ACT, PLAN, OR EXPLORE

As with the pre-test, the post-test is an official, retired ACT, PLAN, or EXPLORE. Official post-tests contain problems from a previously administered test. Only a second official, retired test can provide the necessary data to gauge student progress and target student strengths and weaknesses throughout the rest of the course. Cambridge recommends administering an official ACT, PLAN, or EXPLORE post-test (not included with this package). If you did not order two tests (one for pre- and one for post-), you can contact your Cambridge customer service representative at 847-299-2930 to order additional official retired tests. Do not confuse the ACT Science Reasoning Practice Tests (Step Four) with the Step Five and Step One official tests. Remember that Step One and Step Five tests are official normed and curved exams, whereas the ACT Science Reasoning Practice Tests (Step Four) are used to reinforce problem-solving, concepts, and strategies (Step Three). In Step Five, students are able to use these strategies to "show what they know" on the actual test, under actual test conditions.

2. ASSESSMENT REPORTS

Just as with the pre-test, schools should use their Diagnostic Post-Test Reports to gauge improvement and current ability in Science Reasoning. You will receive a second Student Summary, Item Analysis, and Error Analysis (high, medium, low error analysis for locations ordering more than 150 student sets), as well as a Pre-/Post- Instructor Summary. Using the data within these reports, decide whether to continue to review selected basic skills (Step Two), further practice selected applications of test-taking strategies to certain problem-types (Step Three), and/or finish administering the practice tests (Step Four). The Diagnostic Post-Test Reports are briefly explained below:

ACT • PLAN • EXPLORE Student Summary (page one of two): The student summary indicates the number of right, wrong, and omitted problems. It gives a score and general item descriptor. This summary is used to diagnose whether a student needs to return to the Step Two: Skills Review. It also indicates a student's relative strengths and weaknesses and provides a snapshot of the level at which he or she has tested.

ACT • PLAN • EXPLORE Student Summary Item Analysis (page two of two): The item analysis report indicates the student's individual response to each question. Many times, a student will think that he or she has performed better on the exam than what has been assessed by the computer—given the coding of the answer sheet. Time spent coding problems, mental exhaustion, cheating, or a lack of sustained effort are all made evident by examining this report. We recommend that this report be mailed to each student's parents. It is an excellent communication piece for parents so that they can realistically assess their son or daughter's performance on the exam. Parents may determine the necessary additional steps that can be taken at home in order to achieve the desired score for entrance to the college of the student's choice and to qualify for scholarships.

ACT • PLAN • EXPLORE Instructor Summary: If you are using the Cambridge Assessment Report, the instructor summary proves invaluable to show how individual students have improved from pre- to post-test. In addition to providing the class average, this report can also be used to compare different classes, spot overall trends, and determine what adjustments must be made during the following year in order to meet the desired goals.

ACT • PLAN • EXPLORE Error Analysis: The error analysis is perhaps the most important scientific report available to test preparation. This report not only determines the specific problems with which students

STEP FIVE

performed the most poorly, but it also relates the specific incorrect answer choices that were most frequently chosen by these students. Rather than simply explaining the correct answer choice to students, greater results are obtained by also showing them why their most frequently chosen incorrect answer choice ("distractor") is wrong. The report lists each test problem number and a corresponding percentage of students who chose each of the given answer choices. In order to prevent these trends from reoccurring, teachers should focus on problems (as they pertain to each ability level) that students answered incorrectly but could have answered correctly had they concentrated their efforts a little bit more.

In addition, for locations ordering more than 150 student sets, your program reports include:

ACT • PLAN • EXPLORE High, Medium, and Low Error Analysis: Data is grouped according to three levels: high, medium, and low. Students within each group tend to make the same types of errors as other students within that same group. By targeting specific problems within a specific group, school improvement can be accomplished more easily and on a more widespread and permanent basis. In addition, it makes the most sense to target frequently missed problems that skills (low) students, average (medium) students, and gifted (high) students can get right. If 90 percent of your students get a particular problem wrong, skills students will have the greatest difficulty getting this problem correct regardless of what measures are taken. These problems are targeted for gifted students who should be capable of getting all of them correct.

B. HOW TO USE STEP FIVE AS A TEACHING TOOL

1. PREPARING TO TEACH STEP FIVE

a. KEEP STUDENTS MOTIVATED

After putting forth a great deal of effort to complete Steps Two, Three, and Four, student motivation may subside when the time comes to administer the post-test. They are probably not looking forward to taking another test. As students' attitudes are often reflective of their environment, it is important to remind them of the significance of the post-test. The ACT Science Reasoning Practice Tests (Step Four) will help make the actual testing experience much easier on them. To keep students motivated, plan something fun in order to reward them for all of their hard work and dedication. For example:

- throw a post-test pizza party;
- hand out prizes to everyone who shows up for the post-test; and
- distribute student-designed t-shirts so that students develop pride in their accomplishments.

b. KNOW THE TESTING AND ADMINISTRATION CONDITIONS

It is absolutely necessary that students take the test in one, unbroken session. Due to administrative and scheduling constraints, we realize that many schools can only give one section of the test at a time. It is important to understand that this form of administration does not reflect the actual testing experience and does not produce a valid score. The test score would be inflated since it is easier to take one part at a time. A full-length test requires a student to produce at a high level throughout the entire testing experience. Accuracy and concentration tend to decline during the final hour of the test because students become fatigued. When practicing, it is necessary to finish the entire test in order to develop the physical and mental stamina that are necessary to obtain a high score. If your test prep sessions are typically scheduled for less than the required amount of time that it takes to administer the entire exam, then you might consider holding a special long session after school or on a Saturday.

- ACT: Allow at least 3 hours (add 10-20 minutes for 1 break and proctoring time).
- PLAN: Allow at least 2 hours (add 10-20 minutes for 1 break and proctoring time).
- EXPLORE: Allow at least 2 hours (add 10-20 minutes for 1 break and proctoring time).

Be sure that you are familiar with the proctoring instructions found in Step One of this teacher's guide (p. 23) and that you notify students ahead of time that they need to bring several No. 2 pencils and an acceptable calculator. ACT defines an acceptable calculator as a four-function, scientific, or graphing calculator (see **http://www.actstudent.org/faq/answers/calculator.html** for more details on prohibited calculators).

OVERVIEW

c. ADMINISTER THE CORRECT TEST

If you are using the Cambridge Assessment Service, look at the Assessment Reports Request Form (included with your materials) to determine which of the two official tests students should take as a post-test. It is absolutely necessary that students take the tests as they have been designated, either as a pre- or post-test. **Do not administer the same test as both a pre- and post-test.**

2. STEP FIVE CLASS SESSION: PROCTOR AN OFFICIAL ACT, PLAN, OR EXPLORE

During the Step Five class session, you will proctor an official ACT, PLAN, or EXPLORE. Use the proctoring instructions found in Step One of this teacher's guide (p. 23) to administer the test. It is very important to simulate actual testing conditions as much as possible.

If you are not using the Cambridge Assessment Service, students should use the Post-Test Bubble Sheet on page 177 of the *Cambridge ACT • PLAN • EXPLORE Science Reasoning Victory Student Textbook*.

3. TRANSITION TO STEP SIX

Use assessment data to create Step Six individual student study plans, evaluate your test prep program, and further the larger goal of school improvement. According to the multi-year school improvement model below, you have completed or are about to complete the final phase of your program.

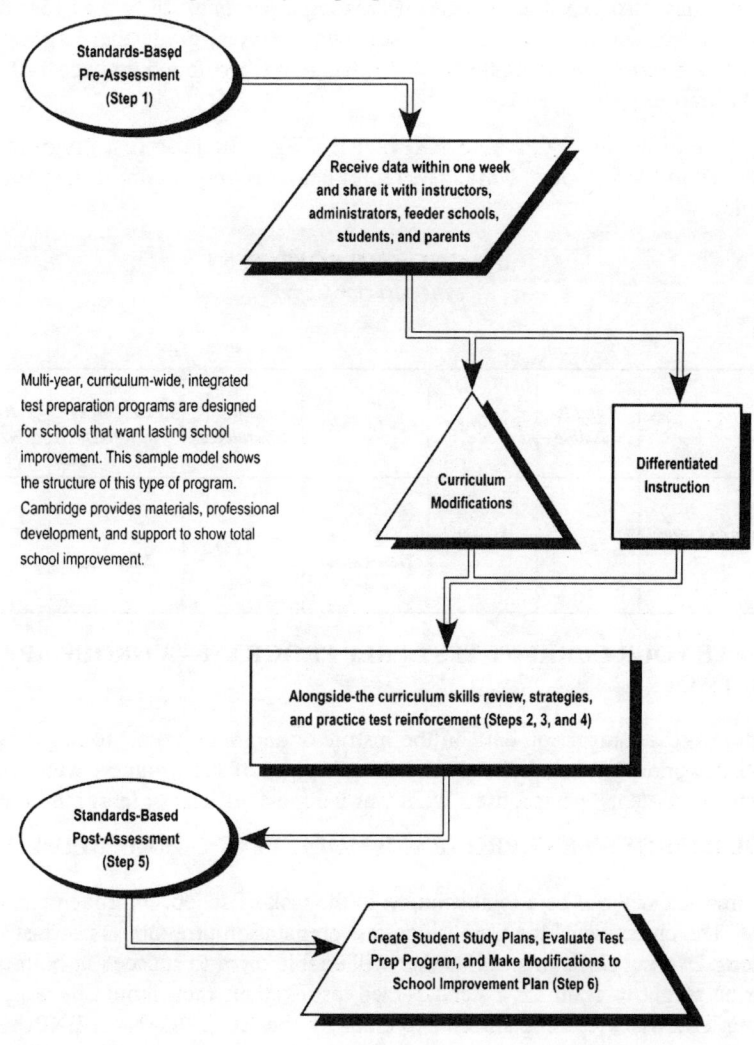

Multi-year, curriculum-wide, integrated test preparation programs are designed for schools that want lasting school improvement. This sample model shows the structure of this type of program. Cambridge provides materials, professional development, and support to show total school improvement.

- Standards-Based Pre-Assessment (Step 1)
- Receive data within one week and share it with instructors, administrators, feeder schools, students, and parents
- Curriculum Modifications
- Differentiated Instruction
- Alongside-the curriculum skills review, strategies, and practice test reinforcement (Steps 2, 3, and 4)
- Standards-Based Post-Assessment (Step 5)
- Create Student Study Plans, Evaluate Test Prep Program, and Make Modifications to School Improvement Plan (Step 6)

STEP FIVE

At this stage of the model, there are three levels with which to be concerned.

Level One: What to do with the student on an individual basis

Level Two: What to do with your class on a group basis

Level Three: What to do with your total school improvement plan

a. STUDENT PROGRESS REPORTS AND STUDY PLANS—AN INDIVIDUAL APPROACH (LEVEL ONE)

Student and instructor ACT • PLAN • EXPLORE Diagnostic Post-Test Progress Reports are on pages 139 and 141, respectively. These progress reports are also found on pages 173 and 175 in the *Cambridge ACT • PLAN • EXPLORE Science Reasoning Victory Student Textbook*. Students should use these forms to record how many and what percentage of problems they answered correctly on the post-test. This information should match that which is presented on the post-test assessment reports.

Ask your students to transfer the information from the student copies to the instructor copies. (These directions are repeated at the top of the student progress reports.) Collect the instructor copies from your students and indicate whether students need additional review. If they do, assign specific sections and problem numbers. File the reports in your students' in-class portfolios. These progress reports give students, parents, and instructors quick and accurate snapshots of student improvement. They also expedite the task of creating a personal study plan for each student in Step Six. If your school has chosen not to use the Cambridge Assessment Service, grade the diagnostic post-tests and convert students' raw scores to scaled scores, by using the Scale Conversion Chart found on page 140 in this teacher's guide and page 174 in the student textbook.

The following portion of the ACT • PLAN • EXPLORE Diagnostic Post-Test Progress Report demonstrates how you might complete the report for a student. **Note:** The report below is only a sample. Use the reports on pages 139 and 141 in this teacher's guide.

DIAGNOSTIC POST-TEST
(Instructor Copy)

Test Section	Total # Possible	# Correct	% Correct	Date Completed	Problem #s to Review	Skills Review Needed? (Y or N)	Section and Problem Numbers Assigned
ACT, PLAN, or EXPLORE SCIENCE REASONING	40	25	63 percent	5/1/05	7, 11, 12, 20	Y	Section One: 4, 7, 11, 12, 20, 23

The last two columns fall under *Instructor Skill Evaluation*.

b. EVALUATE YOUR CURRENT TEST PREP PROGRAM—A GROUP APPROACH (LEVEL TWO)

Use the pre- and post-test comparison data on the instructor summary report to begin evaluating your Cambridge test prep program. What worked? What didn't work? Which parts of the program were most effective from both a teaching perspective and the students' perspective? What was the most difficult or least intuitive aspect of the program?

c. SCHOOL IMPROVEMENT PROGRAM: MODIFYING CURRICULUM (LEVEL THREE)

The Cambridge program will not be a total solution to the task of school improvement, but it will be a strong and effective starting point. The objective of the Cambridge test preparation program is not just to raise overall test scores but also to instill lifelong learning skills in students that will enable them to succeed in both college and the workplace. Students should never be taught to cram for a standardized test. Rather, they should be taught that real success comes from long-term learning. Likewise, teaching students to cram for the ACT, PLAN, or EXPLORE will not lead to actual total school improvement. Only curriculum and instruction that foster long-term learning will accomplish this goal.

If a majority of your students exhibit science deficiencies, it is perhaps due to the fact that they have not received the proper scope and sequence of courses. Students are a product of their educational environment. This educational environment begins at home and continues throughout the various stages of schooling. Although you cannot control the family environment, you can certainly exert a positive influence on your students that may set the stage for future success and afford them many great opportunities.

Modification of curriculum can greatly increase your long-term effect on an individual student. Many students benefit from a more demanding environment of comprehensive, sequential, and rigorous curriculum. This type of environment tends to facilitate their college experience. In fact, there are quite a few schools in which Cambridge finds this scenario to be true. Schools that excel above others in certain subject areas usually have a more rigorous curriculum in one or two specific subject areas. Ideally, all students in grades 6 through 11 would take the same sequence of required courses. If students were to master the skill sets taught at their level, then they would advance on to the next level.

As you look to the next school year, you should imagine the total picture of school improvement that would result in lasting and even permanent change. This program is typically designed in a multi-year format. If this is the first year of your program, then you are to be congratulated for starting something really special. We commend your commitment to the educational achievement of your students.

In order to ensure even greater school improvement, your school can store all of its site data and retrieve it twice or more per year by using Cambridge Data Warehousing. This service enables programs to compare data from year to year in order to implement the proper multi-year, school improvement model. All changes to curriculum and instruction must be carefully tracked on a year-to-year basis by means of individual student progress reports in all the standards-based skill set areas.

d. BUILDING COMMUNITY SUPPORT: HOLD ADMISSIONS AND MOTIVATIONAL WORKSHOPS

Parents want their children to get into the colleges of their choice, but they often do not know the best way to help them achieve this goal. Cambridge will present an on-site college admissions workshop for parents and teachers in your school community. This workshop will put students' test preparation experience into context for your community, thereby helping guarantee the most effective test prep program possible. If your school did not hold an admissions workshop at the beginning of your course, Cambridge recommends that you hold this workshop after administering the post-test.

Although your school has a guidance department, Cambridge-trained specialists are able to speak with parents and students from a third-party perspective in order to provide further insight. Students are more prone to neglect the advice of their parents and teachers because they have a closer "day-to-day" relationship with them. However, students and parents are more receptive to Cambridge's motivational approach that sets out to raise the bar to a point where it makes sense to everyone. School should be viewed as a place to attain a higher level of educational achievement, but far too many students make their way into college only to drop out soon after they've begun. A regularly scheduled regiment of homework should begin in 6th grade so as to prepare students for the demands of college.

You are not only teaching your students standards-based testing points, but you are also establishing discipline, focus, and study habits that will help them succeed both in college and in the real world. In order for your efforts to succeed, students must apply themselves. Even those students who are demographically less fortunate than others can certainly be presented with the opportunity to help themselves move on to the next academic level with your assistance.

Please remember to emphasize to your students the guiding formula for college admission:

- Grades count toward 45 percent of the evaluation.
- Test scores count toward 45 percent of the evaluation.
- Other factors (extracurricular involvement) count toward 10 percent of the evaluation.

While work, athletics, and other extracurricular activities are important, they only make up 10 percent of the equation. The Cambridge test preparation program will help to raise the bar and inform the public as to how much of their children's lives should be spent studying for good grades and good test scores.

Step Five

Call your customer service representative at 847-299-2930 to arrange an on-site admissions or motivational workshop.

C. FAQ

Q: *What do I do if my student's post-test scores did not improve when compared with the pre-test results?*

A: **Don't worry.** Many factors affect test scores, which is why students often take the real test twice. It may be the case that a student answered fewer questions on the post-test, but answered a greater percentage of those questions correctly than he or she did on the pre-test. In that case, the student might need extra practice dealing with pacing, timing, and guessing. Of course, other factors can contribute to a bad test day: fatigue, attitude, inadequate preparation, over-preparation leading to test anxiety, or too little preparation too late.

PROGRESS REPORTS

ACT • PLAN • EXPLORE
DIAGNOSTIC POST-TEST PROGRESS REPORT
(Student Copy)

DIRECTIONS: These progress reports are designed to help you make sense of your ACT, PLAN, or EXPLORE Science Reasoning Diagnostic Post-Test results. Complete the diagnostic post-test and record both the number and percentage of Science Reasoning problems answered correctly. Refer to your Cambridge Assessment Report when recording this information if your program has elected to use the Cambridge Assessment Service. Identify the date on which you completed the Science Reasoning section of the post-test, and list the numbers of any problems that you would like your instructor to review in class.

Transfer this information to the Instructor Copy, and then give that report to your instructor.

Name _____ Student ID _____ Date _____

DIAGNOSTIC POST-TEST
(Student Copy)

Test Section	Total # Possible	# Correct	% Correct	Date Completed	Problem #s to Review
ACT, PLAN, or EXPLORE SCIENCE REASONING					

Photocopying not allowed without Cambridge licensing agreement.

STEP FIVE

SCALE CONVERSION, DIAGNOSTIC POST-TEST SCORE CALCULATION, AND STUDY PLAN AID
(Student Copy)

DIRECTIONS TO INSTRUCTOR: This % Correct Chart will help your students translate the number of problems that they answered correctly into an accurate representation of their abilities. Record both the number and percentage of Science Reasoning problems that your students answered correctly, circling the percentage correct in the chart below. Be sure they look under the proper column as each test section has a different number of problems. Your students will need to compare the percentage correct in each of the four ACT subject areas (assuming they took a complete, official ACT test). Students should allocate the greatest amount of time to the subject in which they scored the lowest percentage correct and the least amount of time to the subject in which they scored the highest percentage correct. Next, to determine their scale scores, have students use Table 1 in the back of the official, retired test booklet to convert their raw scores to scale scores.

Remind students to transfer this information to your instructor copy.

DIAGNOSTIC POST-TEST SCORE CALCULATION				
	Total # Possible	# Correct	% Correct	Scale Score
SCIENCE REASONING Diagnostic Post-Test				

% CORRECT CHART

Raw Score	40 Questions Total	60 Questions Total	75 Questions Total	Raw Score	40 Questions Total	60 Questions Total	75 Questions Total
1	3%	2%	1%	39	98%	65%	52%
2	5%	3%	3%	40	100%	67%	53%
3	8%	5%	4%	41		68%	55%
4	10%	7%	5%	42		70%	56%
5	13%	8%	7%	43		72%	57%
6	15%	10%	8%	44		73%	59%
7	18%	12%	9%	45		75%	60%
8	20%	13%	11%	46		77%	61%
9	23%	15%	13%	47		78%	63%
10	25%	17%	14%	48		80%	64%
11	28%	18%	15%	49		82%	65%
12	30%	20%	17%	50		83%	67%
13	33%	22%	18%	51		85%	68%
14	35%	23%	19%	52		87%	69%
15	38%	25%	20%	53		88%	71%
16	40%	27%	21%	54		90%	72%
17	43%	28%	23%	55		92%	73%
18	45%	30%	24%	56		93%	75%
19	48%	32%	25%	57		95%	76%
20	50%	33%	27%	58		97%	77%
21	53%	35%	28%	59		98%	79%
22	55%	37%	29%	60		100%	80%
23	58%	38%	31%	61			81%
24	60%	40%	32%	62			83%
25	63%	42%	33%	63			84%
26	65%	43%	35%	64			85%
27	68%	45%	36%	65			87%
28	70%	47%	37%	66			88%
29	73%	48%	39%	67			89%
30	75%	50%	40%	68			91%
31	78%	52%	41%	69			92%
32	80%	53%	43%	70			93%
33	83%	55%	44%	71			95%
34	85%	57%	45%	72			96%
35	88%	58%	47%	73			97%
36	90%	60%	48%	74			99%
37	93%	62%	49%	75			100%
38	95%	63%	51%				

Photocopying not allowed without Cambridge licensing agreement.

PROGRESS REPORTS C

ACT • PLAN • EXPLORE
DIAGNOSTIC POST-TEST PROGRESS REPORT
(Instructor Copy)

DIRECTIONS: Transfer the information from your Student Copy to the Instructor Copy below. Leave the last two bolded columns blank. Your instructor will use them to evaluate your progress. When finished, give these reports to your instructor.

Student Name _____ Student ID _____ Date _____

DIAGNOSTIC POST-TEST
(Instructor Copy)

Test Section	Total # Possible	# Correct	% Correct	Date Completed	Problem #s to Review	**Review Needed? (Y or N)**	**Section and Problem Numbers Assigned**
ACT, PLAN, or EXPLORE SCIENCE REASONING							

Instructor Skill Evaluation applies to the last two columns.

Photocopying not allowed without Cambridge licensing agreement.

–141–

STEP FIVE

SCALE CONVERSION, DIAGNOSTIC POST-TEST SCORE CALCULATION, AND STUDY PLAN AID
(Instructor Copy)

DIAGNOSTIC POST-TEST SCORE CALCULATION

	Total # Possible	# Correct	% Correct	Scale Score
SCIENCE REASONING Diagnostic Post-Test				

% CORRECT CHART

Raw Score	40 Questions Total	60 Questions Total	75 Questions Total	Raw Score	40 Questions Total	60 Questions Total	75 Questions Total
1	3%	2%	1%	39	98%	65%	52%
2	5%	3%	3%	40	100%	67%	53%
3	8%	5%	4%	41		68%	55%
4	10%	7%	5%	42		70%	56%
5	13%	8%	7%	43		72%	57%
6	15%	10%	8%	44		73%	59%
7	18%	12%	9%	45		75%	60%
8	20%	13%	11%	46		77%	61%
9	23%	15%	13%	47		78%	63%
10	25%	17%	14%	48		80%	64%
11	28%	18%	15%	49		82%	65%
12	30%	20%	17%	50		83%	67%
13	33%	22%	18%	51		85%	68%
14	35%	23%	19%	52		87%	69%
15	38%	25%	20%	53		88%	71%
16	40%	27%	21%	54		90%	72%
17	43%	28%	23%	55		92%	73%
18	45%	30%	24%	56		93%	75%
19	48%	32%	25%	57		95%	76%
20	50%	33%	27%	58		97%	77%
21	53%	35%	28%	59		98%	79%
22	55%	37%	29%	60		100%	80%
23	58%	38%	31%	61			81%
24	60%	40%	32%	62			83%
25	63%	42%	33%	63			84%
26	65%	43%	35%	64			85%
27	68%	45%	36%	65			87%
28	70%	47%	37%	66			88%
29	73%	48%	39%	67			89%
30	75%	50%	40%	68			91%
31	78%	52%	41%	69			92%
32	80%	53%	43%	70			93%
33	83%	55%	44%	71			95%
34	85%	57%	45%	72			96%
35	88%	58%	47%	73			97%
36	90%	60%	48%	74			99%
37	93%	62%	49%	75			100%
38	95%	63%	51%				

Note to Instructors: This chart has each test's student data, not just Science Reasoning, in order to show you your students' performance throughout the test and in comparison with each test subject. Ask students for a copy of all of their Step One reports to complete this chart and assign the appropriate ranking for each subject area. Assign a "1" to the subject-area that students scored the lowest percentage correct.

DIAGNOSTIC POST-TEST SCORE CALCULATION

	Total # Possible	# Correct	% Correct	Ranking	Scale Score
SCIENCE REASONING Diagnostic Post-Test					
ENGLISH Diagnostic Post-Test					
MATHEMATICS Diagnostic Post-Test					
READING Diagnostic Post-Test					

Photocopying not allowed without Cambridge licensing agreement.

STEP SIX: PERSONAL STUDY PLAN

CAMBRIDGE
EDUCATIONAL SERVICES

ACT • PLAN • EXPLORE
SCIENCE REASONING

STEP SIX: PERSONAL STUDY PLAN

CAMBRIDGE
EDUCATIONAL SERVICES®

AMERICA'S #1 STANDARDS-BASED SCHOOL IMPROVEMENT

Cambridge Course Concept Outline
STEP SIX

I. STEP SIX OVERVIEW (p. 149)

    A. WHAT IS STEP SIX? (p. 149)

    B. HOW TO USE STEP SIX AS A TEACHING TOOL (p. 149)
        1. PREPARING TO TEACH STEP SIX (p. 149)
        2. STEP SIX CLASS SESSION (p. 150)

    C. FAQ (p. 152)

II. ACT • PLAN • EXPLORE SCIENCE REASONING STEP SIX PROGRESS REPORTS (p. 153)

    A. ACT • PLAN EXPLORE SCIENCE REASONING STEP SIX STUDENT PROGRESS REPORT (p. 153)

    B. ACT • PLAN EXPLORE SCIENCE REASONING STEP SIX INSTUCTOR PROGRESS REPORT (p. 155)

III. ACT • PLAN • EXPLORE ENGLISH STEP SIX PROGRESS REPORTS (p. 157)

    A. ACT • PLAN EXPLORE ENGLISH STEP SIX STUDENT PROGRESS REPORT (p. 157)

    B. ACT • PLAN EXPLORE ENGLISH STEP SIX INSTUCTOR PROGRESS REPORT (p. 159)

IV. ACT • PLAN • EXPLORE MATHEMATICS STEP SIX PROGRESS REPORTS (p. 161)

    A. ACT • PLAN EXPLORE MATHEMATICS STEP SIX STUDENT PROGRESS REPORT (p. 161)

STEP SIX

    B. ACT • PLAN EXPLORE MATHEMATICS STEP SIX INSTUCTOR PROGRESS REPORT (p. 163)

V. ACT • PLAN • EXPLORE READING STEP SIX PROGRESS REPORTS (p. 165)

    A. ACT • PLAN EXPLORE READING STEP SIX STUDENT PROGRESS REPORT (p. 165)

    B. ACT • PLAN EXPLORE READING STEP SIX INSTUCTOR PROGRESS REPORT (p. 167)

STEP SIX OVERVIEW

A. WHAT IS STEP SIX?

Based on the data gathered from administering the post-test in Step Five, collaborate with your students to develop their personalized study plans. These plans provide each student with a guide that outlines the final adjustments that are necessary to target the remaining areas in which they need improvement. This method of organization helps students hone the necessary skills to reach their true potential and ability. They may return to Step Two: Skills Review; target specific test-taking strategies; or focus on pacing, timing, and guessing.

In Step Six: Personal Study Plan, you will review your students' progress report forms (both Science Reasoning and cross-curricular), pre- and post-test item analysis, attendance, and homework completion throughout the course and identify the areas in which they need the most help and/or in which they have not made a total effort. Meet with students individually to discuss their performance and effort, and help them to develop a personal study plan.

In addition to focusing on areas that still need improvement, it is important to note that students who have not completed the four ACT Science Reasoning Practice Tests (Step Four) achieve score improvements of 30 percent less than students who do complete all four homework modules. Students who have access to the Cambridge CD-ROM should also go through any practice tests that weren't already completed. Problems that proved to be challenging throughout the student textbook may require extra review time. Students may also wish to read through the explanations to all four practice tests, as well as the explanations to problems answered incorrectly in the official pre- and post-tests.

B. HOW TO USE STEP SIX AS A TEACHING TOOL

1. PREPARING TO TEACH STEP SIX

To help your students create successful study plans, you must be familiar with their post-test data. Take the time before your Step Six class session to review their post-test results and assessment reports. If you are using the Cambridge Assessment Service, the reports that you receive from your post-test can help you as follows:

ACT • PLAN • EXPLORE Student Summary (page one of two): The student summary indicates the number of right, wrong, and omitted problems. It indicates a student's current, relative strengths and remaining weaknesses to address in Step Six.

ACT • PLAN • EXPLORE Student Summary Item Analysis (page two of two): The item analysis report demonstrates the student's post-test response to each question. This report will also tell you if a student still needs to address coding problems, exhaustion, cheating, or a total lack of effort. Cambridge highly recommends that the first two pages of this report be mailed to the parents of each student. It is an excellent communication piece and will help parents determine the type of skills that are still necessary for their child to achieve college entrance or qualify for scholarships. It will show the parents how far their child has improved and which remaining areas still require greater attention.

ACT • PLAN • EXPLORE Pre-/Post- Instructor Summary: If you are using the Cambridge Assessment Report, the instructor summary proves invaluable to show how individual students have improved from pre- to post-test. In addition to providing the class average, this report can also be used to compare different classes and spot overall trends in order to determine Step Six instructional adjustments.

ACT • PLAN • EXPLORE Error Analysis: The error analysis report indicates group performance on each question and specific answer choices that were common incorrect answers. It will also help your school modify instruction for your next course in order to prevent these common errors from reoccurring. This report serves as a major indicator of whether a multi-year school improvement plan is working.

In addition, for locations ordering more than 150 student sets, your program reports include:

ACT • PLAN • EXPLORE High, Medium, and Low Error Analysis: Data is grouped according to three levels: high, medium, and low. Students within each group tend to make the same types of errors as other students within that same group. By targeting specific problems within a specific group, school improvement can be accomplished more easily and on a more widespread and permanent basis. In addition, it makes the most

STEP SIX

sense to target frequently missed problems that skills (low) students, average (medium) students, and gifted (high) students can get right. If 90 percent of your students get a particular problem wrong, skills students will have the greatest difficulty getting this problem correct regardless of what measures are taken. These problems are targeted for gifted students who should be capable of getting all of them correct.

If you are not using the Cambridge Assessment Service and required your students to complete their ACT • PLAN • EXPLORE Diagnostic Post-Test Progress Reports, you can use the instructor copy of their reports to review their post-test results and record specific review assignments for each student. In addition, be prepared to review some of the most frequently missed problems in class.

Step Six is also a good time to do course and instructor evaluations/surveys. Such evaluations will help you make decisions for future test prep programs. Prepare these evaluations ahead of time, and ask students to complete them on the last day of class. Call your Cambridge customer service representative at 847-299-2930 to receive a sample evaluation.

2. STEP SIX CLASS SESSION

The ACT • PLAN • EXPLORE Science Reasoning Step Six Progress Reports are an important tool for creating an effective personalized study plan. These reports provide an opportunity for students to evaluate themselves over the course of the entire Cambridge program. Student and instructor ACT • PLAN • EXPLORE Science Reasoning Step Six Progress Reports are on pages 153 and 155, respectively. These progress reports are also found on pages 185 and 187 in the *Cambridge ACT • PLAN • EXPLORE Science Reasoning Victory Student Textbook*. In addition, Step Six contains English, Mathematics, and Reading forms that are used as cross-curricular tools in order to reference students' overall progress (pp. 157-167). The forms provide a table in which you can help your students rank their ability levels in each of the different test section problem-types. In addition, they require you to help your students to specify strategies and skills on which to focus and additional review sections and problem numbers to study

Ask your students to transfer the information from the student copies to the instructor copies. (These directions are repeated at the top of the student progress reports.) Collect the instructor copies from your students and file the reports in your students' in-class portfolios. These progress reports give students, parents, and instructors quick and accurate snapshots of a solid and well-organized plan for further study.

The following portion of the ACT • PLAN • EXPLORE Science Reasoning Step Six Progress Report demonstrates how you might complete the report for a student. **Note:** The report below is only a sample. Use the reports on pages 153 and 155 in this teacher's guide.

STUDY PLAN
(Instructor Copy)

Problem-Type	Rank (1 = Weakest)	Strategies and Skills on Which to Focus	Additional Review Sections and Problem Numbers
Data Representation Passages	1	Indirect Relationships, Line Graphs	Science Skills Review, Exercise 2
Research Summary Passages	2	Independent Variables, Control Groups	Science Reasoning Review problems #15-25

Students should complete the progress reports in class, enlisting your help when necessary. You should then work with your students to create a study schedule based on the content of these reports. They should focus on improving in areas where they would have the greatest chance to improve and move to the next skill level. A sample one-week personal study plan appears below. Your students' study plans should be arranged in either a daily or weekly format, depending on how much time they have before they take the real test.

SAMPLE ONE-WEEK STUDY SCHEDULE

DAY OF THE WEEK	ASSIGNMENT	WHERE TO FIND IT
SATURDAY	Last class day. Formulate your study plan with your instructor after reviewing the post-test assessment report.	N/A
SUNDAY	Revisit Conflicting Viewpoints.	*Cambridge ACT • PLAN • EXPLORE Science Reasoning Victory Student Textbook*, Science Skills Review (Step Two)
MONDAY	Review Direct and Indirect Relationships.	*Cambridge ACT • PLAN • EXPLORE Science Reasoning Victory Student Textbook*, Science Skills Review (Step Two)
TUESDAY	Review Parabolic Curves.	*Cambridge ACT • PLAN • EXPLORE Science Reasoning Victory Student Textbook*, Problem-Solving, Concepts, and Strategies (Step Three)
WEDNESDAY	Review the Science Reasoning Section of CD-ROM Practice Test II.	CD-ROM Practice Test
THURSDAY	Review Science Reasoning explanatory answers to timed ACT Science Reasoning Practice Tests III and IV.	*Cambridge ACT • PLAN • EXPLORE Science Reasoning Victory Student Textbook*, ACT Science Reasoning Practice Tests III and IV (Step Four)
FRIDAY	Day off. Relax. Get a good night's sleep.	N/A
SATURDAY	Test day. Eat a healthy breakfast.	N/A

STEP SIX

C. FAQ

Q: *What should I do if my students are very resistant to the idea of creating and sticking to a study plan?*

A: **Many students won't get overly excited about studying for the ACT, PLAN, or EXPLORE (especially after your class has ended). Remind them of the progress that they've made so far as a result of their dedicated efforts, and talk to them about the test in terms of their future (*e.g.*, getting into the colleges of their choice or getting the kind of jobs that they really want). Explain that taking the time to create a focused, prioritized study schedule will make the whole studying process much easier and more effective. Also, if you are offering the Cambridge CollegePrep™ program, the chapter on effective studying will assist with your efforts.**

Q: *How can I arrange for my school to hold an admissions workshop?*

A: **Call your customer service representative at 847-299-2930.**

Q: *What should students do with their books at the end of class?*

A: **Students should keep their books so that they can successfully complete Step Six: Personal Study Plan by reviewing the problems indicated in their personal study plans.**

Q: *What should I do with student portfolios?*

A: **Portfolios are useful tools as you proceed to make decisions about future test prep programs and school improvement plans. Keep a copy of all reports associated with this program in these portfolios (all pre-/post-assessment reports and instructor copies of the progress reports for each step). Pass them on from year to year so that the scientific data can be continually used to further benefit future test prep programs and enhance school improvement. You may also wish to give a copy to students and parents, as well as keep a copy for yourself.**

ACT • PLAN • EXPLORE SCIENCE REASONING
STEP SIX PROGRESS REPORT
(Student Copy)

DIRECTIONS TO INSTRUCTOR: This progress report is designed to help your students assess their overall course progress, evaluate their test-taking strengths and weaknesses, and create a study plan that will help them maximize their test score.

Help your students complete this report. Refer to the last column of their Steps One through Five Progress Reports, entitled "Problem Numbers to Review" to assess their performance on each problem-type. Have your students fill out this progress report by ranking their performance by problem-type and subject-area. Rank their weakest area as number 1, and then help your students to identify specific skills and strategies. Finally, work together with your students to identify problems in the textbook, on the CD-ROM, or in the web course that will allow students to hone the skills necessary to improve in their weakest areas.

Instruct students to work through as many of the additional review problems as possible before their test in order to perform to their potential on the actual exam.

Have students transfer this information to their Instructor Copy, and then give that report to you.

Name _____ Student ID _____ Date _____

STUDY PLAN
(Student Copy)

Problem-Type	Rank (1 = Weakest)	Strategies and Skills on Which to Focus	Additional Review Sections and Problem Numbers
Data Representation Passages			
Research Summary Passages			
Conflicting Viewpoints Passages			

PROGRESS REPORTS

ACT • PLAN • EXPLORE SCIENCE REASONING
STEP SIX PROGRESS REPORT
(Instructor Copy)

DIRECTIONS TO INSTRUCTOR: This progress report is designed to help your students assess their overall course progress, evaluate their test-taking strengths and weaknesses, and create a study plan that will help them maximize their test score.

Help your students complete this report. Refer to the last column of their Steps One through Five Progress Reports, entitled "Problem Numbers to Review" to assess their performance on each problem-type. Have your students fill out this progress report by ranking their performance by problem-type and subject-area. Rank their weakest area as number 1, and then help your students to identify specific skills and strategies. Finally, work together with your students to identify problems in the textbook, on the CD-ROM, or in the web course that will allow students to hone the skills necessary to improve in their weakest areas.

Instruct students to work through as many of the additional review problems as possible before their test in order to perform to their potential on the actual exam.

Have students transfer this information to their Instructor Copy, and then give that report to you.

Student Name _____ Student ID _____ Date _____

STUDY PLAN
(Instructor Copy)

Problem-Type	Rank (1 = Weakest)	Strategies and Skills on Which to Focus	Additional Review Sections and Problem Numbers
Data Representation Passages			
Research Summary Passages			
Conflicting Viewpoints Passages			

Photocopying not allowed without Cambridge licensing agreement.

PROGRESS REPORTS

ACT • PLAN • EXPLORE ENGLISH
STEP SIX PROGRESS REPORT
(Student Copy)

DIRECTIONS TO INSTRUCTOR: This progress report is designed to help your students assess their overall course progress, evaluate their test-taking strengths and weaknesses, and create a study plan that will help them maximize their test score.

Help your students complete this report. Refer to the last column of their Steps One through Five Progress Reports, entitled "Problem Numbers to Review" to assess their performance on each problem-type. Have your students fill out this progress report by ranking their performance by problem-type and subject-area. Rank their weakest area as number 1, and then help your students to identify specific skills and strategies. Finally, work together with your students to identify problems in the textbook, on the CD-ROM, or in the web course that will allow students to hone the skills necessary to improve in their weakest areas.

Instruct students to work through as many of the additional review problems as possible before their test in order to perform to their potential on the actual exam.

Have students transfer this information to their Instructor Copy, and then give that report to you.

Name _____ Student ID _____ Date _____

STUDY PLAN
(Student Copy)

Problem-Type	Rank (1 = Weakest)	Strategies and Skills on Which to Focus	Additional Review Sections and Problem Numbers
Parts of Speech			
Common Grammatical Errors			
Analyzing Sentence Structure			
Problems of Logical Expression			
Idioms and Clarity of Expression			
Punctuation			
Capitalization and Spelling			

Photocopying not allowed without Cambridge licensing agreement.

PROGRESS REPORTS

ACT • PLAN • EXPLORE ENGLISH
STEP SIX PROGRESS REPORT
(Instructor Copy)

DIRECTIONS TO INSTRUCTOR: This progress report is designed to help your students assess their overall course progress, evaluate their test-taking strengths and weaknesses, and create a study plan that will help them maximize their test score.

Help your students complete this report. Refer to the last column of their Steps One through Five Progress Reports, entitled "Problem Numbers to Review" to assess their performance on each problem-type. Have your students fill out this progress report by ranking their performance by problem-type and subject-area. Rank their weakest area as number 1, and then help your students to identify specific skills and strategies. Finally, work together with your students to identify problems in the textbook, on the CD-ROM, or in the web course that will allow students to hone the skills necessary to improve in their weakest areas.

Instruct students to work through as many of the additional review problems as possible before their test in order to perform to their potential on the actual exam.

Have students transfer this information to their Instructor Copy, and then give that report to you.

Student Name _____ Student ID _____ Date _____

STUDY PLAN
(Instructor Copy)

Problem-Type	Rank (1 = Weakest)	Strategies and Skills on Which to Focus	Additional Review Sections and Problem Numbers
Parts of Speech			
Common Grammatical Errors			
Analyzing Sentence Structure			
Problems of Logical Expression			
Idioms and Clarity of Expression			
Punctuation			
Capitalization and Spelling			

Photocopying not allowed without Cambridge licensing agreement.

ACT • PLAN • EXPLORE MATHEMATICS
STEP SIX PROGRESS REPORT
(Student Copy)

DIRECTIONS TO INSTRUCTOR: This progress report is designed to help your students assess their overall course progress, evaluate their test-taking strengths and weaknesses, and create a study plan that will help them maximize their test score.

Help your students complete this report. Refer to the last column of their Steps One through Five Progress Reports, entitled "Problem Numbers to Review" to assess their performance on each problem-type. Have your students fill out this progress report by ranking their performance by problem-type and subject-area. Rank their weakest area as number 1, and then help your students to identify specific skills and strategies. Finally, work together with your students to identify problems in the textbook, on the CD-ROM, or in the web course that will allow students to hone the skills necessary to improve in their weakest areas.

Instruct students to work through as many of the additional review problems as possible before their test in order to perform to their potential on the actual exam.

Have students transfer this information to their Instructor Copy, and then give that report to you.

Name _____ Student ID _____ Date _____

STUDY PLAN
(Student Copy)

Problem-Type	Rank (1 = Weakest)	Strategies and Skills on Which to Focus	Additional Review Sections and Problem Numbers
Arithmetic			
Algebra			
Common Equations			
Geometry			
Trigonometry			

PROGRESS REPORTS

ACT • PLAN • EXPLORE MATHEMATICS
STEP SIX PROGRESS REPORT
(Instructor Copy)

DIRECTIONS TO INSTRUCTOR: This progress report is designed to help your students assess their overall course progress, evaluate their test-taking strengths and weaknesses, and create a study plan that will help them maximize their test score.

Help your students complete this report. Refer to the last column of their Steps One through Five Progress Reports, entitled "Problem Numbers to Review" to assess their performance on each problem-type. Have your students fill out this progress report by ranking their performance by problem-type and subject-area. Rank their weakest area as number 1, and then help your students to identify specific skills and strategies. Finally, work together with your students to identify problems in the textbook, on the CD-ROM, or in the web course that will allow students to hone the skills necessary to improve in their weakest areas.

Instruct students to work through as many of the additional review problems as possible before their test in order to perform to their potential on the actual exam.

Have students transfer this information to their Instructor Copy, and then give that report to you.

Student Name _____ Student ID _____ Date _____

STUDY PLAN
(Instructor Copy)

Problem-Type	Rank (1 = Weakest)	Strategies and Skills on Which to Focus	Additional Review Sections and Problem Numbers
Arithmetic			
Algebra			
Common Equations			
Geometry			
Trigonometry			

ACT • PLAN • EXPLORE READING
STEP SIX PROGRESS REPORT
(Student Copy)

DIRECTIONS TO INSTRUCTOR: This progress report is designed to help your students assess their overall course progress, evaluate their test-taking strengths and weaknesses, and create a study plan that will help them maximize their test score.

Help your students complete this report. Refer to the last column of their Steps One through Five Progress Reports, entitled "Problem Numbers to Review" to assess their performance on each problem-type. Have your students fill out this progress report by ranking their performance by problem-type and subject-area. Rank their weakest area as number 1, and then help your students to identify specific skills and strategies. Finally, work together with your students to identify problems in the textbook, on the CD-ROM, or in the web course that will allow students to hone the skills necessary to improve in their weakest areas.

Instruct students to work through as many of the additional review problems as possible before their test in order to perform to their potential on the actual exam.

Have students transfer this information to their Instructor Copy, and then give that report to you.

Name _____ Student ID _____ Date _____

STUDY PLAN
(Student Copy)

Problem-Type	Rank (1 = Weakest)	Strategies and Skills on Which to Focus	Additional Review Sections and Problem Numbers
Prose Fiction			
Social Science			
Humanities			
Natural Science			

PROGRESS REPORTS

ACT • PLAN • EXPLORE READING
STEP SIX PROGRESS REPORT
(Instructor Copy)

DIRECTIONS TO INSTRUCTOR: This progress report is designed to help your students assess their overall course progress, evaluate their test-taking strengths and weaknesses, and create a study plan that will help them maximize their test score.

Help your students complete this report. Refer to the last column of their Steps One through Five Progress Reports, entitled "Problem Numbers to Review" to assess their performance on each problem-type. Have your students fill out this progress report by ranking their performance by problem-type and subject-area. Rank their weakest area as number 1, and then help your students to identify specific skills and strategies. Finally, work together with your students to identify problems in the textbook, on the CD-ROM, or in the web course that will allow students to hone the skills necessary to improve in their weakest areas.

Instruct students to work through as many of the additional review problems as possible before their test in order to perform to their potential on the actual exam.

Have students transfer this information to their Instructor Copy, and then give that report to you.

Student Name _____ Student ID _____ Date _____

STUDY PLAN
(Instructor Copy)

Problem-Type	*Rank (1 = Weakest)*	*Strategies and Skills on Which to Focus*	*Additional Review Sections and Problem Numbers*
Prose Fiction			
Social Science			
Humanities			
Natural Science			

Photocopying not allowed without Cambridge licensing agreement.